The Indie Band Bible

Canadian Cataloguing in Publication Data

Makoway, Mark, 1966–
The indie band bible

Includes index
ISBN 1-894160-03-7

1. Popular music--Vocational guidance--Canada. 2. Rock
music--Vocational guidance--Canada. 3. Music trade--Canada. I. Atkinson,
Toren. II. Title.
ML3795.M235 2000   781.64'023'71   C00-911362-2

Published by Madrigal Press Ltd., 1650 West 2nd Avenue,
Vancouver, BC V6J 4R3 Phone (604) 654-2929 Fax (604) 654-1993
Email: books@madrigalpress.com

Distributed in Canada by Raincoast Books,
9050 Shaughnessy St., Vancouver, BC V6P 6E5
Printed in Canada

For Nicola, keep the pettalon my darling...

Thanks to:

Jeff Pearce, David Usher, Paul Wilcox, Kevin Young, Graeme McDonald, Don Carmichael, Dan Cassar, Brent Clark, Marc Crain, Mark Finkelstein, Craig Finlay, Anthony Greenham, Keith Maryanovich, Duncan McTavish, JP Newton, Gord Reddy, Glen Reely, Dave Retson, Mark Vreeken, Stan Wardle

Ralph Alfonso, Cathryn France and everyone at Madrigal

Terry McBride, Dan Fraser, Chris Fisher, Coleen Novak, Pierre Tremblay and everyone at Nettwerk

Michael McCarty, Barbara Sedun and everyone at EMI Music Publishing Canada

Deane Cameron, Tim Trombley, David MacMillan and everyone at EMI Music Canada

Bruce Allen, Andrew Atkins, Toren Atkinson, Joe Bamford, Dave Betts at Socan, Steve Blair and Steve Jordan at Warner Music Canada, Blanche, Karen Bliss, Albert Chambers, Derek Danielson, Denise Donlon, everyone at Much Music and Musique Plus, Adam Drake, Dorothy at En Tour, Bobby Gale, Kevin Hamilton, Craig Martin, Jeff MacKay at Canadian Musician Magazine, Mitch Joel, Andrea Knoblauch, David Leonard, Yvonne Matsell, Mark Milne and Tim Potocic at Sonic Unyon Records, Paul Northfield, Phillip Rambow, Paul Sanderson, Shaw Saltzberg, Mary Boutette and everyone at S.L. Feldman & Associates, David Steinberg, Chris Taylor, Gregg Terrence, The Agency Group

Nicola, Sara, Beverly, Barry, Sean

My family, friends and everyone who has helped along the way

Mark Makoway
The Indie Band Bible

Publisher: Cathryn France
Managing Editor: Ralph Alfonso
Original manuscript editing: Nicola Makowy
Book design: John Rummen
Cover design: Ralph Alfonso
Typesetting and editing assistance: Kim Kinakin
Cover photo: Anthony Greenham
Back cover photo: Al Robb
Illustrations: Toren Atkinson
Photo on page 29: Daryl Harapiak
Author photo: Ralf Strathmann

Contents

Foreword

Sometimes when I sit down to talk with new artists (and even established veterans), I wish that I had some sort of book or manual I could present them with that they could take home and study and have with them as a source of information. Well, *The Indie Band Bible* is that book. It has an independent artist's point of view, but is grounded in the reality of the music business as a whole, including the major labels, publishers and the Internet.

As the manager of many bands, one of the biggest challenges I have when communicating with artists is getting them to understand that the music business is exactly that: the business of music. It's important to have a good understanding of how things work and to make educated decisions, not just emotional ones.

The music industry has changed dramatically in the past few years. Technology has had a major impact, and has enabled artists to communicate with fans via their websites. The direct feedback artists get from their fans gives a sense of weight in discussions with their managers. Managers in turn are now able to feed vast amounts of information to the artists, through advances in tracking album sales and radio airplay.

The Indie Band Bible is a great way to gain an understanding of how this all works. The bottom line is, the more educated you are about the music business, the more you'll be able to have valuable working relationships with the many professionals you'll be coming into contact with.

I'm also happy to say I'm the author's manager, and he definitely got more secrets out of me than he should have!

Terry McBride
Nettwerk Management

Introduction

Welcome to *The Indie Band Bible.*

Why are you reading this book? You've probably got this crazy idea you want to be a rock star or at least play in a successful band. Is it worth it? Definitely. Being a musician is both the best and the worst job in the world. The workload is unbelievable and much of it doesn't really have anything to do with playing guitar or pounding the drums. The more successful you become, the more you find yourself being business guy or interview master or postering superman or diplomatic wizard. You'll be busier than you've ever been before. But it's your baby—your band—so there's a sense of adventure to the whole thing. It's your calling and you're doing something most people envy but can't get it together to do. Let's face it, it's cool to play in a band.

So you decide to take the plunge. Will you make it? If you make the decision to really go for it—persevere, dedicate your life and make informed decisions along the way—you have a decent chance. Your greatest assets are your brains and your dedication. But success doesn't happen overnight.

People have said to me "Man, you really got lucky, didn't you?" It's true. But I was also prepared. I'd put in ten years of hard work, nobody knew who I was, and I think it's really important to devote and make a decision and stick with it... Find something you love and go after it.

- Daniel Lanois,
artist and veteran producer

Read any of the hundreds of rock star biographies out there and the story's always the same: Everyone started by sleeping on someone's floor. It takes time to build a following, develop some momentum and quite simply to "get good."

This isn't a "get-rich-quick" book. If you think you're going to get rich, choose another business, chump. People do get rich in the music business, but for every megastar there are literally thousands of bands struggling to sell out a small club. Even platinum-selling artists in Canada don't really get rich. It's better to think about it this way: doing what you love, travelling, and experiencing the rush of live performance makes for a great job.

Money, however, is an issue for any band. There are many expenses, such as PA rentals, rehearsal space charges, Gibsons and Fenders, studio fees, photocopying for posters—the list goes on. Where does the money come from? How should it be spent? How can you make more of it? These questions loom pretty large for struggling bands that are always low on funds.

The Indie Band Bible will help you realize your band is a small business. By playing in a band you're selling your music and more than that, you're selling yourself: your ideas, your skills, your face, your name, your attitude. To use a word all artists hate and all industry people seem to use, you're selling a product. In a weird way, you're the salesman and the merchandise, which can be a difficult thing to accept. This might sound a little jaded and the p-word has nothing to do with the rush of an awesome jam, but the music business is a business.

Ultimately, it's business that brings you and your music to an audience. It starts at the level of the bar gig and moves right through to the monster rock stadium shows. Don't fall for the line that successful people are simply lucky. Microsoft or McDonalds didn't get where they are because of luck, so don't think for a second that U2 got to be U2 by chance. A successful band is a finely tuned artistic and business machine.

★★★

Before I sat down to write this guide, I had no idea what a huge undertaking it was going to be. To assemble the required material and ideas I had to conduct interviews, do research and speak to pretty much everyone I've ever met in the business. I also drew on many of my own experiences (both good and bad) as a professional musician in Moist.

Moist has done some pretty cool things over the past few years. We've signed record contracts, toured worldwide, and made hit records and videos. I guess you could say we've "made it." For better and sometimes for worse, we've always controlled almost every aspect of the band. We've made many mistakes, but we've also constantly tried to move forward and learn from those mistakes.

For years we were managed by a friend who had no more experience in the music business than we did. He did an amazing job with very few resources and remained our manager until we released our second album *Creature*. In the beginning we were all very green, so we always talked through every move, every decision and managed to learn a lot about the music industry along the way. Now that we have an established manager we're a real hassle. We ask tons of questions and need to be in the loop on everything, and we wouldn't have it any other way.

I can remember not knowing anything and, worse, not knowing anyone who knew anything about the music business. There were always people who said they knew someone who had sort of, kind of, talked to a real industry player once, but there were never any real answers. I could play guitar, write songs, jam and perform, but the music business was like a black hole. There seemed to be a huge divide between where we were and where successful bands were.

In the music business, it's vital to start on the right foot and make smart moves along the way. Think of *The Indie Band Bible* as a road map to get you started and lead you on to the next level. It will cover everything from band fundamentals and basic promotional strategies to making contact with the music industry giants.

There are many pitfalls bands can fall into and never really get past. Knowing what those pitfalls are and how to avoid them will only increase your chances of success. And increasing your chances of success is what this book is really all about.

There are no guarantees in the music business. However, more often than not, success comes to those who have prepared themselves to succeed. You've got to educate yourself and be smart.

★★★

This guide can be used in a number of different ways. It can be read all the way through or used as a reference book for specific problems or questions. There will be times when you'll say, "wait a minute, I already know this." Cool. Skip that section or read it to confirm what you already know. You can also just read the blurbs contained in the margins. They're snapshots of the music world which I hope will add some humour and dimension to the read. Who knows, this book could find a permanent place in jam-space bathrooms across the country.

★★★

Let me paint a lovely picture for you. Imagine a beat up, unreliable fifteen-passenger van hurtling down a snowy highway in the dead of winter, in the middle of the night. Imagine five unwashed musicians, a pile of maps, a mountain of amps and drums and bags and everything else you can think of squeezed into said van. Imagine sleeping sitting up, and having to crank the windows down to ventilate because someone's passing gas. It's like being in grade eight again, but without the discipline. Our longest drive was from Detroit to Vancouver via Thunder Bay, non-stop except for gas and 7-11 burritos (see above). This is the reality of being in a band. If you think you can hack it, read on. Hey, it's got to be better than your day job...

Chapter One

Band Basics

Band Philosophy

I can't help being a bit idealistic about bands. In a perfect world, a band is a team of like-minded individuals on a collective adventure. Everyone shares similar goals and a common sense of dedication. I believe in band democracy and a shared workload. Band members work to make things happen and take responsibility for things they are naturally good at. Some people are natural artists and take on the design of posters and logos, while others deal with club owners and the shmooze. Everyone is driven and focused, working towards the common goal, and sharing in the rewards.

However, this may not be an appropriate way for all bands to operate. In the real world, some people are more driven while others are naturally lazy. Nothing is ever completely fair or perfectly even. The point is, whatever agreement you come up with in terms of sharing the workload and money, it takes a massive amount of dedication from every band member to become successful.

As an indie band, you have to do everything yourself, which requires time and energy. If there are a couple of people in the band who aren't that bothered about the project, there will be problems down the road. Often, when the time comes to make sacrifices—monetary or otherwise—it will be the half-committed members who bail out.

It's good to decide early on if you're going to be a team that will share the work and the rewards evenly. This democratic spirit makes it easier to manage things like band money and the purchase of new gear. Everyone in the band should have a clear understanding of the way the band is going to work. Then you can be up-front and honest about everyone's contribution and responsibilities. Over time, you might agree to modify the way the band works, but having a basic understanding is an important starting point.

A band is a tight social unit. Band members will often spend more time with each other than with anyone else. It's quite possible to spend weeks on end together, packed tightly into an old van—so you'd better get along. It takes a lot of cooperation and compromise to survive such an intense relationship. You have to learn to recognize and avoid sparking each other's fuses. Believe me, it takes hard work to keep a band healthy and together. You have to be able to trust each other and respect each other's space.

Our band has meetings from time to time to let everyone talk about things that are getting under their skin. It may sound pretty flaky, but it helps. We've found that these meetings help relieve some pent-up pressures and aggravations. It's amazing how much it helps to get things out in the open. Stupid little things can fester and become big issues if they're not dealt with early on. Basically, every cliché you've ever heard about marriages can be applied to bands. (I like the image of four long-haired speed metal dudes sitting in the office of a marriage counsellor: "Man, it really pisses me off that you always disappear at load out time. If I have to move your amp one more time...")

Getting Together
Auditions & Auditioning

Finding band mates is rather like going out on a series of blind dates. When you're looking to join a band or putting your own band together, you'll probably run into some pretty bizarre individuals. Music attracts a really amazing diversity of people and, invariably, you'll meet the weirdest of the weird. Sometimes it's a relief to come across someone even remotely normal, even boring. Of course, if you're one of those total weirdos, then everyone out there seems pretty tame to you.

Musical ability is a big concern when looking for band mates, but equally or more important are non-musical characteristics. It's crucial to find people you vibe with and enjoy hanging out with. A band is a social unit. The keyword here is compatibility.

Things to Consider on Band Mate Blind Dates
- **Personality:** I'm talking about basic social compatibility here. The more success your band has, the more time you'll spend together. At the very least, you have to be able to get along. This seems obvious, but many bands are plagued by personality conflicts that end up poisoning the experience for everyone. Putting up with jerks simply because they have a place to jam probably isn't going to create a lasting chemistry.
- **Musical Influences and Tastes:** Diversity in musical tastes and backgrounds can yield some really great results and you can end up with some great original music. However, there must be a degree of common ground, otherwise some players simply aren't going to like the band's music, which is definitely a problem.
- **Commitment/Goals:** It's very important that everyone has a similar level of commitment. If some players want to focus and play full-time while others are only interested in being weekend warriors, there will be difficulties. Everyone should more or less share the same basic musical goals and work together as a team, otherwise the really dedicated members will become frustrated and resentful from doing all the work.
- **Reliability:** This is related to the idea of commitment. Unfortunately, musicians have a real reputation for being unreliable. There has to be a basic trust in the group.

If members don't show up for rehearsals and/or gigs, you can't move forward.
- **Skill Level:** You obviously want to play with good musicians, but it generally works best when everyone has a similar skill level. The players with the best chops aren't necessarily the ones with the most interesting ideas. Watch for musical chemistry and creativity.

You'll likely go through a few players before you end up with a unit that works really well. It's difficult to know someone's strengths and weaknesses from a quick audition and a few hours of hanging out. Serious personality flaws sometimes take time to reveal themselves. The early history of most bands involves at least a couple of personnel changes. Just getting a band up and running takes time and compromise.

Typical Places to Find Potential Musicians
- **Classified Ads:** Many weekly arts-oriented papers like *Now* in Toronto or the *Georgia Straight* in Vancouver offer free ads in the "Musicians Wanted" and "Musicians Available" sections.
- **Posters:** Music stores and schools often have notice boards for musicians seeking musicians.
- **Music School:** If you take lessons, ask your teacher about other students wanting to join/form a band.
- **Word of Mouth:** Talk to everyone you know and spend some time at new talent/alternative nights.

Getting Moist Together

Moist was formed in September 1992 at a raging house party in Vancouver. Jeff Pearce, David Usher, Kevin Young and I were all there and the conversation quickly turned to the frustration we all felt in getting bands together. It seemed impossible to find musicians who were good players, good people and serious about getting something happening.

So after a few tequila shooters, we grabbed acoustic guitars and started jamming. The party had been raging for hours, but it was only after we started playing that the neighbours decided to call the police. We knew we must be on to something (or else we really sucked). I'd been playing with Jeff for years, and David and Kevin had been working together as well, and the idea of us all getting together seemed pretty exciting. We all seemed to be in the same headspace of wanting to make something happen.

Soon after, we all got together to start writing songs and put together a live set. Things quickly fell into place and over the next three months we wrote and recorded our indie cassette (containing half the songs later released on our first CD, Silver, including "Push," "Believe Me" and "Picture Elvis"). We were energised by the momentum we were starting to feel.

Unfortunately, the hardest part was still ahead of us: finding a permanent drummer. We auditioned many—some were pretty good players with horrendous personalities, while others simply couldn't keep time. The couple of guys we did like didn't want to play with us. We even phoned a friend of ours from Kingston, Ontario literally four times a day for a month, begging him to move out west and drum for us; he never caved in. He couldn't see a future in it. You can never underestimate the importance of having a strong drummer. We went through dozens until we finally found Paul (Wilcox).

Gear

I started playing guitar in grade nine after I watched my friend's band play at an old church hall in Toronto. It was their first gig and they sounded terrible. Feedback cut through every song; their singer was off-key and the band was really loose. But, they were great: a true punk band. Totally cool. It didn't hurt that someone drove a car through the front window of the hall shortly after they finished their set. I was hooked.

That year my sister got a cheap classical guitar for her birthday. It had a rudely wide neck and no tone at all, but it was a guitar. So I liberated it and immediately started playing pick and strum songs like "On Top of Old Smoky." Not my musical taste, but Rush seemed a little bit ambitious at the time (I did manage to figure out the main riff in "Smoke on the Water"). Soon, I discovered that Neil Young songs were the perfect teach-yourself-to-play material (Nirvana songs are also good for this). So, I bought a Neil Young songbook and went to town.

After a few months I was pretty fast with my open chord changes; I had D, G, and A minor down to a science. The only problem was my sister's classical guitar had nylon strings, and sounded nothing like the guitar on my Neil Young CDs. Young played a steel string acoustic (a Martin D-28). It was time to upgrade. I had to have a better guitar, a real guitar.

My first trip to Steve's Music Store was typical of any visit to any music store in any city. Before entering the shop,

I thought I was getting pretty good—I could play simplified versions of "Powderfinger" and "Hey Hey My My."

When I walked into the store, however, everyone seemed like Eddie Van Halen shredding through monster licks and speedy little blues solos. There was one guy doing a stirring rendition of "Stairway to Heaven" while another character played effortlessly through some Guns 'n' Roses song. And there I stood, in awe, more than a little intimidated. Everyone had an attitude and I had the fear—I couldn't even play my open chords very well. Everyone's had this experience. It's a rite of passage. Are you worthy? Well, I didn't feel too damn worthy. The thing to remember is everyone sucked at their instrument when they started. It takes time to become a good player. You have to really practice all the time. And no matter how good you get, there will always be someone better. It's a fact of life.

Get What You Need

On our first tour across the country, we encountered dozens of different bands. One band that comes to mind is "Big Kit." I can't even remember their real name. They were pretty good, sort of in the Pearl Jam vein. Anyway, their drummer saved up several thousand dollars and bought himself the most amazing, expensive, incredibly massive drum kit in the city. It had seven mounted toms, twelve different cymbals, two bass drums, a cow bell, roto-toms, a gong and more. It was all put together with a very complicated, state-of-the-art jungle gym construction that would put Neil Peart of Rush to shame (if he could understand it).

We played a double bill with Big Kit at a small Toronto venue. They had forty-five minutes to set up and sound check and then it was supposed to be our turn. Now, with a team of professional technicians all wearing numbered T-shirts, that drum kit could've been assembled in a couple of hours, maybe. Let's just say, there wasn't a lot of sound checking going on that day, although there was a lot of standing around, worshipping the almighty kit. Of course, no one was actually allowed to touch it.

As a young band that plays for beer, you have to be guerrilla performers. You have to learn the art of the surgical strike. The faster you can load in, set up and be ready to go, the more time you'll have for sound check and preparing mentally for the show. Basically, if you want to throw your gear into someone's beat-up Volkswagen van and show up for a quick basement jam, you're going to want to travel light. Having portable, road-worthy, reliable equipment is essential.

You also don't want an instrument that's so expensive that you're scared to take it anywhere. Your instrument is a tool to express your creativity; it's going to go everywhere, do everything and definitely take a few knocks, cigarette burns and bruises along the way. This doesn't mean you have to buy a piece of crap. You need a solid, reliable instrument that doesn't cost three month's salary or a lifetime's allowance.

Many rock stars don't pay for their instruments; they have endorsement deals where they receive instruments for free. Rock stardom definitely has its privileges.

Try not to overbuy and get the biggest, most expensive gear. Get what you need. Resist the temptation to buy an instrument just because it looks cool or resembles the one you saw your idol with on TV. Play it, listen to it, feel it in your hands. Buy the instrument that sounds and feels right to you. This seems pretty obvious, but people make some pretty bizarre instrument choices, especially when they're just getting started.

Be very careful not to get too blown over by the unbelievable number of products advertised in the music mags. The number of heavily hyped new effects and gadgets out there can be pretty overwhelming. Have some fun and try things out, but remember the basics. A new ten-pedals-in-one effect unit is not going to transform you into Jimi Hendrix, even if their ad says it will. Your sound is determined by your abilities—not by some new piece of gear. Great players can play a piece of crap guitar and make it sound amazing.

Used vs New

Buying a new instrument made by a known, reputable company is a pretty safe bet, particularly if you don't know much about gear (you can't go wrong with a manufacturer's warranty). I bought my first electric guitar new and it served me well for quite a few years. There are a million great used instruments out there if you look around, but you must exercise caution. Instruments can suffer from serious problems that aren't immediately apparent to the untrained eye. Buying used from a reputable music store usually gives you at least a short-term warranty, whereas buying through the newspaper is strictly a buyer beware situation.

Saturdays at the Music Store

When you make a serious visit to your local music store, try to avoid Saturday afternoons like the plague. The store will be crowded and the staff inattentive and full of attitude. Plus, there will be so much noise that you'll never be able to tell how an instrument actually sounds. There really is nothing like Saturday at a big music store. If you're not seriously looking for gear, the experience can be a real trip. Try going in and making as much noise as you can and watch the employees' heads actually turn right around.

I recall being at the house of a guy who was selling off his gear. He didn't really know much about gear and obviously wasn't playing, so he was selling his amp (a 50 watt Marshall JCM 800) which I was interested in, and his guitar, a Les Paul. While I was there, someone called him about the guitar. I overheard him say he hadn't played it much and that it was in great shape—all the usual seller's bull. When he got off the phone, I asked to see the guitar because it sounded pretty great. Wrong. It was a Les Paul all right, but the neck was twisted, it needed new frets, and one of the pickups was completely microphonic, all of which would have cost big bucks to fix. The funny thing was I don't think the guy even knew his guitar was crap. To him it was simply a Les Paul and any Les Paul was a good guitar. The amp, however, turned out to be a real bargain and I bought it on the spot.

There's no point in my endorsing any specific gear. Yamaha, Fender, Gibson, Marshall, Peavey, Roland, Korg, Pearl, and Tama are all pretty well-known, reputable names, but every company makes some products that are better than others. Instruments are a very personal thing. What feels right for me may not be right for you. Look for product recommendations in music magazines that do product ratings, although, I don't very often see negative reviews in these mags. I guess you should just look for the unusually positive reviews.

PA Equipment

If you're a budding young Bono, you're going to need something to amplify your voice. I've seen people sing through whatever they could get their hands on, like bass amps, pieces of cardboard rolled into the shape of a cone, whatever could lift the vocals up to compete with that screaming Marshall. Singing through a spare bass or keyboard amp can be a reasonable short-term solution, but if you're going to be doing some serious jamming, you'll need some real amplification. The singer's amplifier is called a PA for public address system and it's an expensive proposition.

A rehearsal PA consists of a power amp, a small mixing board, a graphic equalizer (known as the graph), a couple of monitors (those wedge speakers you see on the front of the stage), and some microphones with stands. Smaller systems (often referred to as combos or powered mixers) combine the power amp, mixing board, and graph into a single unit. While typically less powerful, combos are portable and pretty simple to set up and use. (You don't need a university degree in sound engineering to get things sounding okay.)

Even smaller combo systems are quite expensive to buy, so most bands end up renting, or in some cases, renting to own. To rent a PA, just pop by your local full-service music store (i.e. a music store that has a rentals department). They'll be expecting you. Rehearsal PA equipment is a common rental, so stores are generally well stocked.

An alternative to renting a PA is rehearsing in a full-service, by-the-hour establishment. This type of setup provides a working PA, microphones, monitors and even guitar/bass/keyboard amps if necessary. (See Rehearsal Spaces, p.18)

Improving Your Chops

When I was growing up, there were many other kids in my neighbourhood learning to play guitar. Some were better than others, some had been playing longer than others, some practiced harder than others. The ones that kept with it are now solid players, without exception. The ones who didn't, are not. It's that simple. There is a belief out there that great players are born that way. That's not the case, ever. Some people learn faster than others, and some have a better ear than others, but great players are great because of dedication; they play everyday.

I used to know a guy named Andrew who hung out with some friends of mine. He was pretty shy and unassuming. I didn't even know he played until one day he picked up a guitar at our jam space and surprised everybody. He could play Stevie Ray Vaughan note-perfect and with that *feel*. I was later floored to learn that Andrew was tone deaf. Determination made him good. Whenever you read the words "musical genius" in a magazine, it probably came from a bio written by the record company hype machine. There are a few genuine geniuses out there, but you don't have to be one to be an astounding player.

There are other ways to progress, beyond the usual determination and playing everyday. Everybody falls into a rut from time to time and needs a kick to break new ground. Invariably the usual pattern is to learn a whole bunch of new material, practice the hell out of it and improve quickly. Then you plateau for a while until you hit a new pocket of things to learn and you're back to improving.

Watch for strong turns of phrase and try to express universal ideas in your own, unique way. I keep a journal with me all the time to keep track of my ideas. Then, when I am working with a melody, those ideas will pop up in ways that I wouldn't have thought of.

- David Usher, singer for Moist on lyric writing

The songwriter must look upon his work as business, that is, to make a success of it, he must work and work and then WORK.

- Irving Berlin, 1920

Lessons

When starting out, lessons are a very good idea. It's very helpful to have someone point you in the right direction. Lessons push you and keep you from falling into learning ruts. Good instructors will expose you to a variety of techniques and styles of music, and steer you away from bad habits that can hamper your progress later on. It's amazing how quickly you improve if you play every day, and instruction definitely strengthens that improvement.

Teachers give you material to practice during the week. Many teachers will ask you to bring in a cassette tape so you don't forget everything you just learned on the way home. If they don't ask you to bring in a tape, suggest it, because it's very helpful.

Lessons last from half an hour to an hour, so there's a lot to forget. They're also fairly expensive ($20-$40 a week), so you may not be able to afford to go all the time. Practicing hard and going to the occasional lesson is absolutely fine. Use lessons as a rut-breaker. Whatever suits your playing and your wallet.

One potential danger with lessons, that isn't really an issue at first but can really matter later on, is becoming a clone of your teacher. If you take lessons from the same teacher for years, chances are that's who you'll sound like when you play. It's important to develop your own style. You are unique and, if allowed to develop naturally, your style will be too. Take lessons from different teachers, learn songs by a variety of artists, and write your own twisted original parts. Andrew was amazing at the Stevie Ray Vaughan style, but he couldn't really play anything else. The world already has a Stevie Ray Vaughan (RIP). Lessons are great for developing skills, just don't let them screw with your creativity.

Jamming

One of the best ways to learn is playing with other people. Take every opportunity to meet with other players. A jam can involve playing songs you all know, learning new songs or making up songs as you go along. An evening of jamming can do a lot for your playing—far more than a night of playing by yourself. Playing with others teaches you to listen and play in time (also known as playing in the pocket) and gradually gives you more confidence. Don't be afraid to play with people better than you, because you'll learn a lot from the experience.

Using Your CDs

You probably already own the best possible treasury of lessons in the world—your CD collection. It can be difficult to learn to play a song from a CD, but that too is a learned skill. The more you use your ear to figure out the parts, the more accurate you will become. No matter what you play, there are great lessons to be learned from the right CDs. Even the best players do it, because getting it right is pretty educational.

I like to throw the stereo on and play along with my favourite bands. It's great to jam with Ben Harper or Jamiroquai. If you're a drummer, jamming with the stars works best if you wear a walkman. If you play guitar, bass or keyboards, plug into your amp, turn on your stereo and play along. Bass players and guitarists will have to tune their instruments to a true E (a tuner is helpful). Also, beware that sometimes bands tune their instruments down to D sharp (particularly blues artists like Stevie Ray). Like everything else, the more you do it the better you'll get.

Books & Magazines

There are hundreds of books and several different magazines on the market dedicated to teaching you how to play your instrument, particularly if you play guitar. These are no match for personal instruction geared specifically to your needs, but you can pick up interesting tidbits. Many publications have sheet music for various songs. This can be very helpful even if you can't read music because most use tablature, a notation that's easy to understand and great for stringed instruments. Tablature shows you which notes to play and how to play them—where on the neck, with bends, and other effects.

Songwriting

Original songs are the fundamental currency of all bands. Without strong songs, even a group with unbelievable chemistry will fail to achieve lasting success. Unfortunately, songwriting is very difficult to teach and takes a lot of time to master. The art of writing, even identifying, strong songs is anything but scientific. Nobody can tell you how to write songs; you can only be given the tools to find out for yourself.

A strong song can usually be played in any format, from a single voice and guitar to elaborate arrangements for a symphony orchestra. Regardless of the presentation, the

It never crossed my mind to be a songwriter until Andrew Oldham [then manager of the Stones] came to me and Mick and said, "Look, how many good records are you going to keep on making if you can't get new material? You can only cover as many songs as there are. And I think you're capable of more." We had never thought of that. He locked us up in a room about the size of a kitchen and said, "You've got a day off, I want to hear a song when you come out."

– Keith Richards

strength of the song will shine through. Hit songs are a little more tricky, because their mass appeal can come from other factors such as personality, arrangement and timing.

In the hit-driven climate of the music industry, the ability to write hit material is an asset for any band, regardless of genre. Record labels often keep a band writing until at least two or three songs with obvious hit-potential are generated. To label executives, hits are what will sell an album and propel an artist's career forward. Strong songs are important, but hits are essential. The first step to writing hits is to develop the ability to write strong songs. The idea is that out of a body of strong material, a couple of hits will emerge.

Like learning to play an instrument, the more songs you write, the more you'll refine and improve your writing skills. Typically, new songwriters tend to be derivative and cliched; they gradually gain originality as they develop their own style or voice. Learning the craft of songwriting begins with understanding the classic structure of most successful pop (as in popular, rock or alternative) songs.

Classic Song Structure

At its simplest, the classic pop song consists of a series of verses, choruses and a bridge, ordered something like this:

- (a) verse
- (b) chorus
- (a) verse
- (b) chorus
- (c) bridge
- (b) chorus

Generally, the verses establish the mood, theme and tension of the song and the chorus works to resolve and pull everything together. The role of the bridge is to break up the a, b, a, b sequence and provide a sense of movement and departure from what has come before. Listen to your favourite songs and identify each section and how it works. You'll find that some songs deviate from this, but not usually by very much.

The Bells & Whistles

To further develop a song, some of the following optional sections can be added to the basic song structure: intros, pre-choruses, post-choruses (also called tags), and solos.

An intro is usually a musical introduction that starts the song and each verse. It typically consists of either the verse music without vocals or some minor variation of the verse music. A pre-chorus is a short segue between the verse and the chorus; it sets up the chorus. A post-chorus, or tag, is usually a small shake-up to the chorus and often involves the repetition of lyrical and/or musical elements to drive home the chorus hooks. A solo is an instrumental section of a song played over the chord progressions from the verse or sometimes the chorus.

A fully developed song might look something like this:

- intro
- verse
- pre-chorus
- chorus
- re-intro
- verse
- pre-chorus
- chorus
- bridge
- solo
- chorus x 2

To understand how each of these elements is used, listen carefully to different songs. Some songs will omit the pre-choruses or solos, but all will stick pretty closely to the fundamental structure. The art of songwriting comes down to manipulating the structure in interesting ways while keeping the basic formula more-or-less intact.

Once you understand the basic building blocks, beware of over-writing. Great songs have a simplicity and flow to them. A great verse and chorus can be obscured when extraneous sections are added. The song is an organic whole; each section should advance the song and lead naturally to the next.

Lyrics

Writing lyrics is relatively easy for some and can be a monumental challenge for others. Great lyrics are often very simple and yet suggest deeper more meaningful ideas and themes. Like anything, lyric writing skills develop over time. The more you write the more you'll find your own unique

The number one things that are missing in new songwriters' work are good strong choruses and structure that has a dynamic and a flow to it. And then secondarily, catchy and/or immediately meaningful lyrics that hopefully have some meat to them if you start to analyze them.

- Michael McCarty, president of EMI Music Publishing Canada

I always do demo critiques at conferences like NXNE and Canadian Music Week. This involves two or three people sitting in the front of the room and listening to a minute or so of thirty songs and giving feedback to the audience at large, because most people are too shy to identify themselves. People always leave after their songs are reviewed (of course, not immediately afterwards as they don't want to be identified). The last time I did one of these, I told everyone that they should stay as it's a perfect time to network. There might be a writer in the room whose work they really like and they might

voice. It takes a great deal of time and effort to express ideas in fresh and compelling ways.

Many writers keep a notebook with them at all times to jot down interesting ideas, turns of phrase or even unusual rhymes. Sift through the works of other songwriters to see how they work with lyrics. Watch how they express ideas in unique ways, use different sounding words and repetition to create tension and hooks, and craft chorus (refrain) lyrics in relation to verse lyrics. The best advice I can offer is to write, write, write...

A Final Note on Songwriting

From an industry perspective, the most important part of a song is the chorus. This is obvious, but the most common weakness in songs is substandard choruses. As a general rule, chorus writing is the hardest part of the songwriting process; it's difficult to come up with catchy and appealing choruses. Usually strong songs have strong, memorable choruses and weak songs have weak, forgettable choruses.

Extracurricular Songwriting Activities

Interacting with other songwriters can really help you develop as a songwriter. It can be very rewarding to both hear constructive criticism about your work and offer your thoughts on other people's work. Networking with other writers can lead to some amazing collaborations.

In a major centre it's easy to attend songwriter's open mic nights at downtown clubs. You can just sit back and listen or jump in and perform your own songs. These events are usually pretty casual and the more you participate the more you'll get out of the experience.

Songwriting workshops, designed to help writers develop skills and network with other writers, are put on by The Society of Composers Authors and Music Publishers of Canada (www.socan.ca) and the Songwriters Association of Canada (www.goodmedia.com/sac).

Music conferences like NXNE and New MusicWest offer demo critique panels where industry professionals listen to demos and discuss them in front of an audience. These critiques aren't always super intensive due to time constraints, but the panel often includes the same industry people (i.e. A&R and publishing execs) you would love to have hear your tape. It's quite illuminating to see how these people listen and think.

Money

One of the few absolute truths of the music business is: bands lose money. In the beginning, your band may not have many expenses, and later, once you become that rising star making fat headliner dollars, you might just make enough to balance your books (maybe even make a profit). However, in between, your band will have a ton of expenses and won't earn very much, so you'll most likely be seriously in the red.

Expenses can mount up in a hurry. You'll have charges for the rehearsal space, PA rental, guitar strings, photocopying, blank tapes (to record those legendary jams), sticker printing, demoing, gas for the van, drum skins, T-shirt printing and so on. Gigs you'll play from time to time probably won't pay very much. Your little band business will cost a lot more than you'll make. The truth is, like any new business, it costs money to prime the pump and get things rolling.

Band Tax

Welcome to the world of what I call band tax. Band tax is the money each band member forks over every month to pay for all the little expenses that come up. In this plan, everyone pays the same amount per month into a collective band pool. Consider it an investment in the later success of the band. When you hit that awkward big costs/no revenue period, you can get into some pretty heavy tax. I remember putting as much as $300 a month into the band. It sucked, but we couldn't have made anything happen without it.

Depending on your needs, you can get by with a pretty low tax rate. However, it's good to tax as heavily as band members can afford to build up a surplus in the band treasury. Many band expenses can appear out of nowhere and hit hard. Studio costs or T-shirt printing, for example, require a fair chunk of up-front change.

If there's a nice big treasury, there won't be a big panic when a bill deadline hits. In a five member band, a $100 per month tax rate will raise $6,000 a year. Few bands are forward thinking enough to tax themselves before the money is needed, but it does make a lot of business sense.

The Treasurer

Pick the most responsible band member as the "money lord"—the member least likely to drink, smoke or otherwise

be able to set up a collaboration. I suggested they might want to identify themselves, as then we can offer them direct feedback and they can ask questions of us—some did. I also suggest people go to songwriter open mic nights to perhaps find people they might want to work with.

- Barbara Sedun, EMI Music Publishing Canada

squander the precious band treasury. This person will collect and hold (guard) the band money.

The money lord also keeps the band's books, which is a basic record of money coming in and going out. At this stage of your career, it's not a big job and won't require an accounting degree. However, bookkeeping should be taken seriously as it shows that you take your business seriously.

The books also come in handy when someone in the band asks the inevitable question: "What do you mean, we're out of money again?"

At this stage, you won't be able to open up a business chequing account for your exciting new band treasury. You have to be a registered business to do this. You can always register your band as a business, but it doesn't offer you any big legal advantages or stop other bands from using your name. It mostly allows you to open a business chequing account and write or cash cheques made out in the company name. If you're interested, contact the provincial (or state) office in charge of business registration (see Business, Registration in the blue pages of your phone book). This involves conducting a rudimentary name search, filling out some forms, and paying around $100.

Another option is a joint chequing account with each band member's name attached to it. Withdrawals and cheques

Band X

Register

	Payee	Description	Bank Account	Show Income	Merch Sales	Hotel	Gear Rental	Crew Wages	Gas	Meals	GST
1-Sep		Open balance	727.14								
5-Sep	Long & McQuade	Amp Rental	(80.25)				75.00				5.25
10-Sep	Petrocan	Gas to drive to Vancouver	(42.00)						39.25		2.75
10-Sep	Travel Lodge	Hotel in Kamloops	(128.40)			120.00					8.40
10-Sep	Travel Lodge	Band meals	(53.50)							50.00	3.50
11-Sep	Esso	Gas to drive to Vancouver	(45.55)						42.57		2.98
12-Sep		Show proceeds for gig	1,650.00	1,500.00							(150.00)
12-Sep		Merch sales	267.50		250.00						(17.50)
12-Sep	Bob	Sound guy	(100.00)					100.00			-
12-Sep	Holiday Inn	Hotel in Vancouver	(187.25)			175.00					12.25
13-Sep	Petrocan	Gas on return trip	(44.00)						41.12		2.88
14-Sep	Petrocan	Gas on return trip	(43.75)						40.89		2.86

must be authorized by more than one band member. If you can't be bothered to set things up at the bank you can just pick up an over-sized pickle jar to hold your band treasury.

Deadbeats ← *n)ch†u que no pAnn*

The band will have to collectively decide how to deal with deadbeats. Deadbeats have chronic cash-flow problems and try to skip tax payments or borrow from the treasury. "I need to get my money out of the treasury otherwise my landlord is going to kick me out onto the street." I know this refrain very well—I was once a deadbeat myself. There are no easy solutions to this problem.

Financial responsibility can be a rare characteristic in musicians, but it's an absolute necessity. I can't emphasize enough that successful bands are successful businesses.

You'll have to find your own unique solutions for "deadbeat-itis." It doesn't take long for a couple of skipped tax payments to throw a member pretty deeply into debt. In fact, you can quickly reach a point where, realistically, the member won't be able to make up back-payments. Nothing can breed resentment in a band faster than some members paying in and others getting a free ride. Decide on a band money policy and stick to it before serious problems arise.

Band Gear & Band Debt

It's a big deal the first time you pool your money, go out together as a band and buy gear that belongs to all of you. It demonstrates a level of commitment and seriousness about the project. It might very well be the first time real-world business enters into your band's existence: Suddenly you enter the realm of assets and liabilities. Most bands' first taste of the real business world is going into debt, so get used to it.

Band Gear

You'll have to agree on which equipment should be designated band gear as opposed to personal gear. For example, it's very unusual for bands to use collective band money to buy the guitar player a fancy new amp (which is a drag for us guitar players) because it's clearly personal gear. In the event of a band breakup, that type of gear goes with the player. Later, when you're making more money or spending large album advances, you can get into gear bonuses to help cover the expense of new personal gear. In that case, everyone receives a cheque for the same amount of money with which they can buy gear. That way, personal gear stays personal.

Every band has a slightly different band gear policy depending on things like how much money they make or how hard they tour.

Items Generally Designated as Band Gear
• PA equipment.
• Touring van.
• Road cases.
• Replacement gear (if a drum pedal, for example, wears out on the road, the band will replace it).
• Heavy duty staple guns (a must for those late-night guerrilla postering expeditions).
• Wear & tear accessories (guitar/bass strings, drum heads, and microphones).
• Backdrops.

Band Debt

When you buy something expensive like a rehearsal PA system, you'll probably take on some liability, otherwise known as band debt. Unless your band has socked away a small fortune, you'll probably get into a rent-to-own or installment deal, which will require a contract with a band member's name and credit rating on it. Usually, it ends up being the member who has the best job or still has a good credit rating (this is also the person left holding the bag if everyone else takes off). Taking on band debt is one of the first times trust enters your band life in a very serious way (most particularly if it's your name on the contract).

If a member leaves or the group splits up, band gear can be the subject of some nasty divorce arguments. Try to agree way ahead of time on what would happen in a nightmare scenario, as it could save heartache and hassle down the road. This is especially true if your band gear purchases are going to ring up some serious band debt. (See Partnerships, p.24)

Rehearsal Spaces

The term *garage band* implies that you can just set up and jam in any old garage. I wish. Maybe you can if you live a quarter of a mile from your closest neighbour, but in reality, it's very hard jamming in residential areas (or anywhere within city limits) without getting shut down by noise complaints. I've heard of bands that put tons of work into soundproofing their jam spaces, only to have the cops show up twenty-five minutes into their first rehearsal.

A lot of high frequencies, like guitars, vocals and snare, can be blocked with minimal sound insulation, but the low frequencies, like bass drum and bass guitar, travel through just about anything. My friend Albert operates a professional rehearsal facility in an office tower in downtown Montreal. The soundproofing cost him several thousand dollars per room, but it works. It has raised floors, double walls and double doors—the same techniques recording studios use to create sound-proof booths. Unless you have a degree in carpentry and piles of money or a VISA Platinum card burning a hole in your pocket, better to rent a room for $15 an hour from someone like Albert rather than build your own.

Lock-outs

Lock-out rehearsal spaces are usually rented on a monthly basis. They generally provide twenty-four hour access, although the actual jam times can be limited by noise restrictions. The most common lockout spaces are warehouse lofts that are rented out like apartments, or rooms in multi-room rehearsal facilities rented on a monthly basis.

When renting out a warehouse loft make sure you can actually crank up and play in it. Many warehouse buildings may contain artists and small businesses that might not appreciate your, uh, music. On the other hand, beware of nasty sound leakage from other bands. I've rehearsed in band buildings where twenty bands played simultaneously in adjoining rooms without sound insulation. It's a big drag getting drowned out.

However, these spaces have their advantages in that you can leave your gear set up, decorate your room to set the mood, and party in it. They have their disadvantages though—be very careful about security. You may have to supply your own PA system and, of course, there's always having to deal with the mess you'll make.

The cost can be anywhere from free (if your lock-out is actually your parent's basement) to over $1,000 a month. Expect to pay around $500-$800 a month for a seven-hundred square foot loft on the seedy side of town.

Hourly Spaces

There are many rehearse-by-the-hour facilities across Canada that cater to bands who only rehearse a few hours a week. The spaces are usually kept in decent repair, with reasonably good monitor systems. They often come equipped with back line gear like drums and amplifiers.

The advantage to these spaces is that a PA and other gear is usually provided. Security isn't an issue, and many offer locker space for anything you don't want to take with you. However, hourly rooms can be pretty sterile. You have to set up and tear down your own gear before and after each rehearsal. The cost ranges from $5.00 to $25.00 an hour. Fifteen dollars an hour is average for a rehearsal room equipped with the basics. Also available at a higher cost is what is called a tour pre-production room, where you get a simulated stage performance with front of house PA, multiple monitor mixes and lights.

Sharing

If you want the luxury of a lock-out space but don't have enough cash, consider sharing with another band. We've shared rehearsal spaces with other bands and it's always worked well. Of course, we chose our roommates carefully and didn't connect up with bands that would screw around with our gear or throw massive parties in the space (around and on top of our gear). If the room is big enough, each band can be set up at opposite ends so that gear doesn't have to be moved around. If you share a PA, you just shift and rotate the monitors and everything should be ready to go. The biggest issue with sharing is the security of your gear, so be careful.

Security

Band gear is very popular in the thieving community. It's reasonably valuable, difficult to trace and very easy to unload. Everyone I know who plays in a band has been ripped off at one time or another. Occasionally thieves will wipe a band out and take everything. The problem is that it's hard to be inconspicuous when people on the street can hear you jamming loudly inside. It's like you've hung out a neon sign saying: "Valuable Band Gear Inside; Come Back Later When It's Quiet." Unfortunately, thieves have well-trained ears. So if you don't take all your gear home with you after rehearsal, security should be a huge concern. Here are a few ways that you can minimize the risk:

When judging a potential jam space, examine the doors and windows to make sure they're solid with functioning locks. Also beware of fire escapes and adjoining roofs.

Does the room have a security alarm? Is it actually wired into a central security company or does it just make noise? We had a nasty surprise once when we found out our expensive-looking alarm system didn't actually alert anyone.

Is there anyone around at night or is the space located in a desolate warehouse district where you could set off dynamite and not bother anyone?

Put yourself in the headspace of a burglar: How easy would it be to break in and clean you out?

The Great Flood

I'm convinced that over the years I've had more bad experiences with rehearsal spaces than anyone else, ever. When I was at university, I shared a house with four other students. The band I was in at the time rehearsed in the basement. The ceiling was only six feet high, so it was very loud, and jumping came with its own set of perils. It was nice to rehearse at home though. Things were working out fine: not too many noise complaints, and, we were getting pretty good. In fact, we got so good that we were hired to play a gig at another university, a day's drive away. This was quite a big deal and the whole household drove up with the band to witness the event.

One of my house mates, who was in charge of the heating oil money, had a particularly good weekend, buying rounds of beer and shooters for everyone. A few days later, when we ran out of heat, we knew why. It took about a month for him to scrape together enough pop and beer bottle change to get some more oil and get the heat back on. In the meantime, to survive, everyone bought, borrowed or stole electric space heaters to heat their rooms enough to avoid dying in the night (actually, another house mate rented an industrial strength propane heater and almost burned down the living room).

The problem with running several electric heaters simultaneously in a house with old wiring is that fuses tend to blow. And when you blow a fuse in a student house, you don't install a new one in its place; you move another fuse from somewhere else in the fuse box. So sometimes I would come down to the kitchen and find the fridge didn't work or suddenly the TV wouldn't turn on. There are always two or three fuses in every box that seem to run nothing at all. You unscrew them and nothing happens. Obviously these are the first to go and, because no one missed whatever the mystery fuses were supposed to be for, they never got replaced. One of them was for the pump that keeps the basement (our jam space) from flooding in the spring time.

It was a Tuesday and we hadn't jammed for a week or so because exams were in full swing. I happened to go down to the jam room to get something only to find it swimming waist deep in water. As if that wasn't enough, the light was burned out, so we had to wade through ice cold water with candles to try and rescue whatever hadn't been ruined by the great flood. There wasn't much; it's amazing how badly electrical gear and water get along.

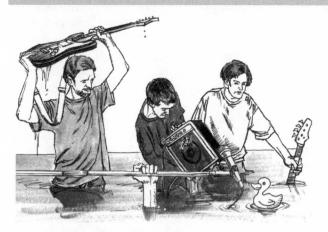

Naming Your Band

All I can say about this is good luck; you're going to need it. Naming a band is much harder than you might think. It drives me crazy. I've been involved in naming bands about five or six times and I'm still not very good at it. Consider some of my bands: Asparagus Lozenge & the Men of Pause, The V.K. (i.e. Victor Kayam, the guy who "bought the company") Fanclub, Cacaphonic Karma, Buffalo Rome and Moist.

After your band breaks into the big time and becomes a household word, your name becomes less crucial. You could be called anything and it would simply be a label for your sound (and an angle for merchandising). Think about the name Pearl Jam. After you've heard it a million times, you don't think about what Pearl Jam actually means. Now it means a five piece band from Seattle—the sexual reference is lost.

However, a name is extremely important to an unknown band. There's less opportunity to get into people's heads because DJs and VJs don't say your name twenty times a day. You want people to remember your name when they see it on your posters and stickers. Having a memorable or catchy tag can really help. By the same token, a tremendously stupid name can handicap you. A memorable catchy name can really help your T-shirt sales when you start gigging. Look at the various names you're considering; would you want to wear a T-shirt with any of those names emblazoned across it? Would anyone else? I saw a band once called Bloody Urine. Memorable, yes, but a name is very personal—only you know what works for you.

One advantage to having a short name like Moist is that it often ends up being bigger on posters than a longer name would. Poster designers want to fit one name to a line, so they use larger lettering for short names and smaller lettering for long ones. Unfortunately, this didn't seem to hurt The New Kids on the Block!

A lot of names are taken from songs, books, movie titles, or road signs—whatever. The Tragically Hip took their name from the Monkees movie *Head* in which the Institute for the Tragically Hip caters to the needs of terminal hipsters. My friend Jeff has a computer programme that randomly puts together groups of words. It created a pretty amazing list of nonsense and actually named one of our songs: "This Shrieking Love." Other memorable combos included: "Mother's Gun," "Twilight Candy," and "Pepper Horse."

A friend in Vancouver suggested the name Moist as a naughty name for an all-girl band, which it actually was for a group of women in Southern California. In fact, there were at least two other bands in North America using the name Moist: one in Toronto and the other in San Diego. We didn't know this at the time. We figured that Moist would be a strange (and therefore memorable) name for an all-male band to use.

There were two basic reactions to our name: the first was the nod and smile of amusement (usually from people under twenty-five) the other was "that's disgusting. It makes me feel funny." The fact is, the name was memorable because it prompted a reaction.

Partnerships

So, you're at the point where your band is pretty much together. You haven't started gigging, but you're writing and rehearsing and generally getting things going. Guess what? In the eyes of the law, your band is a partnership, governed by the rules and regulations outlined in partnership legislation. You may not be familiar with these regulations, but one little tidbit you might find interesting is that, without an agreement to the contrary, all your profits and losses must be divided equally between the partners.

This leads me to a very important point: As soon as you get your band together, draw up a partnership agreement that outlines exactly how your band is going to work. It can be as simple or complex as you want. The whole purpose is to avoid serious, potentially band-destroying conflicts down the road. Just because you all get along famously right now doesn't mean that problems won't arise later, particularly when money enters your lives.

Key Issues of Band Partnership Agreements
- **Band Name:** If a member leaves or the band breaks up, who keeps the rights to the band name? If you have a following and name recognition, your name and logo may become extremely valuable commodities. Some bands work with a majority rules agreement where, for example, if three members of a five member band want to keep using the name, they retain the rights. Others use a variation of the majority rules agreement where certain key members, like a lead singer or principal songwriter, must be involved.
- **Profits and Losses:** How are profits and liabilities (debt) divided between the band members? In a perfect world, all profits and losses are divided equally. However, this may not be appropriate for your band. Some bands divide income from live performances equally but opt for other divisions for songwriting income. Either way, outline these divisions in your partnership agreement.
- **Capital Contributions:** This includes band tax and any other financial contributions made by band members to the band. If profits and losses are divided equally, then your capi-

tal contributions should be equal as well. If profits are not divided equally, consider setting contribution requirements accordingly. A member who only receives 10 percent of the band's profits should only have to contribute 10 percent of the band's internal tax.

- **Band Gear:** Outline how the band will invest in equipment, such as a PA or a touring van, and how that equipment will be paid for. Many bands require unanimous or at the very least majority consent for large equipment purchases so one band member can't buy a big ticket item on the band's behalf without the rest of members' knowledge or consent.
- **Going into Debt:** Under what circumstances can the band take on liability?
- **Division of Duties:** Partnership agreements may outline responsibilities for each band member. One may be in charge of finances; another looks after booking shows and so on. But, since people often discover aptitudes and grow into responsibilities over time, it's better to leave things open and flexible.
- **Leaving Members:** What happens to the partnership when a member leaves? One person's departure shouldn't dissolve the partnership. When members leave, how will they be compensated? The leaving member probably has a share in both the assets and liabilities of the band.

Considerations for Leaving Members

- **The band treasury:** How to divide funds.
- **Band gear:** Assigning a value to band gear can get a little tricky. It depreciates, meaning that it will not be worth what it was worth new.
- **Loans:** Taken out for the band (bank loans or personal loans from a rich uncle).
- **The balance owing on a PA or van purchase:** How will this be divided up?
- **Songwriting credits:** a member who participated in the writing of your original songs is entitled to a percentage of any of the future earnings of those songs.
- **Inventory:** A garage or warehouse full of T-shirts and CDs counts as assets. There is no guarantee these items will ever be sold, so leaving members should not be entitled to any value attached to inventory. At the same time they should not be held responsible for any debt incurred in the manufacturing of that inventory.

Bringing in a Lawyer

Once you've decided on the terms of your partnership agreement, it's extremely advisable to hire a lawyer to put it in writing. It doesn't have to cost a fortune, especially if you know what you want and just need an expert to look it over and draw it up. Drafting a reasonably simple partnership agreement is a straightforward process for any lawyer. Taking the time to do this now could save you an unbelievable amount of money and heartache later. (See Entertainment Lawyers, p.197)

Chapter Two

Introduction to
Promotion

Promotion is a collection of different activities that turns you, your music and your show into something everyone is talking about. Big bands spend as much time on promotion, like interviews or personal appearances, as they do making music. Their record labels spend millions of dollars on various types of advertising. When you hear about a new album, it's because a team of people has worked long hours to get that CD in your face.

The most effective promotion can't be bought or manufactured; it's word of mouth. The best possible sales pitch comes from someone who isn't trying to sell something. When a person tells ten people how great your show was, it creates a buzz. Being a buzz band is worth more posters than you could ever possibly staple to a wall. The goal of all promotion is to generate a buzz—the most effective form of promotion.

A young, unsigned band obviously doesn't enjoy the luxury of a multinational corporation flogging their music on the public. You can, however, do some amazing things both locally and regionally. If you've been involved with and taken an active interest in your local music scene, you probably understand the music audience in your town better than any of the major labels do. You've got to use that knowledge.

Micromarketing

Writing great songs, playing great shows and making great records will always be the cornerstones of your success. Your music must be your primary focus. Marketing can't make up for weaknesses. The creativity, skill and energy you channel into your music are what makes your band great. But your music and stage presence alone are not enough—there are too many great unknown bands out there. The goal of promotion is for you to become known.

I'm going to cover the fundamental areas of grassroots promotion: postering, stickering, busking and merchandising. These are things that everybody does (and you should too). They're a starting point from which to add your own creative marketing ideas. Ultimately, your own unusual, original ideas will create the most buzz. Your promotional creativity can out-shine the major labels.

Terry McBride, one of the Moist managers and CEO of Nettwerk Productions, has a philosophy on breaking bands that can be boiled down to one central theme: micro-marketing. The basic idea is that a significant result (like national success) is the sum of countless small (usually local) promotional activities. Alone, these activities may seem to be insignificant, but together they have a cumulative effect. Postering alone won't get people out to your gig, neither will stickering or an afternoon of busking, but together they might. McBride uses micromarketing on a national scale. He'll keep a band on the road to work an ever-growing circuit of cities. His bands return to cities repeatedly for small shows, in-store appearances, and radio interviews.

An executive at EMI in England once told me that in order to sell a record to Joe Smith, you have to hit him from at least five different directions. A typical onslaught might go something like this:

• Joe hears a song on the radio.
• He sees the band interviewed on TV.
• He reads an article in some music magazine.
• He notices a concert poster or ad.

• His friend Jessica tells him how much she's into the group.

This might seem like a lot of pounding, but there are many new records competing for Joe Smith's money. Joe is more likely to buy an artist with a track record, like REM or Lauryn Hill, than to take a chance on an unknown band.

Micromarketing will help your band get a buzz going. Record company executives look at your hometown buzz as a measure of your potential on a larger scale. The buzz you create now can play a huge part in determining whether or not you'll be successful later.

Busking

I've seen people playing every possible combination of instruments, from guitars and violins to bizarre Ukrainian folk instruments, performing almost everything from zydeco, speed metal, classical, rock, folk, to jazz, on street corners, outside liquor stores or in subway sta-

tions. This is called busking, which can be a very effective promotional tool; a direct way of taking your music to the people, rather than waiting for the people to come to you.

Certain musical styles are better suited to busking than others, but with a bit of ingenuity, anything is buskable. The novelty of seeing speed metal performed on the street with furious violins makes for a more memorable spectacle than a folk duo.

Remember, busking is a promotional tool, a means to get your name and music into people's minds, so the more memorable, the better. There's even a little perk to busking: you can actually make a surprising amount of money.

The Busk

- **Location:** A heavy pedestrian traffic zone is a must. Passersby are your audience, so the more foot traffic, the larger your audience. Some areas, like subway stations and malls, require that you apply to the management for a license, and often, an audition is necessary.
- **Performance:** You're performing, so put on a show. Over time you can develop a great busking show that will probably even affect the way you approach your regular gigs.
- **Your Name:** Make it easy for people to identify you. Set up so that passersby will be exposed to your band name. Think of yourself as an interactive poster advertising your band.
- **Attitude:** Be approachable. If people want to talk to you, be open. If you're friendly and relaxed, you'll connect better with the audience.
- **Promo Tools:** Pass out stickers and gig flyers. It's better not to hard sell, but have them handy. If you have a tape or CD, display it. Don't expect monster sales, but a CD can make the public take you more seriously.
- **Gear:** Acoustic guitars and basses are the classic combination. Cellos and violins also work well. A mini drum kit (even a lone snare drum) is a nice touch. Keyboard players may have to resort to battery-powered mini-keys and amplifier (it can be a little tricky setting up an acoustic piano on the street). Battery-powered amplifiers make any electric instrument a possibility, but they can sound pretty lame. Sometimes it's better to keep it simple with acoustics.
- **Money:** A good busker can make over $100 from a long afternoon outside the liquor store. Don't expect to make quite this much on your first busking adventure, but it's quite feasible once you refine your busking skills. It's a little ironic that you can sometimes make more playing on the street than at an actual gig, don't you think?

The Great Flatbed Truck

The year is 1993. It's June and the MusicWest conference in Vancouver is in full swing. Three-hundred bands from all over North America are vying for attention at showcases all around the city. Industry players dash from showcase to cab to showcase to meeting. There's so much happening in such little time that it all becomes a blur. No one can even remember who they saw or what they did.

On Friday evening around 6:15 PM, Nettwerk Productions is hosting a MusicWest barbecue. It's a large, well-attended affair with all sorts of industry folks gathered in front of the old Nettwerk offices on 6th Ave. It's a who's who of the Canadian music industry and the place is jammed. Everything is going according to plan until Tank Hog shows up. And when the dust settles from another MusicWest, Tank Hog is all anyone wants to talk about or can remember. They are, in fact, one of the few bands mentioned in the *Globe and Mail* coverage of the conference.

Tank Hog wasn't awarded a MusicWest showcase that year, so they made their own. The band rolled up to the Nettwerk barbecue on the back of a flatbed truck, all set up and ready to wail. They had volume to spare and became the unofficial soundtrack to the barbecue. They played three or four songs and drove off. Advanced Busking.

Stickers

Disclaimer: I should state that the activity indicated as follows is not condoned or advised since some of it is illegal and could get you a free night in jail, a fine, and a possible criminal record (not good for trans border gigging). I'm simply relating personal experiences from early in my career. Be responsible, please, and think about the consequences of your acts. A sticker is a powerful thing.

Stickers are the ultimate tool of self-promotion (and vandalism). Over the years we've stuck (and distributed to be stuck) so many stickers that I really couldn't guess how many are out there. We'd go to a bar, drink, pass out stickers, drink some more and then go on a stickering rampage through downtown. No bus shelter, mailbox or signpost was safe. You'd get extra points for stickering in extra-hard-to-get-the-sticker-off places, obscene places (Moist is an awfully good name for this one), and places where the sticker would sit undisturbed in the public eye for months. My personal favourite stickering site was the back bumper of police cruiser 117 while it sat waiting for the lights to change.

We've always managed to avoid capture by the authorities and have enjoyed a pretty successful stickering career. We had trouble one night though, when we passed out about five-hundred stickers before a show. We played the show. No problem. The club closed after last call and the people left. No problem, except, there were about four-hundred and ninety stickers stuck all over the bar—on tables, on the bar itself, in the toilet stalls, on the walls, on the floor. Big problem. It was the aftermath of an all-out sticker rampage. And of course they were Moist stickers, so you can guess who took the blame. Needless to say, we were never invited back.

Stickers should be simple, legible and cool. Your band name should be readable from a distance. Use colours and designs that stand out among other stickers. There's no room for subtlety in the sticker game.

Buy the least expensive stickers available; just make sure they have good glue. Until a record label started picking up the tab for deluxe vinyl, full-colour stickers, we always went for the cheap paper crack-and-peel ones. It's all about volume and getting your name out.

Typical Sticker Costs

Paper stickers with black or white print on a solid colour background: 60¢ per sheet—three stickers per sheet (20¢ per sticker). Vandalism fines: $500–$1,000 per offence and up...

The Fine Art of Postering

Postering isn't exactly rocket science. A lot of what I'm about to say is common sense, but postering is important, and there really is a bit of an art to it.

Whenever your band plays a show anywhere, you've got to put up posters. Sometimes bars will put up posters automatically and sometimes (you being just a lowly local band) they just don't care. Either way, you must poster; it's essential. The more posters on the street, the better it is for you.

It's a war out there. A promoter friend of mine, Duncan, estimates that the average life span of a poster, until it's covered over by new posters, is about twenty-four hours (if you're lucky). The competition for space, particularly in high visibility areas, is intense. Every city has professionals who poster all day, everyday, for a living. You must poster very aggressively just to keep up and be noticed.

Be creative about postering in unusual ways and places; go for spaces high above the rabble of all the other posters; create cool multiposter blocks; go after heavy traffic areas like transit stops. Since posters get covered so quickly, be prepared to be repostering a few times to replenish the supply.

Three Basic Tools of the Postering Trade
• A heavy duty staple gun with staples to spare.
• Many posters.
• Something to stand on (recycling bin; plastic milk carton).

There's only one real rule to postering: Don't poster over other indie bands' posters unless their show has passed. The real enemy is the big glossy corporate postering machine, with those huge wall size glossy posters all in a row. You know the ones (although big glossy Moist posters don't seem to bother me as much these days).

Also, beware of the law. Some cities have ordinances and laws about how and where posters can be posted. The penalty is a steep fine. It's difficult for the police to track down bands and fine them unless they happen to catch them in the act. However, if there's a venue name on the poster (i.e. Friday May 20 at The Pig & Whistle), the venue can get fined. Since your name is on the poster as well, the venue will know who's responsible. Let's just say that you may not get another gig at the Pig & Whistle for awhile.

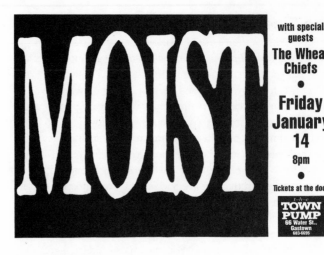

with special
guests
**The Wheat
Chiefs**
●
**Friday
January
14**
8pm
●
Tickets at the door

**TOWN
PUMP**
66 Water St.,
Gastown
683-6695

Poster Design

The most important part of your concert poster is your band name, because the majority of people are not necessarily interested in coming to your show.

You're promoting a performance, but the primary goal of postering is to create an awareness of your name. Make your band name big. Many posters masquerade as works of fine art. While they can be very beautiful, it's as if the band name is an imposition to the design. Don't stick your band name at the bottom of a poster in small type for the sake of artistic effect. Most people are in a hurry or driving by on the bus and you have five seconds to get their attention. They've got lives; they're not lowly rock musicians hanging around all day looking at the innovative design of the Bleeding Heads poster on Hastings Street. Catch people's attention with big letters that can be seen from a fast-moving bus.

Poster Production

Once you've designed the ultimate poster, find a super-cheap photocopy place and bargain with them. Tell them you'll be using their services for tons of copying in the future. Use 11"x 17" sheets of paper. Try different colours—neon paper is extremely eye-catching, if you're willing to pay a little extra. Don't even think about full-colour poster printing at this point because it's ten times the price.

Typical Photocopying Rates
B&W on 11"x 17" colour paper: about $65 for 500 posters.
B&W on 11" x 17"neon paper: about $85 for 500 posters.
Full four-colour printing on regular 11"x17" paper: about
$1,000 for 500 posters.

One final note: Don't expect any miracles. Postering alone seldom prompts people to attend a show, unless they already know who you are and are waiting for your next show. If you're a young band that no one has ever heard of, no amount of postering is going to fill up that club on a Tuesday night. Your audience will be your friends and anyone else you've begged, browbeaten and otherwise forced to come out to your show.

Postering is just one of the micromarketing tools you should use to create awareness of your band. It's time-consuming and hard work, but it does have a long term cumulative effect. It's a sort of investment in the future. Later on, when strangers do start coming out to your shows and then tell other strangers about you, those other strangers will say: "Oh yeah, I've heard of them," and the ball will be rolling.

Merchandise

Done right, merchandise (merch) can become a sizable supplement to your band income. On small-scale tours T-shirt and CD sales can make the difference between success and failure, or at least eating and not eating. Beyond the monetary benefits of merch, selling things that advertise your band is a powerful promotional tool. You must, however, take care to handle your merch effectively, otherwise you can make some extremely costly mistakes, like being stuck with a garage full of moldy T-shirts that cost a fortune to make.

The Five Golden Rules of Merch
• Don't even think about going into the T-shirt business unless you can reasonably expect to sell shirts at your gigs. If you've never played to more than about ten people, you can probably afford to wait a little while before getting into the merchandising business.

- Bands often make more money on merch than they make playing the show. This is especially true of arena bands that play to 5,000 or more people.
- Design is crucial. Most people would rather buy beer than T-shirts. To compete with beer, your shirts have to look pretty cool. The designs should appeal to the type of audience you attract; think of something you would wear. It really helps to have a great band name, an eye-catching logo and/or a clever slogan. If no one in your band is a budding Picasso, ask an artistic friend or, if you want to spend the money, a professional graphic artist.
- All-ages crowds buy more merch. Drinking crowds are faced with the inevitable beer verses merch dilemma—and you can guess how that usually turns out.
- Price your merch to sell. It's better to sell more shirts and make less money per shirt. Don't forget that T-shirts are a form of promotion. T-shirts turn the general public into walking billboards and the more billboards out there walking the streets, the better.

T-Shirt Production
The Three Stages of T-shirt production

- Transferring camera-ready artwork to film.
- Using the film to create a silkscreen.
- Using the screen to apply the artwork with the desired colour of ink to a T-shirt.

A printer creates the screens of your design which are then kept on file for future orders. You will be charged a onetime setup fee. For each additional colour involved in your design, the printer must create an additional film and screen. Setup and printing costs rise as more colours are involved.

The Raw Materials
There is a wide variety of T-shirts on the market, that come in different sizes, styles, colours and weights and range quite dramatically in price. The success of your merch operation can have a lot to do with the kind of shirts you choose. Unfortunately, fashion is constantly changing, so it's impossible to make any hard and fast rules; a successful T-shirt last year may not be as successful this year.

Size: T-shirts are available in sizes ranging from "baby" to XXX-Large. For us, XL, L and baby T-shirts are the best sellers by far. The breakdown is roughly: 45 percent XL, 35 percent L, and 20 percent baby. I'm always surprised that baby T's sell as well as they do (they were originally manufactured with small children in mind), but they've become big sellers with women over the last few years.

Weight (thickness): T-shirts come in a variety of thicknesses. Heavier T-shirts (6.5 ounces) are more popular than lighter ones. They last longer, but are more expensive.

Fabric: T-shirts are available in 100 percent cotton and cotton/polyester blends. All-cotton shirts are more popular but more expensive.

Style: Shirts come in crew neck, v-neck, ringer, tank-top, long-sleeve, turtle-neck, bowling shirt, and waffle. The popularity of each style depends on current trends. The basic crew-neck T always sells and never really goes out of style. Long-sleeve and deluxe items cost more to make, so you'll sell less because of their higher price.

Colour: T-shirts are available in many colours, the popularity of which changes from year to year. White T-shirts are the least expensive, but black T-shirts are the classic choice and sell the most. Navy blue, maroon and khaki shirts are also popular. A colour's success often depends on the design printed on it; some designs work better on different colour backgrounds.

T-shirt Alternatives: Ball caps, toques, patches (good for people who only want to spend a couple of bucks), buttons, condoms, matches, and the list goes on and on. Safe to say, you should probably steer clear of leather tour jackets until you become the next Aerosmith.

The Artwork

Camera-ready: This refers to a design that is finished and ready to be put onto film for printing. Your artwork can be saved as a Photoshop™ or Illustrator™ document, or it may be as simple as a clean drawing on white 8.5" x 11" paper.

Printing: Several different techniques are available for printing artwork on a T-shirt. While silk-screening is by far the most common and most affordable, some designs are better suited to embroidery or heat transfer (iron-on) techniques.

Colours: The only limit to the number of colours is cost. Limit yourself to two colours—you'll make more money on shirt sales. Save the super-deluxe sixteen colour designs for your stadium tour.

Number of sides: Printing on both sides of the T-shirt can double printing costs. If it involves different artwork, it involves twice the screens and additional set up.

Sample production costs for one-colour designs on medium weight, 100% cotton shirts (including the T-shirt and printing):

Setup fees: $25 per screen
Graphic artist: $35 to $60/hour
(if artwork must be created or isn't camera-ready)

T-shirt colour	12 units	48 units	250 units
White	$7.10/unit	$5.50/unit	$5.00/unit
Light colours	$8.00/unit	$6.40/unit	$5.95/unit
Dark colours	$8.40/unit	$6.80/unit	$6.45/unit

T-shirt costs will vary from company to company, so shop around. Compare the unit cost (price per shirt) for different order sizes for the same type of shirt. The more shirts you order the less they'll cost per unit. However, resist the temptation to order more shirts than you can sell. The last thing you need is a basement full of unsold and unwanted T-shirts.

Questions For the T-shirt Printer

What is the minimum order size?
What are the setup charges?
Are there discounts on repeat orders (once screens are made)?
How long does production take?

Selling Your Merch

It's important to set up a visible and well-positioned merch table at all your shows. If possible, hang a sign and a few sample T-shirts on the wall behind the table. You want to attract as much attention as possible to your merchandising operation.

Some venues have permanent merch stands set up to sell merch. These same venues can demand a cut of your sales, even if you take care of everything yourself. This doesn't happen too often at the club level, but large theatres or concert halls can take a fairly significant cut, even if you're the opening band.

Treat merch they way you'd treat a big bag of cash. Before handing over any merch to people outside of the band to sell on your behalf, make sure you have an exact count of everything put on sale. At the end of the show, double check that money earned equals merch sold.

The Merch Salesperson

In the beginning, have band members work the merch table; it's a good opportunity to connect with your audience and you don't have to pay anyone. When you play bigger shows, hire a merch person who can sell your wares while you're actually on stage.

Merch salespeople usually perform best when they get a cut of the profits rather than a flat rate for the night. This gives them added incentive to do a good job.

Having a friendly, cool, trustworthy, business-minded person selling your merch can have a huge impact on sales. Our friend Jonathan used to staff our table and he was amazing. People would hang out, talk to him and invariably end up buying stuff. He wasn't a hard-sell dude, he was just laid-back and personable—in other words a great T-shirt salesman.

One night we were playing a show in Kingston, Ontario and another friend of ours was looking after the merch. He decided to enlist the help of his cousins: two unusually attractive twenty year old girls. These girls went crazy and approached everyone in the bar that night. It was a new

kind of hard sell! Afterward, when we found out what had been going on, we were a little embarrassed (after all we were used to the super laid-back Jonathan sell), but we were also absolutely amazed. They had managed to sell over two-hundred T-shirts in a bar that held only three-hundred and fifty people. That's the wonderful world of merch.

Mailing Lists & Newsletters

Bands at all different levels of success make amazing use of mailing lists; I'm currently on three or four mailing lists, and every so often indie bands send me things. A mailing list is a tool for periodically reminding people that your band exists (and for giving them a taste of your winning personality).

A newsletter or homemade magazine brings information about your band directly into the homes of people who are

at least somewhat interested. In the real world, where mailing lists are bought and sold, this is called direct marketing, and it's considered an extremely powerful and effective sales tool.

Compiling Your List

Building a good-sized mailing list takes time, so your first few mailings might be pretty small and inexpensive. The mailing list is basically an unofficial fan club, but in the beginning don't call it that, because the term "fan club" often scares people away. It makes them think of excitable teenage groupies.

Place an address book on your merchandise table so interested people can fill in their names and addresses. Every time you perform, a few new names will be added to the list. Some bands place blank address cards on all the bar tables and collect them at the end of the night. This strategy gets the mailing list sign-up into everyone's face, but too many people fill out joke cards with names like Mickey Mouse and I.P. Freely. This is a particular drag if you don't recognize the joke and end up paying good postage for mail sent to fake people at bogus addresses. People are less inclined to fill out joke responses if you or your merch person are standing right there when they fill in their vital information.

The Newsletter

Now that you have a growing mailing list, you should probably send something to the brave individuals who chose to sign up. Enter the newsletter. Your newsletter is basically a photocopied, homemade magazine about you. It should include information about what you've been doing, the shows you've performed and are going to perform, upcoming recordings, and anything else you believe the reader will find interesting. Be sure to include your complete mailing address, email, and website information. Ask for the subscriber's contact information as well; include change of address blanks.

Make the newsletter entertaining, and don't take yourself too seriously. If you try to come off as big rock stars when you're clearly not, you'll probably turn people off. It might be a better idea to let people in on your struggles as an indie band. Sarcasm and humour work very nicely in Moist's newsletters. Include artwork and graphics to make it as palatable and easy to read as possible.

When a member of your mailing list gets a copy of your newsletter in the mailbox with the rest of the bills and pizza flyers, it's likely to float around the apartment until they decide to read it while sitting on the can. If your writing is shortlisted for the Booker Prize, they'll stay on the can a little longer. If not, it's wasted time for both of you. It'll probably end up in the garbage before they get to the all-important merchandise section.

- Toren Atkinson, *vocalist for The Darkest of the Hillside Thickets*

Pretty well everyone has access to the word processing and layout power of home computers, so people expect legible, visually appealing material. (Don't forget the spell check.)

Many bands include a mail-order form for their merchandise. In the beginning, don't expect many T-shirt sales, but, if you sell a few, it could pay for the operation of the mailing list. Later, when you develop more of a following, your mailing list can account for some sizable merchandise sales.

Depending on your budget, try to include free stuff, like stickers and postcards, with your newsletter. People love free stuff. A Vancouver rockabilly band called The Rattled Roosters sent me a calendar once, which was pretty original. Each month featured another photocopied picture of the band on the road. Be creative—the more original and cunning you are the more you'll win people over, and the more they'll talk about you: "you wouldn't believe what this band sent me..."

Once your newsletter is up and running, send a copy to *Broken Pencil*, a cool magazine dedicated to reviewing indie magazines, zines, CDs, and newsletters. If *Broken Pencil* gives your publication the thumbs up, you can expect to receive some mail asking for your newsletter.

Broken Pencil
PO Box 203, Stn P,
Toronto, ON
M5S 2S7
www.brokenpencil.com

The Internet

The Internet has become very significant for bands. The big labels are redirecting a lot of their focus to cyberspace as more people turn to the net to discover and purchase new music, so establishing a presence early in your career makes a lot of sense. If you create an interesting, entertaining website and properly promote and link it up with others, you'll be surprised at how many people will stop by for a browse, especially if the site is one of several promotional activities you engage in. If people see your posters and hear about you on campus radio, they'll often investigate you on the web.

Pretty much every band you can think of has a site, either operated by the band (or people working for them), or

created by fans. Often a band will have an official page and several fan pages. Depending on the time, effort and sometimes
money invested, websites range from the plain and simple to
colourful, comic book-like adventures with real-time audio,
video, animation and stunning graphics.

The Moist page at www.moist.ca generally receives
over three-hundred visitors per day. When we tour and do lots
of press, the number of hits goes sky-high.

It takes time to develop a large volume of traffic. When
you first set up your page, expect only ten to twenty hits per
week (or even per month) for a well-linked page. If you create
an interesting experience, people will tell their friends to stop
by and come back themselves.

Setting up Your Site

There are a number of different approaches to setting
up a website. Large corporations often farm out the design and
maintenance to a company that specializes in Internet promotion. Big corporate websites consist of a network of different
pages and links and get an astronomical numbers of hits. Just
updating and maintaining one of these sites is a huge undertaking. Fortunately, your first site will be a much simpler animal, so
you won't be requiring the services of expensive professionals.

Try to set up and operate your own site, or find a
friend to do it for you. If no one in your band is a computer
wizard/budding webmaster, remember that most band sites,
even official ones, are operated by fans. It's a great opportunity
for someone who wants to start a career in website design. Most
bands that hire friends to design and operate their website will
pay for expenses, but not the friend's time.

The Do-it-Yourself Approach: Getting Hooked Up

When you open an account with an Internet service
provider (ISP), they'll give you a few email addresses and two to
five megabytes of space for a website. This isn't a lot, but it's
enough for a fairly basic website. Bells and whistles, such as
audio and video, cost extra because of the additional space
required. Most site operators avoid hosting their sites on AOL
or CompuServe, because they tend to be way too slow.

Rates for Internet access are always changing and
often depend on how much time you spend on-line. Expect to

You can develop a really good on-line site and a relationship with your audience so that they feel that you are them and they are you, but ultimately you have to advertise it, otherwise you're living in the nether lands out there. People have to be pushed towards it.

- Denise
Donlon,
president of Sony Music Canada (former VP/GM MuchMusic/ MuchMore Music)

spend somewhere in the neighbourhood of $20 to $30 per month. Companies like Geocities and Tripod provide free space for websites (about 15 mb) but the downside is they paste advertising banners for other companies and services on your page. But, as an indie band, it's hard to argue with free stuff.

The next step is to register your domain name, which allows you to have an easy www.yourbandname.com web address. If someone already has the name registered, you're out of luck, unless you can talk the holder into giving up the rights to the name. Moist, for example, only recently got the rights to use www.moist.ca. There are many sites to register your domain name and the prices vary from $17 to $100, often in US funds, depending on the services of the registrar. A couple of domain name registries are: www.networksolutions.com and www.domainnameregistry.com.

Hardware

You don't need state-of-the-art computers to create and maintain a website hosted by an ISP. In this context, "host" means that your pages are stored on your ISP's computer and served out to the public from there. If you have a full-time connection to the Internet rather than a dial-up phone line you could even host your pages on your own home computer, though it's usually more cost-effective to pay an ISP to do it for you. Whatever you do, be sure to shop around. Pricing varies wildly from one ISP to the next, and most also charge extra for hosting custom domain names (eg: www.yourband.com).

Software

HTML (hypertext markup language) is the language or code of the website, and working with it is not brain surgery. There are a number of shareware and freeware programs available that allow anyone to create a page using a near idiot-proof drag and drop method; you just type in the information and the program converts it to HTML.

There is a growing variety of dedicated website operation and design software on the market. However, it's difficult to recommend specific packages, because the software world is changing by the day. As I write this, Claris Homepage and Dreamweaver are both fairly user-friendly packages, while more advanced webmasters (i.e. people with some knowledge of HTML) may prefer Microsoft FrontPage.

Content

The most important thing to remember when designing your website is to make it entertaining.

Typical Content

- **Contact information:** mailing address, email, and phone and fax numbers. (Too many bands set up elaborate websites and neglect to provide the means for people to contact them).
- **Photographs:** standard band photos, bizarre candid shots.
- **Biographical material:** what you're up to, who you are.
- **Reviews:** excerpts from any media coverage your band has received (don't reprint the whole thing, just the best bits).
- **Gig/tour dates and venues.**
- **Audio clips:** from your demo/album, rehearsal recordings.
- **Games/contests:** people naturally love contests.
- **Merchandise:** promote those super-cool T-shirts.
- **Message boards:** visitors can leave messages for the band or feedback about the website.
- **Mailing list sign-up information.**
- **Newsletters:** post back-issues of your acclaimed newsletter.
- **Website exclusives:** offer cyber treats, such as your band's own screensaver, desktop theme or even video clips, that can be downloaded.
- **Links:** link your website up to other, similar websites to increase visitor traffic; the more links, the better.

Upkeep & Maintenance

It's important to update your website frequently to keep people coming back. It drives me crazy when sites sit idle for more than three weeks. If nothing's going on with the band, say anything: "The band is rehearsing and making progress on the new album," or "our drummer is slowly getting over his bowel disorder," or get quotes, add pictures, whatever comes to mind. Just don't let the site sit there, or people won't come back. Andrea, the keeper of the Moist page, spends at least ten hours a week doing updates, checking links, and doing routine emails and mailing list stuff.

Multimedia

Multimedia (audio and sometimes even video) is pretty much standard on most websites. People love to hear audio clips. There are a number of audio platforms available.

Once you establish your site, you have to be communicative. Give them a reason to keep coming back. You engage in dialogues, little contests. Tell them what's going on. Give them digital snapshots of what your tour was like. Give them inside information. Give them the opportunity to be the first in line to buy a ticket to your next gig. All the little incentives so that they feel like you're their band. Because if they adopt you and you disappoint them, they're fickle.

*- **Denise Donlon,** president of Sony Music Canada (former VP/GM MuchMusic/ MuchMore Music)*

One of the most common and user-friendly is RealAudio. With RealAudio, visitors listen to samples of your music in real time on their computers; this is called streaming audio. They can't, however, copy the samples as files onto their hard drive to listen to off-line.

You can download the RealEncoder software for making RealAudio files for free at the RealAudio website (www.realaudio.com). Anyone can download the RealAudio player software for free, so your multimedia will be accessible to all. Be sure to link through to the website of the company whose platform you're using.

MP3

The most popular music platform on the Internet is called MP3, and, unlike RealAudio, it allows the audio track to be saved. MP3 offers a range of sound levels from poor to CD quality; the quality level affects the size of the file and the time it takes to download. The mp3.com site contains encoding and decoding (i.e. recording and playing back) software, much of which is free to download.

MP3 exemplifies the potential and limitations of the Internet as far as indie bands are concerned. That is, in theory, an MP3 file is a free demo that can put your music into the hands of millions. In reality, however, Internet users typically look for things they already know about to download. This means that in order to tap into the Internet's potential, bands must first do all of the regular, real world promotional activities to get noticed. The general public is never going to stumble onto an indie band's website—first they have to know it's there.

There are many unresolved copyright issues with MP3; it's opened up an entirely new arena of music piracy and has prompted controversial services like Napster. Don't make your whole album available for downloading. Instead, feature one full song and provide shorter clips of a few others. Place a song or two in a variety of music library sites around the Internet, including the mp3.com website.

Video

Some websites offer video clips that can be streamed or downloaded from the site. Unfortunately, video clips require lots of extra space from your ISP, which will greatly increase the cost of operating your website. Video is also notoriously slow to download and most people simply avoid it. Unless you have some video footage that simply must be posted, stick to the world of audio.

Promoting Your Site
Ways to Promote, In and Out of Cyberspace

- Include your web address on posters.
- Hand out flyers advertising your website at your shows.
- Contact other band website operators and get to know them.
- Post messages about your band and website on relevant Internet newsgroups: Newsgroups are essentially virtual bulletin boards. There are newsgroups devoted to just about any topic you can imagine.
- Link your site to relevant webrings: A webring links related websites so visitors can navigate easily from one to the next. Whenever sites join a ring, an official ring banner is added to their site, which automatically links them to the related pages. Webrings are a free, effective way of increasing visitor traffic. Try some web searches or visit other bands' sites to see if there's a webring that's relevant to your music.
- Check out Webpromote: This is a site and newsletter with free advice for promoting your website, www.webpromote.com.

Register with:

- The Ultimate Band List (UBL) at www.ubl.com, a massive database of bands.
- *Chart* magazine at www.chartnet.com: Link your site, and add a RealAudio clip to let people hear a sample of your music.
- The large mainstream search engines (like yahoo.com or altavista.com, for example). There are some sites that will link you to all the engines for free or for a small fee. There is no guarantee that your site will appear at the top of any search conducted. There are several websites, magazine articles and full books that deal with how to get your site to the top of the search list.

One of the newer things that's out right now is setting up a "street team" on the Internet. There are physical street teams flyering at events and such, but now we also have these web chat teams that are being put together where you get five kids and they go into chat rooms and talk about the new release, the artist, and so on.

–David MacMillan, marketing manager, EMI Music Canada

Websites to Check Out and Perhaps Link To
- www.mp3.com: Huge archive for on-line independent music.
- www.goodnoise.com: Large repository for on-line music.
- www.listen.com:On-line music source for indie bands.
- www.sonicnet.com: Music news. Got news? Let them know.

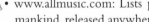

- www.allmusic.com: Lists pretty much every CD known to mankind, released anywhere in the world.
- www.musicvideos.com: Send a copy of your video. If they like it, they'll make it available for viewing or downloading.

The Email List

Collect email addresses of friends, contacts, and fans— people you know want to be informed of your band's activities. When people email you out of the blue for information, ask them if you can keep their email address on file for your monthly announcements. But resist the temptation to barrage people with piles of useless information and photographs that take twenty minutes to download. Try to keep your emails succinct, relevant and personable. Otherwise, you risk turning your new friends into enemies.

medio   comentario de press *(handwritten)*

Press Releases

Press releases are often overlooked as a way for indie bands to attract attention from the press. Whenever you play a plum opening slot, participate in a benefit show, even play a second stage spot on a festival show, send a press release out to the media. Local media are actually reasonably interested in noteworthy achievements of hometown bands. Sending out press releases will often get you a mention in the "what's going on" column—sometimes even an interview and feature article.

To hit all the media in your city all you need is access to a fax machine and a list of the fax numbers for the entertainment desk/editors at the various newspapers, radio stations and TV stations. It goes without saying that it may take a week or so to accumulate this information. Consider it a good way to improve your phone skills as you call everyone to get the info you need.

After you fax your press releases, wait a day or two and then make follow-up calls to ensure your fax was received. In actuality, you're phoning to make personal contact, but checking to see if they received the fax is your excuse. When you do get someone on the line, be sure to stress that you're available for an interview and/or to provide additional information.

Writing a Press Release

An effective press release is structured a lot like a newspaper article. Newspapers sometimes reprint segments word for word, so make sure your release is lively and well-written. Start with an attention-grabbing title, printed in large, bold type. This is very crucial because the media receive countless press releases and will quickly scan through them, looking for interesting titles. Make it a grabber. Additionally, if you can personalize each fax with the recipient's name (Attn: Johnny Rock Critic c/o *The Morning Fishwrap*), it won't have the appearance of a mass fax-out and may score some bonus points. It's a little extra effort, but worth it.

The very first paragraph should briefly encapsulate the overall gist of the release. The following paragraphs should then provide more detailed information, such as names, dates, times, places (the who, what, where, when, why of journalism).

Always write in the third person, meaning that you write: "The Red Devils have been working to support AIDS

> *There is nothing worse than getting a fax from a band you've never heard of to your attention, without a personalized message. It's kind of like batch fax.*
>
> *- Mitch Joel,* Montreal-based freelance journalist

awareness..." instead of "We have been working to support...." Providing quotes from the band can also liven things up.

A press release should clearly show why the subject is of interest to the audience. While it's very important to put an interesting spin on your message, please resist the temptation to exaggerate or downright lie. If you get caught in a lie, the media will give your band a wide berth in the future.

A press release should be no longer than one page in length, with "For Immediate Release" printed at the top. The next line should contain a contact name and telephone number. At the bottom of the page add: "For additional information, contact..." and include contact name and number, email address and URL. You want to make it as easy as possible for journalists to connect with you.

If the media do bite at your press release and call for more information, make sure you have a promo pack handy to send their way. (See Promo Packs pg 90)

Interviews

Interviews are a powerful form of promotion. Radio, newspaper, magazine, and television interviews are a means for you to speak to the public. They show off your personality, your wit, yourself. Appearing in the media gives you credibility; it's an extension, if you like, of the "if it's in a book it must be true" mind-set. People are often overwhelmed by the number of bands out there and turn to the media to discover interesting new groups.

When you eventually tour, you'll spend more time giving interviews than anything else (except maybe sleeping). Interesting, entertaining, insightful interviews can play a big role in propelling your career on to the next level, just as boring, inept or unpleasant interviews can really handicap you. Every successful band has learnt to deal effectively with the media. It's important, so start preparing yourself now.

Getting Interviews

It can be quite a challenge for new, unknown, indie bands to attract interview requests, because most don't have a story or a reason for the media to cover them. Typically, even the biggest bands only attract media coverage when they play a big show in town, release an album, or participate in a special event. Simply put, the media don't give you attention without a good reason.

The best place to start in your quest for interviews is to gradually develop relationships with local entertainment journalists and DJs who specialize in independent music. Campus-level media is the most approachable, followed by weekly street publications. Usually, journalists are freelance and write for several publications. Many people view the media as a big, closed organization, when in reality there are many writers genuinely interested in getting to know new, promising bands.

It's actually surprisingly easy to contact journalists directly (unlike entertainment editors). Call them up. Compliment them on their writing and ask if you can send them a demo tape. Invite them out to see you play. You can even

Don't always go after the music editor. Find a writer you like and go after them, because odds are they're not as approached as the editor, because they don't do it full-time. Just say: "Hi, I'm so-and-so from whatever band. I read your stuff and I thought it was cool." Journalists rarely get compliments, you know?

– Mitch Joel, Montreal-based freelance journalist

offer to take them out for a beer, whatever. I can't emphasize enough, the value of the personal touch and the shmooze. Once you do make a connection with someone in the media, keep that connection alive by touching base every few weeks or so. Also, if you have email, use it.

Giving Interviews

Good interview skills develop over time. The more interviews you give, the more you'll come across as natural, spontaneous and interesting. Many television personalities have received extensive coaching to make them seem natural. There are a number of training courses and workshops that cater to people in the media.

Think of interviews as a form of performance. Talking with perfect strangers as if they were close friends about subjects close to your heart has to involve some measure of acting. Picture the scene: You're seated in an uncomfortable chair under bright lights inside the fake walls of a studio set. Technicians and camera operators are running around just outside the halo of lights. A heavily made up interviewer is making small talk. You feel the knot of some nerves in your belly. Suddenly, someone with a clip board says "Okay we're on in 5...4...3...2...1..." and you have to act like you're sitting with a good friend in the comfort of your own living room.

Seasoned interview veterans come to life when the cameras are turned on. They answer simple questions with entertaining anecdotes and stories, and talk with an ease and spontaneity that draws in the viewer. A green interviewee can be spotted a mile away; they appear uncomfortable, look down at their shoes and speak with short, clipped, yes and no answers. Check out a new alternative music programme and watch for tense people and uncomfortable interviews or, better yet, find a local cable access talk show where everybody, including the host, is wooden.

Your interview manner is the most exposed during television interviews, where more of you is on display. TV is a more powerful publicity tool than radio and print, where less of your manner comes across to the audience. Fortunately, bands typically encounter print and radio (usually campus and/or community radio) interviews long before they do television. This gives you a chance to get comfortable and refine your chops before the whole world can see how nervous you are.

Using the Questions

To fully exploit an interview, treat questions as jumping off points for things you want to talk about. This is called leading the interview. Questions can be answered many different ways, so try to manipulate the interview to suit your agenda. Interviews are formulaic, so it's easy to learn how to use questions to your advantage. It's very uncommon to run into a question that falls outside of the roster of standard questions. But be creative—try not to answer questions in exactly the same way as the last ten bands.

Interview questions typically fall into one of four subject categories: your show/tour, your songs/album, your videos, and your history. Each category has a list of standard questions you'll be asked repeatedly. Be well acquainted with them so you can provide interesting and (ideally) original answers. Band experiences are often pretty similar, so most bands have the same old answers to the same old questions. Here's a list of standard interview questions. Get to know them and try to think up original answers to them.

The Questions

History Questions
1. Where did you get your name?
2. How long has the band been together?
3. How did you get together?
4. Do you have any advice for young bands out there?

Performance/Road Questions
1. What can people expect from your show tonight?
2. What's it like to play on stage? What runs through your mind?
3. What shows have you been doing/are you about to do?
4. How do you like playing in [insert city name]?
5. What bands have you played with?
6. Do you have any groupie stories?

Good press and bad press are the same thing. The only bad press is an obituary.

- Mitch Joel, Montreal-based freelance journalist

Songs/Album Questions
1. How would you classify your sound?
2. What are your musical influences?
3. What kind of music are you currently listening to?
4. Who writes the songs? Can you tell me about the songwriting process?
5. What is [insert song title] about?
6. What kinds of things do you write about?
7. How do you find working in the studio?

Video Questions
1. Do you enjoy making videos?
2. Do you think videos detract from the music?
3. What is the video for [insert song title] about?

Bonus Question
Do you have anything you would like to say to your fans?

Most interviewers prepare in advance, and use your bio to prepare their questions. An interesting bio makes for interesting questions. Be prepared to retell stories and anecdotes from your bio; interviewers often structure their questions simply to lead you to regurgitate bio content. From time to time you'll encounter questions that catch you off guard. Enjoy them, because it doesn't happen very often.

Content
Different interview situations demand varying degrees of substance. Different media require different kinds—and more importantly—different depths of information. There's a big difference between an AM all-hit radio station interview and a serious music journal interview. The all-hit DJ wants snappy fun answers to snappy fun questions, while the serious music writer is looking for more in-depth, meaningful answers (substance).

It doesn't take long to learn to automatically cater the depth of your answers to the specific interview situation. You only need to try to talk with Panic Pete, the AM morning man, about angst once before you learn some powerful lessons about depth. It's important to know the style of show or publication that's interviewing you before you open your mouth.

Typical Media Interviews

Hit Radio: superfast-paced, superficial q&a.
Alternative Radio: fast-paced, more content.
Campus Radio: slower-paced, moderate to heavy content.

Mainstream TV: super fast-paced, superficial q&a.
Music TV: (MuchMusic) fast-paced, light to moderate content.

Daily Newspapers: slow-paced, light to moderate content.
Weekly Newspapers: slow-paced, moderate to heavy content.

Music Magazines: slow-paced, moderate to heavy content.
Non-Music Magazines: slow-paced, light to moderate content.

Preparation

Before you step into an interview situation, practice giving a good interview. Have a friend ask you some of the more standard band questions and practice giving smooth, entertaining answers; use a tape recorder or video camera so that you can review your interview performance afterwards. Try to go over different ways of leading the interview from boring topics into interesting stories and anecdotes.

Think of different ways to answer the same question. This is really important if you're doing multiple interviews in one area. It's never good to have the same quotes in several different publications at the same time. Make sure you know all your own pertinent information. There's nothing worse than drawing a blank to: "So, where are you playing tonight?" Answer: "Um, ah, um...jeez, I should know this...um, ah..."

Soundbytes

Soundbytes are short quotable remarks. They often end up being the hooks of an interview; memorable moments that people talk about later. Soundbytes often end up as the headlines of articles. Slick interviewees are sometimes said to talk in sound bytes. It's worth preparing a few soundbytes of your own in advance by thinking up witty or sarcastic answers to some common interview questions. However, try to sound spontaneous and not overly rehearsed. Check out interviews with the Gallagher brothers of Oasis, Marilyn Manson and even Gene Simmons from KISS.

You'll never see an R.E.M. VISA card, because they're scared. What will people think?

- Gene Simmons in RayGun Magazine speaking about the new KISS VISA card in classic Gene Simmons soundbyte

Who Does the Interviews?

Interviewers seldom want the entire group for an interview, because it's generally awkward and impersonal to talk to four or five people at once, and most band members feel the same way. When you receive interview requests, you'll have to decide who is going to speak for the group. It's usually best to send two members. When interviewers don't specify who they'd like to talk to, send the most articulate and entertaining band members or those who simply give the best overall impression.

Different members might be better suited to different kinds of media. Some may do well with more in-depth, cerebral interviews, while others might be better suited for the fast-paced style of hit radio. Whatever your strategy is, make sure that the two selected band members work well together.

If an interviewer requests specific band members (usually the lead singer or songwriter) it's best to comply, at least until you wield some clout. Think of interviews as a privilege and an opportunity. If you try as much as possible to satisfy the media's demands, and provide great, entertaining interviews, you'll ultimately get more interview requests. Bad interviews mean interviewers will be less eager to talk to you the next time.

Bad Interviewers, Bad Press

Sooner or later you'll likely encounter an inept or mean-spirited interviewer who either doesn't have a clue or, worse still, has an agenda. There's nothing you can really do about this; it happens. Stay cool, give your best answers, and try to lead and control the interview. If the interviewer is openly hostile, feel free to ask what's up, but again, try to be diplomatic and stay cool. You can avoid doing interviews with a particular jerk in the future if it's not worth the headache. It's pretty much the same story with bad press; it happens, so get used to it. Not everyone is going to like you, your band or your music. Try not to take it personally.

Chapter Three

Gigs

Gigs and How to Get Them

So, you have a band together and you've been writing
songs and rehearsing. At some point, you'll have to take the
plunge and move on to performance. If you haven't done the
band thing before, it's easy to waffle a lot at this stage: Are we
ready? Maybe we need a few more weeks of preparation.
Maybe, but don't waffle for too long. Getting out and playing in
front of an audience alongside other bands is very good for
your group; it's initiation by fire. It's a good road test for your
new songs and can reveal a lot of strengths and weaknesses in
what you're doing. And mostly it'll be a blast—there's nothing
better than getting on stage and playing for an audience.

When Are You Ready to Perform?
- When you've amassed all your members.
- When the band is reasonably tight and confident i.e. everyone
  knows and remembers their parts.
- When you have forty-five minutes of mostly original songs
  that you can play in a set without a lot of long breaks.

The Age Factor

In most areas you have to be at least eighteen years old to play shows in a bar, and legally of age if you plan to consume alcohol. If you or any band members are under eighteen, this could be a bit of a snag. You can still play all-ages gigs, house parties and bar mitzvahs, but the number of potential venues is limited. Many bars are becoming more strict about minors; it's getting much harder to slip past the border patrol, no matter how great your fake ID is. If you're all fifteen years old, you'll have to be creative and make your own gigs. Sorry, I wish there were a loophole. Let me know if you find one.

Some bands refuse to play anything but all-ages gigs because bar shows discriminate against the younger audience. This is a very good point, but unfortunately, cutting off the majority of potential gigs for the sake of political correctness can really limit your opportunities. It's hard enough to find gigs as it is, especially when you're just starting out. Instead, play a healthy dose of both all-ages shows and bar shows. It's been my experience that there aren't many of-age people attending all-ages venues (with the exception of large concerts and festivals) and vice versa. By playing both kinds of shows, you're doing your audience (and yourself) a favour.

Three Kinds of Gigs

There are basically three kinds of gigs for unknown indie bands (beyond house parties, which I'll come to later):

- Slots on multiband alternative/new talent nights (at some bars, every night is alternative/new talent night).
- Slots in multiband all-ages events (if you're lucky enough to have a permanent all-ages venue that offers live music in your town, all the better).
- Opening for better-known, local, national/international acts.

In the beginning, you'll likely be stuck with the least desirable slots in multiband situations. Monday night at 1 AM can give you a pretty sparse audience, but you have to start somewhere. The music scene at every level is about hierarchy, so when you begin, you'll be at the bottom. Some people call it paying your dues; mostly it's a drag but there isn't a whole lot you can do about it, except play, get good and rise through the ranks. Never put on a loose, slack performance just because there's no one in the audience. Even impressing the bar staff counts, because at the very least, they're probably friendly with the person who books the room.

Opening slots can be amazing opportunities. Depending on the status of the group you're opening for, you could be playing to a full house with media and perhaps even music industry execs in the audience. Plum opening slots for national acts are usually given to more seasoned/popular local bands (something to look forward to), but opening slots are a real possibility, even early on. Often just knowing and hanging out with other bands can lead you to them. You might even find that teaming up with another band to get gigs as a double bill can be effective. Who knows? Be creative.

Booking

Owners or managers of bars or all-ages venues sometimes book bands, and sometimes it's someone who we'll call the buyer (promoter sounds a bit too glamorous and bookie just sounds wrong somehow). If you want a gig, you'll be talking to one of these individuals. Someone at the venue, like a bartender, can lead you to the person you need.

Be patient and reasonably professional (i.e. polite). If you storm in there like Oasis and demand a gig, you might not get one. There are a lot of bands competing for a very limited number of gigs and the buyer has no particular incentive to deal with you and absolutely no reason to put up with any crap no matter how great you may be. Talk to other bands and find out how they've dealt with a specific venue; every buyer and venue is a little different.

Demos

Part of being professional is arriving with a demo. If you don't have a CD, record your band playing live off the floor at rehearsal. Recording with a well-positioned ghetto blaster can yield impressive results. Experiment with your amp and PA volumes to create a decent mix where you can actually hear the vocals reasonably clearly. We used a four track portastudio and two microphones (Shure SM-57s) and recorded the band without vocals. Then we overdubbed the vocals on the remaining two tracks. It wasn't perfect, but it sounded good enough to be played on local campus radio a couple of times (although, admittedly that station would play almost anything).

The smaller the club, the better it is for the band, because it's not going to look too threatening if there's only fifty people out to see you on an early week night.

- Yvonne Matsell,
veteran talent buyer for various Toronto clubs

If you have time to make cool cover artwork, all the better. We used to colour-photocopy our designs. Whatever works for you. Just remember to label the cover and the tape or CD clearly with your band's name and contact information.

Many groups also submit a band photograph or use a picture on the tape cover. If you want to use a photo, don't worry about hiring a professional quite yet. Just find someone who's into photography and try to take interesting group shots. (Please avoid the five guys standing in front of a chain link fence shot.)

When You Get a Gig

When you're offered a gig, remember to take down all the relevant information.

- Date of show.
- Times for load in, sound check and your set.
- Promotion: Are you expected to put up posters, and distribute promo tickets?
- Terms of payment (if applicable).
- Other bands: Are you expected to share equipment like drums and amps? In what order will the bands play and for how long?
- Is a PA supplied with a house engineer?
- How many monitor mixes? Is a monitor engineer supplied?
- Is lighting supplied with an operator?
- The merchandise arrangement: Does the house take a cut? Who provides the merch seller?

Cover Bands

There's usually a big difference in the approach to gigs for cover bands. Cover bands usually play different clubs or at least on different nights than original bands, because the crowd that goes out to original bands usually isn't too interested in cover bands and vice versa.

When I was going to school in Kingston, the scene was different and very accepting of hybrid cover/original bands. Bands would play three 45 minute sets of cover songs and gradually drop in a few of their own original songs. Bands were expected to play covers but no one said anything as the list of original tunes grew. It was around this time that The Tragically Hip gained popularity in Kingston as a cover/original band. They played old Animals and Monkees favourites along with their own songs. Unfortunately, the same opportunities don't necessarily exist in larger cities for this kind of hybrid band.

House Parties

Some of the craziest gigs I've ever played were house parties. There's something about a good barn-burning house party that brings out the best (and the worst) in people. Add a band to the mix and things can go medieval! Keep an eye on your gear. Be aware of potential problems before accepting one of these gigs (noise complaints, police). If you're going to play one, consider adding a couple of rocking cover tunes to your repertoire. It's always been my experience that party-goers love songs they know.

Sound Systems

The nice thing about playing at a bar or all-ages venue is that the sound system, however beat-up, is provided for you. House parties are a different animal; you have to bring your own PA. Your rehearsal PA might be fine, but depending on the size of the party, you might have to rent better gear. Often you'll be paid in beer and PA rental charges.

The PA should be powerful enough for vocals to be heard over the din of the drums and guitars. It should include a pair of monitors so the band can hear the vocals, and a pair of loud speakers so the audience can hear them. Only vocals should be put through the PA (and maybe the kick drum, but that's very optional). Don't mic guitar amps or the snare. You'll need a powered mixer capable of handling four speakers. This set up should be powerful enough to blast most indoor parties. Expect to pay around $75 to $100 for a one-day rental; add a couple of dollars more if you need microphones.

Anything larger than the fifty to a hundred people-in-a-basement sort of party will probably require more PA than outlined here. If the party is in a hall, gymnasium or field, talk to a sound company that rents out full systems complete with a sound technician. They'll supply a system that accepts multiple inputs (to mic the entire band), and includes outboard gear like compressors, equalizers, delays, and full sound board for mixing.

This option is actually simpler than it sounds because the company's tech sets up and operates the system; all you have to do is play. This kind of luxury comes at a price—about $500 plus a night for a small system and engineer. Prices vary, so call several local sound companies to get quotes (look under "Sound Systems" in the Yellow Pages™).

Advancing Shows

Advancing is the process of following up on your booking by calling the buyer and/or house technician a week before your performance to finalize details. It involves double-checking all the performance arrangements. This may seem unnecessary, but there are false assumptions, misunderstandings and grey areas in almost every show agreement. Advancing eliminates the element of surprise and establishes a good working relationship between yourself and the venue.

Allocate the job of advancing shows to the most business-like, organized member of the group. Be thorough and keep notes of all the pertinent details. If you want to be super-professional, fax a copy of your stage plot and input list through to the buyer before you make the advancing call.

The Advance
Confirm the Basic Details
- Payment terms: What are they? If you're opening for someone, make sure it's clear who's paying you—the venue, the headliner, the promoter or someone else.
- The cover charge or ticket price and the ticket sales so far.
- Times for load in, sound check and the show.
- Other bands: Are you expected to share equipment like drums and amps? What is the set order and length?
- Is the PA supplied with a house engineer?
- Monitors: How many monitor mixes are there? Is a monitor engineer supplied?
- Lighting: Is it supplied with an operator?
- The merchandise arrangement: Does the house take a cut? Who provides the merch seller?
- Detailed directions to the venue, parking instructions.
- Back end: Later, when you're headlining and stand to make some money through back end (i.e. ticket sales and/or sell-out bonuses), it's important to find out where sales are at and how much promo is going on. Also, ask for a sales count and request to see receipts or tickets when you settle.
- The key points of the technical and hospitality riders (if applicable).

When you call, be friendly, sound enthusiastic and grateful for the gig. Also, it's really important to remember people's names, including the techs you'll be dealing with. It sounds corny, but knowing the staffs' names really helps; you need them to be on your side for the night.

The Gig

It's time to play when your ten best songs are running like a fine-tuned machine, the band is sounding great and you're bored of rehearsing.

A Typical Gig

• You go into a downtown club or all-ages venue that deals with local original bands. If you don't know of one, pick up a weekly street newspaper and check the listings. You deal with a bit of the "this is my club" attitude when you drop off your demo tape and contact information. Sometimes Mr. Club gives you a gig right away and sometimes he'll listen to the demo and get back to you.

• When you book your first gig, it's a rush. It has that "it's all starting to happen" vibe. Before you quit your day job, however, remember that this is not a headline gig. You'll most likely be one of three bands on a bill on a dead Monday night—but it's a beginning. Rejoice.

• When Mr. Club confirms the date and time of your thirty to forty-five minute set, remember to get all the relevant details.

• Mr. Club will probably give you some tickets to give away. Not all clubs do this, but most of the ones I played did. Here's the deal. You give all your friends, family and acquaintances tickets for $2.00 off at the door. They show up, watch you perform, and drink. Your tickets will differ from the other bands' tickets, so the club knows exactly how many people you brought in. If none of your tickets shows up at the door, don't expect another gig at that club for a while (as much as a year in larger centres like Toronto). However, if a bunch of your tickets comes in, it proves you're worthy and maybe you'll even get to open up for a local headliner on a better night. To Mr. Club your sound is definitely of secondary importance to your draw.

• Arrive for sound check (if you're lucky enough to get one). The soundman will probably have lots of attitude; after all, he deals with an endless line of bands and has his own natural

If the band doesn't show up when they are supposed to (without a VERY good reason), then things will indeed get off to a bad start. One example of a good reason to be late is a vehicle breakdown (you of course would have phoned ahead to let them know you'd be late). An example of a bad excuse is the drummer had to work...

– Mark Finkelstein, *longtime sound engineer for Moist*

defenses. He'll be a lot nicer if you load in and set up on-time and don't have a mountain of gear.

- If you're first on the bill, you'll probably be able to leave your gear set up after sound check. If you're in the middle of the pack, you'll have to deal with a changeover. Multiband night changeovers are fast. One band whips its gear off stage while another races to set up (remember the nightmare of Big Kit).
- Warm-up and pace in the seedy basement dressing room.
- Play your show.
- Strike your gear from the stage and load it into the van.
- Talk to all friends and family that came out to support you.
- Receive whatever small amount of money is coming to you.
- Thank the staff.

The Science of Sound Checking

A sound check is a technical run-through where the band and the sound engineer(s) set stage volumes, mixing and monitor levels before a performance. It usually happens before the doors are opened to the general public. It's a bit of a stretch to say that there's a science to sound checking, but being systematic and making the most of a sound check can have a big impact on your performance. The more organized and cooperative you are the better the stage and front of house sound will be. Also, house engineers love bands that conduct short and efficient sound checks.

The Sound Check
- Band sets up.
- Each member plays alone for a minute so the sound engineer can set EQ's, compressors, effects, and the like.
- Each member asks for a selection of the other players in their monitors.
- Band plays one or more songs to test their monitor mixes and levels and so the sound engineer can get a rough idea of the front of house mix.
- Band tears down (strikes) and stores their gear until showtime.

Small venues will typically have small, simple sound systems with only a few monitor mixes available, so sound checks are not that complicated. Band members have to share mixes. In really small venues, amps may not be mic'd and put through the main speakers. In larger venues, there are usually at least four or five different monitor mixes, so band members can have their own tailor-made mix of instruments and levels. Setting five different monitor mixes lengthens a sound check, making it even more vital to be efficient and systematic.

A System for Setting Monitors

The following system is for a venue large enough to warrant separate monitor mixes for each player. The whole sound check should only take about twenty minutes, but if you have more time, play more songs. When playing a small club with a compact stage, you won't need much more than vocal monitors and in that case you'll probably only have a couple of separate mixes anyway.

1. Lead vocal wedge(s): Listen for clarity, volume and feedback. If the sound is muddy or dull, ask for more top (boosting the high frequencies) or less bottom or low mids (cutting lower frequencies). If the sound is thin and harsh try more bottom or low mids. Ask about headroom (volume before feedback); if you have headroom, you can be turned up without feedback rearing its ugly head.

2. Background singer wedges: This involves the same process as step one. At this point you're only checking the wedges for vocals. Instruments will be added later.

A note about grounding: If you sing and play bass or guitar, test the shock factor by touching something metal on your instrument to the microphone. If it sparks, beware, because you'll get shocks if you touch your lips to the mic while you're playing. Carrying some foam windsocks makes good sense.

3. The "drum fill" (the drummer's monitor): Typically, drummers put kick and snare in the drum fill to clearly hear (and feel) what they're playing. After getting a comfortable kick and snare level, add some bass guitar. Jam a drum and bass groove to get a good level for the bass. To add guitar or keyboards (or any other instrument), jam a drum and bass groove and have other players join in. Adjust as necessary.

4. Bass wedges: Bass players have to lock in with the drums, so the first things in the bass wedges are kick and snare. The bass amp points right at the bass player, so not much bass is needed in the wedges. Jam a drum and bass groove and find a nice balance; add in whatever other instruments you require.

5. Guitar or keyboard wedges: Like the bass player, guitarists and keyboardists have amplifiers pointed right at them, so they don't need a lot of themselves in their wedges, unless it's a very large stage. Typically, a fair amount of kick, snare and bass are required, so start by adding these and then jamming on a groove. Once you find a comfortable balance, add whatever other instruments or vocals you need.

6. Side fills: On large stages, there are large side fill monitors set off to either side of the stage. Side fills are used to create even sound coverage on stage. The most common way to do it is to put a mix of all of the instruments in each side fill.

7. The half-song: By this point, everyone should have pretty much everything they need in their wedges. Play half a song and see how the stage sounds. Some people like to have the front of house speakers muted for this stage, but I find it more revealing to have the mains on for this test. After the half song make any necessary adjustments.

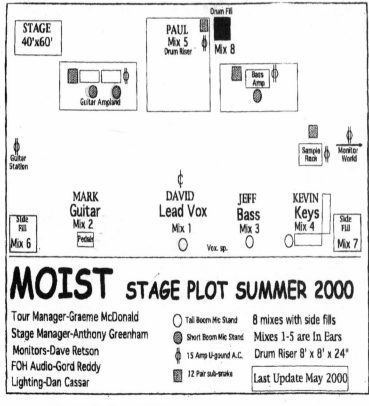

8. Songs: Play as many songs as time allows. This will enable the sound technician to adjust the levels out front and allow you to get accustomed to the onstage sound.

9. The strike: After sound check you might have to strike your gear and stow it offstage until you play. Keep all your gear together and don't leave anything small like mics or guitar pedals sitting out in the open. Consider throwing a tarp over everything to deter would-be thieves.

Ten Tips for Better Sound Checks

Gear: Before leaving your jam space, check your gear. Replace weak batteries, faulty patch cords, broken drum skins, and old strings. Don't show up at a gig with gear that doesn't work.

Input List: Bring a copy of your input list for the house sound technician, even if you've already dropped one off at the bar.

The Sound Board: Never touch the sound board, unless you have the house technician's permission. This goes for the band and your soundman. Breaking this rule will definitely get you off on the wrong foot with the house tech.

Stage Volume: This is a crucial point particularly aimed at guitar and bass players with powerful amplifiers. If you play at reasonable volumes, the stage mix and the sound out front will be much better. If you're taking everyone's head off, you'll drown out the monitors, which in turn means singers will either sing off-key, be forced to scream, or blow out their voices. When your amp is too loud, particularly in smaller venues, the sound engineer out front will be forced to take you out of the house mix. The sound from your amp will not be amplified through the main speakers and the overall sound of the band will be patchy and less cohesive, with some instruments too loud in some places of the house and too quiet in others. Some musicians use plexiglass shields in front of guitar cabinets and drums to control stage volume. I've been told Moist is pretty loud and I only use a 50 watt Marshall set to 3 out of 11.

Simplicity: Keep things simple. Don't put instruments in your monitors just because you can. Only put in things you can't hear clearly. If possible, every player, including the keyboardist, should have an amp, and not rely on the PA for their own stage sound.

Speed: Don't screw around during sound check. Get everything right and leave the stage. This is especially important for multiband gigs where there's usually a rigid time limit. If monitor levels are set quickly, you can play more songs for the house engineer, who will then become more familiar with your sound.

Amp position: Angle the amplifiers inwards so other players can hear you without putting you in their monitors. On monster outdoor and theatre stages this is less effective, but it works great in clubs.

Spiking the stage: If there's more than one band on the bill, you'll likely have to tear down after sound check. Once you find the perfect position for your amps, spike them; get some duct tape and mark the amp positions on the stage so that you can quickly put them back into position.

Cue sheet: If using a house engineer, provide a copy of your set list with simple notes beside each song that outline any special effects you want and which instruments have a solo.

Be nice: Be friendly towards the house engineers even if they're not particularly nice to you. Remember to say thanks for a job well done—you'll definitely get better sound next time.

The Sound Engineer

If you're playing gigs around town, you've probably encountered bands that bring their own sound engineer. A sound engineer is often the first person that bands bring onto their team. Sooner or later, you'll bring a sound engineer on board too. The question is: when?

You need to do everything in your power to make your live show the best that it can be. It makes sense to put your best foot forward when climbing the ranks. In the beginning, your live show is basically the only public dimension of your band. Later, people will know you by your albums, videos, and interviews, but now, your only public face is live performance.

Reasons for Getting Your own Sound Engineer
- Good sound is vital to the success of your live show. Even a riveting performance can get lost in substandard sound.
- Your own engineer understands exactly the sound you want to convey and will make sure that's what the audience hears.
- They know your material and arrangements and can boost solos and apply special audio effects right on cue.
- You get consistent sound night after night, venue to venue.
- You don't have to suck up to house engineers just to get a decent mix.

- Your own engineer brings peace of mind. They're employed by you and dedicated to your interests, so you don't have to wonder if the house engineer is putting in the effort.
- An engineer brings a general technical expertise to your team. If something breaks down, chances are they can fix it.

Finding a Sound Engineer

It's easy to find sound engineers who are, in theory, capable of giving you reasonably good sound at the club level.
- Talk to other bands about their sound engineers.
- Ask a house engineer you like if they do gigs on the side.
- Contact local sound companies.
- Put up a notice at a sound school like Trebas.
- Check the music classifieds in the weekly street papers.

Reality Check: Live Sound

Live sound is an art. In theory, it's pretty easy to grasp: you mic stuff on stage and amplify it through the PA. In practice, live sound is full of pitfalls and challenges that make it extremely difficult to master. Each venue has its own unique set of problems and sonic idiosyncrasies with equipment in various stages of disrepair. It's rare to encounter new gear in full working order. An engineer must have enough experience to know how to deal with these handicaps. If you hire your own sound engineer, choose wisely. Otherwise, you may do more harm than good to your live show.

The Four Flavours of Sound Engineers
The Experienced Professional

Experienced, professional engineers have mixed every style of band using every imaginable kind of equipment. They know what to expect, because they've mixed bands in every kind of venue. Different engineers have different styles of mixing, but professionals generally adapt to any mixing situation.

Unfortunately, good, professional sound engineers are expensive; they charge $175 and up for a gig. We've paid as much as $3,200 a week for a top-flight sound engineer. Occasionally, pros will give young bands a break and offer reduced rates. However, there aren't that many competent engineers around and the good ones are often busy with steady house gigs or out on the road with successful touring bands.

According to longtime Moist sound engineer, Mark Finkelstein, a non-drawing band would almost never bring in an experienced, professional engineer. In the beginning, bands simply can't afford to pay for that level of professionalism. Don't spend $175 on a sound engineer until you can draw at least two-hundred people and you're seeing enough money to offset the expense. However, for a special event, like a plum opening spot that will give you great exposure, it might be worth paying the big bucks for the one-off.

The Trained Rookie

It's common for a young band to hire a knowledgeable, amateur engineer. Amateurs range from inexperienced, recent sound school graduates to studio engineers with limited live experience. The trained rookie is the experienced professional of the future and can be a great option for bands on the showcase circuit. But exercise caution; engineering in the controlled environment of a school or studio is very different than mixing on the live circuit. Before hiring anyone, listen to them mixing another band. All rookies aren't created equal, even if they did graduate from some accredited sound academy.

The charges for this grade of engineer are typically in the $75 to $100 range per gig, but these rates are negotiable, depending on the engineer's experience (and whether they're into your band).

The Friend of the Band

An astounding number of bands hire a friend of the band who has no knowledge of sound. Putting someone who doesn't know what they're doing behind the board is bad. Don't do it. You'll get crappy sound (even if said sound person knows your songs) and you could damage your relationship with the venue. Cost: $75 per show down to, well, beer (or in some cases a punch in the stomach and your reputation).

The House Engineer

House engineers are typically experienced professionals who take house gigs when they're not touring. The house engineer may not know your material, but they have intimate knowledge of the sound system and can make a band sound decent with their eyes closed. Almost all venues employ house engineers and their services come free of charge. They might be jaded, grumpy and full of intimidating attitude, but they're often the best option on the showcase circuit.

Basic Teching

All serious bands carry a handy collection of tools and supplies to get them through any technical emergency. Being professional involves anticipating problems and being prepared to deal with emergencies when they arise. Before you pack up your gear and head to the gig, put together a case of teching items. Murphy's law definitely applies to performing live. Basically, if something can break down, it will. Also, the more important the show, the more things break down.

Although it's expensive to carry spares of every piece of equipment, try to have spares for as much gear as you can, particularly anything indispensable. If you're unlucky enough to have an amplifier blow out, try to borrow one from another band. If your gear is kept in good repair, the chances of a major catastrophe are greatly reduced. Get any problems (like amps that only work sometimes) fixed before you play a show. Remember, if it might not work, then it won't work, guaranteed.

If you know someone who can act as a stage tech for the show, all the better. They can help with change over (set up and tear down), tune guitars and basses and just be there as extra hands in case something does go wrong.

The following is a checklist of essential teching items. Use a case with various compartments, trays or shelves to keep items organized and accessible. Keep this case close by before and during your performance (not in the dressing room down in the basement).

The General Tool Kit
- Screwdrivers (various heads).
- Allen keys.
- Regular pliers.
- Needle nose pliers.
- Soldering iron with resin core solder.
  (If you've never used a soldering iron, learn.)
- AC plugs (2).
- Electrical tape.
- Duct tape.
- Permanent black marker.
- Nine volt batteries (3).
- Cleaning spray.
- Power bars (2).
- Extension cords (2).

Teching Items for Each Instrument

Guitar & Bass

- Spare guitars/basses: Each player should have a backup instrument tuned and ready to play. There's nothing worse than having to stand around on stage while a guitar player changes a broken string and tunes up.
- Guitar stands for spare instruments.
- Guitar strings: two spare sets for each player.
- Bass strings: one or two spare sets; they're expensive, but it's a good idea to have at least one set on hand.
- Nine volt batteries: three or four depending on the number of stomp boxes and active pickups you use.
- Guitar tuner: The Boss TU-12H is the most common.
- Shielded instrument cables (¼" to ¼"): Carry at least one spare cable for each length you use.
- Speaker cables: one or two. Unshielded speaker cables are different than shielded instrument cables. Ordinary shielded guitar cables used as speaker cables can damage your amp.
- Spare fuses: two for each amplifier. Every amp contains a main fuse that can blow out every so often. Each amplifier probably requires a different kind of fuse (i.e. 2 amp slowblo, 3 amp) so carry spares for each type. Always replace a fuse with one of the same rating. Fuses blow because of power surges, low or high voltages, a faulty A/C cord, and old, faulty tubes. Continual fuse blowing is a problem; get it fixed.
- Secret internal fuses: Unlike the easy-access main fuses, many amps also contain internal fuses that can occasionally blow. Open it up, find the internal fuses and get spares.
- Tubes: Some bands carry a spare set of tubes. This is optional, because tubes rarely blow; they just slowly wear out. After moving your amp around, always check for loose tubes.

Drums

- Spare heads: Tom heads aren't critical, but definitely keep a spare snare and kick drum head.
- Drum key: Drummers always seem to forget their drum keys, so keep a spare in the tech case.
- Spare snare: Many drummers carry a spare snare drum, so that if they do break a snare head, they can change the whole drum quickly without disrupting the performance.

Keyboards

- Amplifier and cable issues are the same as with guitars and basses (see previous page).
- Spare keyboard: If you don't have a spare board or can't afford one, make sure your board is reliable and in good repair.
- Backups for indispensable sounds: These can be in the form of a RAM card, sampler or sound module.
- Spare pedals.

Draw & The Gigging Paradox

Draw is the most important yardstick for gauging an indie band's success. If you can attract a bit of a crowd to your performances, the industry will notice you. For bar owners and promoters, draw equals beer and ticket sales. When big touring bands ask for local opening acts, they want bands that have a draw, to augment their draw. When people take a chance and come out to see a local band, they're more likely to come back if the place is happening (i.e. you draw).

Your worth as a band is also measured in artistic terms, but in the beginning, this is secondary to the reality of your draw. There are some pretty great bands out there who haven't developed a draw, so their chances of being discovered and gaining success are not very good. Even a band with an arsenal of potential hit songs waiting to happen can be severely handicapped if they don't attract people to their shows. Draw makes people sit up and take notice.

Building Your Draw

Building your draw takes time. The promotional activities outlined in chapter two are a means of developing your draw. In addition to these, don't forget to be approachable before and after your set. Talk to people, get their feedback, get them to sign onto your mailing list or buy a T-shirt. It's amazing how far the personal approach will take you. And by the way, putting on an electrifying performance that leaves the audience begging for more doesn't hurt your draw either!

Artificial Draw

When you're just beginning to develop a following, you have to rely heavily on friends, acquaintances and family to come out and support you. This is artificial draw, because they're really there as a favour to you. Always make every effort to get everyone you know out to see you play. Think of artificial draw as priming the pump, so that later you'll enjoy real draw. People are more likely to come see you again if your shows are packed; it's a snowball effect. Draw makes your show an event.

Incidental Draw

Incidental draw is the built-in clientele at a venue. These are the people who would be there with or without you. Most live venues don't have incidental draw, especially on week nights when there's a cover charge (however minuscule).

Draw Burnout

The more your band gigs, the better you get. Nothing beats performance for making a band tighter, more confident and more dynamic. You can always spot a band that's new to the stage, just as you can spot a seasoned band. So, the answer would seem to be to play all over town, all the time. Go for opening slots, multiband nights, parties; play anywhere anytime.

Unfortunately, playing too often in the same city burns out your draw. Even successful bands are very concerned about this. A band playing too frequently can literally play themselves out of a following (real and artificial). People get tired of you when you overexpose yourself. You can't expect loads of people to come out every week (they probably have something better to do, even if you don't), so be careful. Your draw is vital.

The Gigging Paradox

In order to improve as a band you must perform all the time; but if you perform all the time, you'll harm your band. I can't really suggest the optimum amount you should play. It depends on the size of your hometown and the kind of shows you're doing. If you play a ton of opening slots in a month, it will have a different effect than headlining your own nights. Feel it out. I've heard of bands that play practice shows under a pseudonym to save their draw for real shows. Beware: this little trick can tick off bar owners if they figure it out.

It's better to play once a month to a hundred people than once a week to twenty. If you fail to draw, the clubs will simply stop booking you. It was the gigging paradox that finally led us to buy the Great White Van and hit the road. On the road, you can play every night in a different city and not burn out your draw. But we'll get to the road later.

Presentation

One of the easiest ways to tell an experienced band from an inexperienced one is presentation. It's amazing how much thought and effort goes into a big band's presentation and how young bands don't even seem to think about it. The way you present yourself has an enormous effect on how the public will think of you, label you and finally, if they'll identify with you and like you. Obviously your music is important; a great image won't make up for shaky songs, but don't underestimate the role presentation plays in your relationship with the public.

Appearance & Self-Styling

Before a professional band films a video or goes for a photo shoot, they invariably meet with a stylist. The stylist arrives with racks of hip, trendy, new, used, and sometimes very stylish clothes for the band members to wear for the camera. A lot of energy goes into crafting a band's visual image. One of the aims is to create a look that suits the band. Watch some videos or pick up a copy of *Spin* magazine and examine the way various bands are portrayed. Look at the way all the band members seem to fit together as a unit. Styling isn't accidental, despite the fact that it's often meant to look that way.

How many times have you seen a local band that looks like a kind of visual history of rock? There's the longhair Led Zeppelin rocker, the punk, the skin head, the Weezer nerd rocker—you get the picture. Perhaps that's the hook, but it's more likely a reflection of the different backgrounds and tastes of the members. Unless you're going for a Village People cross-section of personalities look, you'll want to hone your image with some self-styling.

Styling doesn't have to make you into something you're not. It's more concerned with subtly directing and refining a collection of existing looks so that they work together. It's perfectly acceptable to have a diverse look in the band, but your image should make sense to your audience. Different looks come with a whole set of associations attached to them, and if there are too many contradictory messages happening at once, it can make it difficult for viewers to get their heads around what

A lot of bands come to me directly, fresh, coming straight to the A clubs. I can't help them unless they've got their act together and they are actually drawing crowds. So, find the little bars and pubs that might do live music, where you're just playing to the locals, and do that for several months. You can find all of these places on the outskirts; it's mostly little bars, here there and everywhere. And you just try to build up your audience that way.

- Yvonne Matsell,
veteran talent buyer for various Toronto clubs

you are. There's a big difference between having a unique look and having a confusing, screwed-up image.

Self-styling is not easy to do. People are often quite attached to and protective of their appearances. In most bands styling happens gradually, on its own. The more you hang out with people, the more you begin to grow together into a unit. In a lot of cases, styling can boil down to things as simple as gig shirts and a couple of haircuts.

The Stage

Arena-scale bands employ professional designers to create striking and effective environments for their concerts. A stage designer works in coordination with a lighting designer and the band to create an overall visual theme for a tour. On large tours, bands often have to dedicate several eighteen-wheelers to carry the many elaborate stage sets, risers and props from city to city. The idea is that the visual components will work with the music to create a bigger, more striking and impressive performance.

So what are you doing? You don't need to call up expensive set and lighting designers to work on your show at The Elbow Room on alternative night, but try to do every-thing in your power to make your show as memorable and impressive as possible. It's unusual to see any interesting set dressing at a multiband night; most bands either haven't put any thought into stage presentation or simply can't be bothered. But a few simple, easy touches can really help you stand out.

The Backdrop

A personalized backdrop hung in front of the venue backdrop (if there even is one) is an easy and surprisingly effec-tive place to start. If you want, you can print your name across the backdrop (aesthetics are a personal thing), but the backdrop should somehow make the stage seems like it belongs to you.

A backdrop can be as simple as two dyed bed sheets sewn together, or, if you're itching to spend money, you can pay great heaps of cash (often into the thousands) at a theatrical supply store for the super heavy-duty real McCoy. I recommend the cheap and simple route because you'll want to change your backdrop design periodically for freshness. And by the way, when it comes to backdrops, bigger is always better.

When The Tragically Hip were playing Monkees covers in local Kingston bars, they used to hang 60s flowered psychedelic shower curtains behind them on stage. It worked because it suited the music style they were playing at the time.

Props & Effects

Your stage design is only limited by your imagination (and your bank account). Mind you, if you have a really complicated stage design with all sorts of props, you may have trouble setting up in the allotted changeover time.

Common Stage Props and Effects

- **Candles:** Good, cheap, effective and oh so moody. Everyone from The Tea Party to Jane's Addiction uses candles. Obviously you're not going to get big originality points, but if it works... Also, beware of setting your backdrop on fire (I saw it happen once and it wasn't pretty).
- **Black lights and/or glow-in-the-dark paint:** I saw a band called Blue Dog Pict do pretty impressive, over-the-top things with these tools.
- **Fog:** Used sparingly, fog can be great. Fog machines can spit out a wisp of fog every few seconds to give the lights something to shoot through; it's a subtle effect. You can also get that pea soup Spinal Tap super fog effect, if desired (again, aesthetics are a personal thing). You can rent a fogger from your local musical equipment rental outlet quite cheaply.
- **Dry ice:** The cousin of fog, dry ice creates a hang-at-knee-level type of fog. It isn't used much anymore because it's a hassle and difficult to control.
- **Carpets:** Some bands lay Persian-style carpets on stage.
- **Slide and video projectors:** With the right images to project, these can be extremely effective visual tools. It's amazing that more performers don't get into this, when there's probably a slide projector sitting in the back of their parents' closet right now. Video projectors rent for around $100 to $150 a night.
- **Pods:** Spinal Tap shows how effective pods can be in their *This is Spinal Tap* film.

Canadian artists, more so than American or British ones, buy the hype and don't understand the reality behind images and how much thought, care and, dare I say, contrived elements there are behind the images of their favourite artists. So, they'll read an interview with their favourite artist with credibility and that person will spout off about never caring about hit singles, or never caring about their image or not caring about money and of course it's all crap. Nobody ever made it to the top of the music business without caring about all those things.

- Michael McCarty, president of EMI Music Publishing Canada

The Art of the Set List

Song order has a huge impact on the movement and effectiveness of your live show. You can achieve some intense peaks, but you can also create deadly lulls that are guaranteed to send your audience to the bar en-masse in search of another beer (to ease the pain). The goal is to hook your audience and keep them with you from the first song until the end of the set. Think of it as controlling/manipulating their response to your show. It all sounds a bit sinister, like a form of mind control, and perhaps, in a sense, it is.

There are various theories about crafting set lists. I've even heard that some bands try to have ascending keys: that is, position a song in the key of B after a song in the key of A and before a song in D. Never having tried this particular technique, I can't say if it actually creates a sense of rising intensity. Try it if you feel so inclined, but to be honest, I prefer to think of set design in terms of dynamics and pacing.

Dynamics

Audiences tend to get tired of one dynamic level when it's sustained over a few songs. If you play five slow ballads in a row you'll lose the audience's attention. The opposite is also true. Five fast tempo burners in a row puts the audience to sleep—despite the sonic onslaught. Audiences get bored with sameness; they react to dynamic change. The peaks are only peaks in relation to the valleys and the valleys only make sense in relation to the peaks. Playing a slow, quiet song and then slamming the audience with a burner always makes an audience sit up and take notice.

Your ability to experiment with dynamics is tied to the kind of material you have at your disposal. If you only play two minute, 130 plus beats per minute songs, then varying the song order won't have a huge impact on your show.

Decide what role each song in your set plays: is it high intensity, moderate or low intensity? Then arrange your set to create a sense of dynamic movement. If you slam your audience with a couple of rockers off the top, you can afford to give them a rest with a less intense song before building up the intensity again. And when you do build up the intensity again, the crescendo will have more impact.

The most common (and effective) way to arrange the dynamics in a rock set is to start with a bang and end with a bang. In between, create an ebb and flow of movement. I'm not suggesting you design a rocker-ballad-rocker-ballad set, because a dynamic roller coaster can also hurt momentum. I like to think of a set as a sequence of three song mini-sets, each one consisting of an opener (fast rocker), an interesting middle song (moderate/lower intensity), and a closer (bigger, more epic, more emotional). No set conforms to this perfectly, but it can be a good starting point for arranging your material for a set.

Pacing

The overall flow of your set should have a sense of pacing. As the audience warms to you, gradually turn up the heat so that the end of your set feels like the end—there's nothing left to add. Therefore, it's not a great idea to play all your strongest material first. You'll probably win the audience over, but lose them as you move into the weaker songs. You have to grab the audience's attention but it's equally important to finish strong and leave them wanting more.

It doesn't take long to identify the songs that really connect live; it's usually pretty obvious. Position your strongest material throughout the set to support weaker material. Later, when you've released a collection of hit singles, these will become the supports for lesser known songs. The stronger the material (or singles), the easier it is to design an effective set.

Segues & Breaks

Breaks give you an opportunity to talk to the audience and show off your sparkling personality, explain your lyrics, swear, whatever. Some performers can keep an audience riveted with entertaining banter that goes on and on, while others don't feel comfortable with talk and prefer to keep breaks short. Good between song "shpieling" can create a real connection with the audience. Bad shpieling sends people running to the bar. Get to know your limitations. Like slow, quiet songs, breaks provide breathers and slow your momentum. Breaks also give guitarists and bass players an opportunity for a quick tuning check or instrument change.

When you connect two songs or play them so tightly in sequence that there's no hole, you create a segue. You can use these to increase momentum. Audiences get applause fatigue if you force them to respond after every song. If you run three songs together, you'll usually get more reaction when you finally do take a break. Position breaks and segues to work with dynamics and pacing to increase the impact of the performance.

Moist Set List: 1997 Creature Tour

- **Disco Days:** whisper beginning w/slam into Tangerine
- **Tangerine:** energetic single
- **Kid Conductor:** longer dynamic jam song
  [shpiel break]
- **Kill for You:** energetic album track
- **Resurrection:** energetic single
  [shpiel break]
- **Creature:** w/fanfare trumpet intro
- **Machine Punch Through:** moody single
- **Break Her Down:** longer dynamic epic album track
  [shpiel break]
- **Gasoline:** quiet single
- **Leave it Alone:** single
  [shpiel break]
- **Ophelia:** energetic w/tribal drum intro
- **Silver:** single
- **Miss You:** Rolling Stones cover with harmonica jam
  [shpiel break]
- **Shotgun:** album track
- **Push:** single (extended set closer)
  1st encore
- **Hate:** moody album track
- **Shrieking Love:** epic, dynamic closer
  2nd encore
- **Believe Me:** single
- **1969:** short energetic Stooges cover

Stage Fright

Everyone suffers from stage fright to some degree. When I was a kid, I played goalie in the Pee Wee hockey league; I remember my coach told me about some old-time NHL goalie named Glenn Hall who suffered from severe nerves and vomited before every game. He was also one of the best players around. Stage fright never completely goes away. Nerves are tied to performance and adrenaline.

However, nerves definitely decrease the more you get used to playing in a particular environment. If you play twice a week at local house gig, you'll find that your nerves almost completely disappear. On long tours I find that, after a week or so, the pre-show jitters disappear, even when we're playing to large audiences. At that point, the challenge becomes getting pumped up for the show. Without the adrenaline that pumps through your veins, it's easy to put on a flat show.

Taking nerves as a given, you need to develop your own ways of harnessing them. Rather than hindering your performance and making you feel shaky, nerves should be the catalyst for electrifying performances. You'll discover some tricks, routines and superstitions to help your mind prepare for the job at hand. Learning to deal with nerves is an important part of becoming a great performer.

Everyone in Moist deals with their pre-show nerves in different ways. I like to sit quietly in a calm, quiet space and do guitar exercises for half an hour, whereas Paul, our drummer, is the opposite; he likes to wander around the backstage area talking with people. We both feel nerves, but we deal with it in opposite ways. Over time, most bands develop some unique and often private rituals for getting ready to play.

Exercises

- **Visualization:** Picture the gig unfolding as you want it to. Read over a set list if necessary and imagine the show going the way it's supposed to, step by step.
- **B'Hai exercise:** Half the Vancouver B'Hai community came out to a Vancouver show one time. One of the B'Hais taught me this tension exercise: starting with the tips of your toes, slowly tense up every muscle and move upward until every muscle in your body is clenched. Hold for about ten seconds, then gradually relax each muscle.

A mature person's identity and self-concept are not overly tied to their performance. They understand that a given performance is simply a temporary action or situation, and they know that they are bigger than this one moment and that they will survive regardless of the outcome of the next hour or two on stage.

– Dr. Marilyn S. Miller, registered psychologist in Toronto who has worked with performers since 1981

- **Breathing:** Breath deeply and evenly. Before you start this exercise, exhale fully to expel stale air that might be hanging around in the bottom of your lungs.
- **Sit-ups/Crunches/Push-ups/Stretching:** These gym class favourites get the blood and tension moving.
- **Sanctuary:** Find (or create) a calm and tranquil environment for warming up and collecting your thoughts. This can be quite a challenge at multiband nights where numerous bands are sharing one dressing room.
- **Play through any challenging parts and/or scales:** Beyond warming up your fingers, playing can help focus your thoughts and your nervous energy. Watch bands playing before you go on. Personally, I never do this because it psyches me out, but a lot of people like to get a sense of the venue and the crowd before hitting the stage.

Theft From Venues

Next to the bicycle, band equipment is probably the most stealable merchandise in the world. It's tailor-made for theft: Amps, guitars, pedals, keyboards and cymbals are valuable, portable, and very easy to unload. I wouldn't be surprised if there were sophisticated fencing organizations in major cities to cope with the endless flow of stolen band equipment.

Never leave any equipment in a vehicle, unguarded. Thieves prowl the streets and alleyways around live venues looking for vehicles containing gear. More bands get ripped off after load-out than at any other time. I recently spoke to someone who left his 1970 Les Paul Standard in a locked car, parked on a busy street in the early evening. Ten minutes later he returned to find the window broken and the guitar gone. That very guitar will be for sale in a city three-hundred miles away before the end of the week.

If you don't have insurance, you should jump forward to the section on the union. (Musician's Union, p.98) With insurance you'll still lose your prized guitar, but at least it will take the sting out of your wallet.

The Van, Some Gear, Someone in our Organization and His Date

About a year into the life of the band, someone in our organization (I won't name names) got a hot date. He'd been after this girl for months and when she finally said yes, he put together his plan for the perfect evening: dinner, dancing, a romantic drive… All he needed were some wheels to make it all happen.

He didn't own a car, but he did have keys to the band van, which was loaded up with all our gear—amps, drums, and guitars—the whole enchilada. He picked Ms. Wonderful up and drove to a funky eatery he knew on the wrong side of town. (It's always cool to know hip places in bad neighbourhoods.) After parking our van on a particularly dark and deserted street, he dined in the bliss that only a hot date can offer. From what I can gather, everything was going perfectly. Of course, things started to sour a little upon their return to the freshly unloaded van. He'd been like Santa parking a sleigh-load of goodies, and somewhere children were rejoicing.

I still remember the phone call: "Ah guys, um, well, ah, we have a little problem." By the time we arrived to the scene of the crime, his date, like our gear, was nowhere to be seen. So much for the hot date. Insure your gear!

Performance Contracts

Early in your career, most of your bookings will be based on verbal or handshake agreements. As soon as you start working with a booking agent, join the union, or begin to command big headliner fees, contracts will play a larger role in your life. It's never bad to have even the simplest contract for playing a show; it helps avoid confusion and misunderstandings.

At the most basic level, a performance contract should be written and include the following:

• Signatures of the venue owner or representative and a representative of the band (note that only one band member signature is required).
• The date, time and length of the performance (i.e. seventy-five minutes or two forty-five minute sets).
• The agreed upon payment arrangement, whether it's a guarantee, a cut of the door or a combination of the two.
• The time of payment (i.e. immediately following the show or

50 percent in advance with the balance paid following the performance).

Contracts can also deal with specifics, such as the sound and lighting requirements, promotion responsibilities of both the venue and the band, and hospitality (i.e. beer in the dressing room). As your draw and clout increase, you'll be able to be more specific about the show details; contracts for arena bands are literally pages long. Unfortunately, in the beginning, you'll be lucky to even get a performance contract. By the way, the musician's union provides their members with performance contracts free of charge.

Chapter Four

Getting Down to Business

Self-Management

If you're actively engaged in booking your own gigs, trying to get press, making contacts and generally working your band, I've got news for you—you're managing yourself. These activities, which are basically different angles of micromarketing, are the kinds of things a manager does, particularly for a local band. At the indie level, managing yourself is advantageous because it gives you the opportunity to learn the industry from the ground up. Also, you'll probably put more sweat into it than a professional manager would at this stage of the game; after all, managing a local indie band demands a lot of time and effort and offers very little monetary reward.

There's a school of thought that suggests that bands at any level should have an outside person act as manager. Having an objective third party say how great you are holds more weight than when you say it yourself. This is quite a valid point, particularly if you know of a capable person who can take on that role. This is the route we took with Moist. A friend with a good head for business was brought on quite early on to look after management.

Having said that, people are usually impressed with bands that manage themselves in an aggressive and professional manner. It shows that you take your band and the business of your career seriously, and it's even more impressive if you do manage to reach some level of success. Self-management also saves you a 15 to 20 percent management commission.

If you do decide to go out and actively hunt down a manager, skip ahead to Personal Management section in the Next Level chapter. (page 199)

Contractual Obligations

In a perfect world, a business relationship should be mutually advantageous. A dissatisfied party should be free to leave. A handshake should be enough. Unfortunately, it's not a perfect world; you may be confronted with opportunities that require you to sign a binding contract and give away some of your freedom. In many cases, this is a good move. But be very careful. A contract is usually in favour of the person trying to get you to sign it. I'll come to the subject of lawyers later, but, for now, remember: Never sign anything without consulting a lawyer. Ask your lawyer to explain exactly what you're getting and what you're giving up. Signing rotten business deals has destroyed far too many bands.

One of the most common ways for a band to get into trouble is by falling into debt. Many bands will take loans from managers, benefactors or other investors, and if things don't work out, they're left owing everyone money. This somewhat ugly situation can lead to lawyers, lawsuits and the complete destruction of a band. I've heard of musicians who've had to sell all their gear and have their day-job wages garnisheed (i.e. repayment installments automatically deducted). Resist the temptation to go on a buying spree at your local music store with borrowed money. However, advances from reputable record or publishing companies do not have to be paid back. If things don't work out, you don't owe anyone money. The worst that can happen is that you get dropped.

One of the most important sources of income for a band is from song publishing, which is covered in detail in the Music Publishing section (page 231). You should be aware, even at the beginning of your career, to never sign your publishing over to anyone else.

Signing over future publishing may not seem like a huge deal now, but, believe me, it is. Many well-known artists made this mistake and consequently make nothing from songs written earlier in their careers. It's more common (and fair) to agree on a publishing split, where the publishing company gets a percentage for administering your publishing. Again, consult with a lawyer before signing anything.

Beware of sharks. It doesn't take Einstein to figure out what a young struggling band wants to hear (i.e. you're great and have a bright future) and the things you need (money and contacts). Sharks can be very charming. They'll drop names, push all the right buttons and snow you without you even knowing you're being snowed.

Once sharks get their hooks into you, they'll try to get you all signed up. You'll think that signing over your future for a small short-term gain is an amazing opportunity. In the real world, manipulation and business go hand in hand. There really is no such thing as a free lunch. So, before getting involved with anyone, check their references. Ask everyone you know about their reputation. And, again, have an entertainment lawyer explain all the terms of every contract you're tempted to sign.

Copyrights

A copyright is the legal protection you have for your own original work (otherwise known in legalese as *intellectual property*). Under the law, as soon as your own original ideas are recorded (written down or actually recorded on tape), they become your property. Other people don't have the right to simply steal your property—it belongs to you. The only catch is that you have to be able to prove that it's actually yours.

As soon as you record or write out a song, you own the copyright. However, being able to prove you possess that copyright is not quite so simple. There's a danger that someone will steal your songs and pass them off as their own. In this case, you have be able to prove that you came up with the song before the thief did.

Three Methods to Establish Date of Authorship
- **Registered Mail**: Make a recording of the songs (using a ghetto blaster if necessary), write out the lyrics, package and

A lot of management is an absolute joke out there. Be very wary of it. Don't ever sign anything with management. Management should never have any of your publishing. You should negotiate a term of agreement. Management should not handle your money. You should do all those things— you have a responsibility.

- Jann Arden

send to yourself by registered mail. When it arrives, put the unopened envelope away somewhere safe. While not really rock-solid, this method does help to establish the date of authorship, because the envelope is dated and sealed.

• **The Canadian Intellectual Property Office (CIPO)**
Their registration form only requires the song title and the songwriter(s) name(s). This method, ironically, holds less weight than sending your material by registered mail, because the only information on file is the song title, which won't take you very far in court.

> **Copyright Office**
> Canadian Intellectual Property Office (CIPO)
> Industry Canada
> 50 Victoria Street
> Place du Portage, Phase I
> Hull, PQ
> K1A 0C9
> cipo.gc.ca

• **The Library of Congress**
Even a Canadian indie band is entitled to register songs with the Copyright Office of the Library of Congress in the United States. This is the most fool-proof method of guarding your copyrights, and the extra security might be worth the trouble. You can register each song individually for $20 US a pop (which can quickly add up) or register a collection of songs on a single tape or CD for $20 total. Although it's less specific, the second route should be sufficient to defend your copyright. The form you need is called a "Circular 56: Copyright for Sound Recordings."

> **US Copyright Office**
> Library of Congress
> 101 Independence Ave. SE
> Washington, DC 20559-6000
> Tel: 202-707-3000
> email: copyinfo@loc.gov
> www.lcweb.loc.gov/copyright

Trademarks for Band Names

If you can demonstrate that you've used a particular band name publicly in an area first, you hold what is referred to as common law rights to the name in that area. Proof of usage can be as simple as your band name appearing in a gig advertisement. Therefore, different bands may have rights to the same name in different regions. Touring across the country can establish common law claim nationwide, as long as no one else has publicly used the name before in a particular region.

Another option is to officially register your band name as a trademark. Although costly and time consuming, it protects your name nationally. It involves hiring a lawyer, undertaking an official name search (to ensure no one else holds the rights to the name) and completing a fair amount of legal paper work. While this is the best protection you can get for your band name, it really doesn't shield you from people who have prior common law claim to the name. So even if you register your name, someone can still come out of the woodwork and claim common law rights. Also, in order to maintain your trademark, you have to keep using the name. For example, if you registered the name "Leather Head" in 1985, but haven't done anything publicly since then, someone could come in and take your claim to the name.

Indie bands don't usually have registered names. When a band signs a record deal, the label will often take care of the name registration on the band's behalf. During this process, it's not uncommon to find a few bands with regional common law rights to your name. In this case, you either have to choose a new name or convince the other bands to give up the name (often requiring a buyout).

After we played a couple of cross-Canada tours, we discovered the existence of another Toronto-based band called Moist, except they spelt it Möist. They were a punk band who had a singer with a pink Mohawk, and we found out about them after we heard rumours that we'd moved to Toronto and changed our image. We had the rights of first usage in Toronto (by virtue of our previous touring), so we had our lawyer draw up a cease and desist letter and the problem disappeared. The same thing happened with an all-girl band in California. It's amazing how many bands have the same name, so maybe you should think twice about calling your band "Free Beer." You could probably resolve these disputes amicably, band to band, but a lawyer's letter can definitely speed things along.

To find out if anyone is using your band name, check out the North American Band Name Registry website at www.bandname.com.

The Professional Promo Pack

When you begin to make contacts in the music industry, it's important to have a professional promo pack (also known as a press kit). A promo pack is your calling card; it allows people to learn all about you with a minimum of effort. It shows off your sound, your look and your accomplishments.

Contents of a Professional Promo Pack

• A cover letter written to the recipient of the promo pack.
• A well-labeled demo tape or (preferably) a CD (your sound).
• An 8 x 10 glossy photo of the band (your look).
• A one page band biography written in the third person (your accomplishments).
• Photocopies of all print media coverage you've received.

It's hard to say exactly when to start using a professional promo pack. If you're approaching (or being approached by) agents, lawyers, and labels, you should definitely have one ready. However, submitting a full-on promo pack for new talent slots could be overkill. Promo packs cost money to assemble, so you'll want to be somewhat particular about who gets one.

The Cover Letter

A cover letter personalizes each package you send out. It's the first step in establishing a relationship with the recipient, which is the point of sending out a promo pack. The style and content of the letter should be tailor-made for the person receiving the package. Always make sure your letter is typed and reasonably well-written (i.e. free of glaring spelling mistakes).

The Demo

Your demo should consist of your three very best songs, with the best placed first. No exceptions: three songs, with your best song first. This is the absolute industry standard. Joe music industry won't listen past the first song if he doesn't like it. He figures that if he doesn't dig your best song, then he probably won't dig anything that comes after. This might sound cutthroat, but it's a fact. So if you play hard to get and put your best song last, most people will never hear it. Period.

It's now reasonably cheap and easy to make dubs onto a recordable CD (CDR). Most studios and/or duplication houses have facilities for limited runs. If you're sending your promo pack to someone particularly important, splurge on a CDR rather than a cassette tape. To get people to actually listen to your music, you have to make it as easy as possible for them.

Label everything with your band name, song titles and contact information. This is extremely important, and you'd understand why if you could see the desks and offices of most industry people, piled high with thousands of demo tapes. If you want to create some eye-catching artwork for the case, fine, but make sure the labeling remains clear. Professional demos don't usually come with artwork, but creativity can be effective, or at least refreshing.

As far as the standard of your recording goes, the higher the quality, the better. Your demo is being listened to primarily for vocal melodies, not guitar riffs, so make sure the vocals come through loud and clear.

The 8 x 10 Glossy Photograph

Eight by ten colour glossy photographs are expensive. Typical prices for reproduction are about $4.00 per photo after an initial outlay of around $15, when you provide a 35mm negative. Some companies specialize in reproducing band promo photographs and may charge far less than standard reproduction houses. Talk to other bands and find out where they get their photos reproduced. You can also look in the Yellow Pages™ under "Photographic Reproduction."

Band photos should show off the different personalities in the band. Industry players are looking for a cool look and that illusive star quality. It's hard to get a good group shot. Labels spend thousands of dollars to get really interesting eye-catching publicity photos. Try to get someone you know who's into photography (i.e. owns a 35mm camera) to take a few rolls of photos. You only need one or two cool shots. Check out cool magazines like *Spin* or *Details* for interesting photo ideas.

I can't tell you how many people, even in the industry, send things out without proper labeling. I'm not even talking about complete labeling; I'm talking about any at all. There seems to be a trend now that people have gone to CDR to not put any labeling whatsoever on the CD or on the jewel case or anything. You've got to have every piece of it labelled with the artist name, song titles and as much contact information as you have. If you just put your address on and I want to phone you, I won't be able to phone you.

*– **Michael McCarty**, president of EMI Music Publishing Canada*

The Band Bio

There are two types of band bios: one geared towards the music industry, and the other written for the media. The industry bio should be no longer than one page in length and should only contain information that the industry is actually interested in. The bio is usually the weakest part of a new band's promo pack because there's usually not much to say yet. Sure it's cool that you started singing when you were three and I'm sure that you and your mom are pretty happy about it, but the industry doesn't care. The music industry is really only interested in your penetration into the music industry.

Your industry bio should read more like a fact sheet than your life story, so include things such as:
• What kind of music you play.
• How many indie CDs you've sold (sales of less than 1,000 CDs can probably be omitted).
• How much radio exposure you've had.
• Any media coverage.
• The size of your draw.
• The tours you've done.
• The bands you've played with.
• How long you've been together.
• Other successful bands your members have played in.

Some new bands resort to embellishing their histories (lying). "And then when we finished opening up for Metallica on their eastern swing..." Lying is worse than writing about high school music class. People can spot the bull in about two seconds. If you don't have much to say in the bio, keep it short.

Your media bio, however, should entice the reader to listen to your demo and lead interviewers to ask interesting questions. It's not only concerned with what you've done, but why you do what you do: Your views on music, your influences, your personality as individuals and as a band are relevant. The media bio should intrigue people to find out more.

It's a good idea to hire a music journalist to write your media bio. Journalists read dozens of band bios every week and know what makes an effective, unique bio and what's been written a million times before. Journalists also have a keen understanding of the needs and mind-set of other journalists.

Approach local music journalists whose writing you like. Many journalists will write up a bio for surprisingly little money (i.e. $75 or less). Remember, most music journalists are freelance (i.e. indie) themselves, and are very approachable. They can also use the extra income.

Print Media Clippings

Photocopy any newspaper and magazine coverage you've had, and include it with the promo pack. Press coverage really enhances your credibility. Even a one-line mention in a magazine means something, so include the article and highlight the section about you.

Keep the clippings treasury down to a maximum of five pages, otherwise you risk overwhelming the reader. If you've had a lot of media coverage, choose your most useful pieces. Larger media is more impressive than high school newspaper coverage, even if your school paper says you're going to be the next big thing.

The X Factor

Most music industry people are swamped by demo tapes and promo packs. Making yours different and interesting can give you an edge. Your unique creative ideas are the x factor. Bands deliver promo packs to record labels in all manner of ways: in wooden or giant multicoloured boxes; accompanied by scotch; wrapped in chocolate; or as a balloon-o-gram. In fact, many labels send new releases to radio programmers using similar strategies, because people notice unique and unusual things.

The downside to wrapping your demo in chocolate is that industry professionals may jump to the conclusion that you're trying to hide substandard material with gimmickry. More than a few insiders have told me that they're suspicious of over-elaborate demo packaging.

Using the x factor is most appropriate when you send out an unsolicited promo pack. In this case, your outrageous creativity might be the only thing that prompts someone to listen to your demo. I'll get to the subject of solicited materials later, but be forewarned that many industry professionals (especially record company executives) are so bogged down with unsolicited demo tapes and packages that they simply no longer accept them: They throw them straight into the garbage bin.

The bio can actually be an interesting part of the press kit. The picture says a lot, and the music might speak volumes, but it's always cool to have something to read while you listen to that music.

- Mitch Joel, Montreal-based freelance journalist

Performing Rights Societies (SOCAN)

Copyright law dictates that copyright holders (i.e. songwriters) must be compensated every time their original material (i.e. a song) is performed, whether on the radio, in a TV program or movie, or performed live (even if the performer is the songwriter). Radio stations and venues that play music publicly have to pay music licensing fees.

It would be virtually impossible for songwriters to chase down everyone who is playing their songs to demand money. Fortunately for songwriters, there is an international network of performing rights societies, dedicated to collecting music licensing fees and distributing them to writers in the form of performance royalties. In Canada, the performing rights society is called SOCAN (The Society of Composers Authors and Music Publishers of Canada).

How SOCAN Works

To get a representative cross-section of radio playlists, SOCAN uses a radio station sampling system; this cross-section creates a picture of what songs are getting radio play in different music formats, geographical regions and languages. The more a song shows up in the sampling, the more money is allocated to the songwriter. Although not completely accurate, sampling provides a reasonable survey of what's being played. If you know for a fact that your song was played once on a radio station and you never received any money, you'll know why.

Television stations across Canada provide SOCAN with music cue sheets for all programs they broadcast. These sheets list the songs used and the duration of the use. Money is allocated to songwriters based on how much of their music is used and how widely the show is broadcast.

To receive royalties for a live performance, SOCAN requires that you fill out "Notification of Live Performance" forms, detailing the songs performed, the venue, and the ticket price. You'll also need some other proof of the performance, like tickets or posters. The size of royalty you receive depends on factors like audience size and ticket price.

Foreign performance royalties are collected by the performing rights societies in each territory. These societies are affiliated with SOCAN, so if your song earns income in another country, it will flow through SOCAN. For example, if you earn performance income in England, the UK society, The Performing Right Society (PRS), will pass the royalties along to SOCAN on your behalf. Likewise, if you have a monster hit in Portugal, you'll be covered. We recently received royalties because the song "Push" was featured in a Finnish television program, and we've never even been to Finland!

BDS

Broadcast Data Systems (BDS) is a company that uses a computerized system to monitor the airplay of radio and television stations across North America. Unlike surveys and polls, the BDS information is extremely accurate and is the industry standard for measuring airplay.

When a song is released, the record company sends a copy of the track to BDS where its electronic fingerprint is logged into the computer system. The field computers listen to radio and television stations and log the time, date and station each time that fingerprint shows up. Every twenty-four hours, this data is sent to a central BDS operations facility where the information is then used to create the daily airplay statistics sent out to BDS subscribers, such as record companies or magazines.

Some of the American performing rights societies have already switched over to the BDS system. It's only a matter of time before SOCAN changes over to BDS monitoring. By the way, when you hear someone talking about airplay in terms of spins, they're referring to the number of times a song has been played as measured by BDS. To find out more about BDS, visit their website at: www.bdson-line.com

Registering With SOCAN

Before you can start receiving performance royalty cheques, you and your original songs must be registered with SOCAN. To qualify for membership, your songs must have been performed live or played on the radio or TV. You also qualify if you've signed a publishing or record deal. Registration is free.

SOCAN
41 Valleybrook Dr.
Don Mills, ON, M3B 2S6
Tel: 416-445-8700, Toll free: 1-800-55-SOCAN
Fax: 416-445-7108
www.socan.ca

It takes around 600 spins a week to sell records in Canada.

- Terry McBride, manager of Moist and Sarah McLachlan

When you sign up with SOCAN, you'll be provided with song registration forms requiring the title, duration, names and addresses of writers, cowriters, publishers (if applicable), and writing credit percentages (i.e. Jack gets 33, Bill 50 and Alice 17 percent based on their contribution to the writing of the music and lyrics).

SOCAN Cheques

SOCAN issues royalty cheques four times a year, in February, May, August, and November. It takes about nine months to receive compensation for a Canadian performance, and longer for international play. Until your songs start to receive considerable airplay, don't expect monster SOCAN cheques; my first few cheques were in the $7.00 range.

It's difficult to say how much royalty money a single play generates, but a top ten single in Canada will generate around $5,000 to $10,000 in royalties over the course of its three to five months on the airwaves. This figure is then split between the songwriters and the publisher (if applicable).

Of course, the real fun starts when you get a top ten single in the US; for a rough estimate, simply multiply the above number by twenty-five.

Setting up Your Publishing Company

Setting up your own music publishing company isn't difficult, but you must decide if it's worth the money and effort.

Reasons to Set up a Publishing Company

- Lend a sense of credibility to you as a songwriter.
- Get a copublishing agreement with a larger publisher.
- Act as publisher for your own commercially released material.
- Publish other people's songs and operate as an independent publishing company.

As far as credibility is concerned, it's debatable as to whether anyone actually cares that you've gone to the trouble of forming your own publishing company. Any songwriter, regardless of talent, can form a publishing company, and having your own won't really increase your chances of being heard or noticed. Industry professionals will judge you according to your work and your reputation.

However, to enter into a copublishing deal with a major publisher requires that you have your own publishing company. It doesn't hurt to set it up in advance, but it's not essential. You could quite easily wait until the situation arises to take the plunge.

Some artists will act as publisher for their own commercially released music. In this case they don't have the benefit of a large, well-connected company working to get their music onto film and television, or covered by other artists, but they do save the 25 to 50 percent cut a publisher takes. Many publishers can argue that 50 to 75 percent of something is better than 100 percent of nothing. Self-publishing means no up-front publishing advances, which many artists live on (remember, you keep up-front money whether or not your album sells). If you're up to basic bookkeeping and administration chores, self-publishing can make sense for well connected, motivated people.

Opening up shop as a publisher for other songwriters' material is an interesting avenue, if your dream is to be an indie publisher. Otherwise, why bother? Unless you plan to work around the clock establishing connections to be a real player, you won't have anything to really offer other songwriters. Why should another songwriter sign over the publisher's share of their music to you? By the same token, if you're considering signing to a micro-indie publisher, make sure you know what they have to offer.

The Process

To set up your own publishing company, you have to register the company with the provincial (or state) government as a business (look in the blue pages of your phone book under Business, Registration). This allows you to open a business chequing account and to write and cash cheques made out in your company name. Business registration involves conducting a name search to make sure another business isn't using your proposed company name. There is a fee of around $100. In some provinces you can register on-line; it's that simple. Keep in mind that registering a business is not the same as registering a corporation. Incorporation is considerably more complicated and expensive. (See Incorporation, page 215)

Next, register your publishing company with SOCAN. To qualify as a publisher with SOCAN, you must have either a minimum of five songs cowritten by a SOCAN member (i.e. you) or have at least one commercially released song. Registration involves a $50 processing fee.

You must clear your company name through SOCAN as well. Companies from all over the world are registered with SOCAN, so even though your name search may have cleared in your local area it may not clear through SOCAN. They will not allow two companies to have the same name. Contact your SOCAN office to obtain a publisher registration kit.

The next step is to register and copyright the songs in your catalogue as outlined in the copyrights section earlier in this chapter. This isn't mandatory, but it is recommended.

If you plan to act as the working publisher for songs released commercially by a label, consider registering your company with the Canadian Mechanical Reproduction Rights Agency (CMRRA) and the Harry Fox Agency in the United States. These agencies collect mechanical royalties on behalf of publishers in Canada as well as internationally, if applicable. (See CMRRA, p.125)

The Musician's Union

Every major city across North America hosts a chapter of the American Federation of Musicians (AFM). The AFM is a musician's union that protects the interests of musicians in a cruel world, and for classical musicians, it's an essential service tailor-made to meet their needs. I'm not so sure about indie band musicians. A bass player for a local indie band and the first violin in the symphony orchestra don't have a lot in common; beyond playing varieties of music, the realities of their working lives are completely different. There are, however, a few services that you will find extremely helpful. As your career develops, joining the AFM will become a necessity.

Union Dues

There's an initiation fee of around $175 to join the AFM. A card-carrying union member (you really do get a union card), pays a fee of around $200, broken down into four $50 payments. Before joining you'll have to weigh the $200 in union dues against the value of the services you'll receive.

Wage Scales

Wage scales outline the minimum musicians can receive for playing a gig. This minimum is guaranteed to all members whether they play the piano at the local Ramada Inn, beat a kettle drum for the Montreal Symphony Orchestra, or play guitar in a band performing their first gig at Moe's Tavern. Union scale is good money (around $90 per player and $130 if you're a designated band leader, for a performance under two hours in length).

Of course, the reality is that not one club in North America will pay a young, non-drawing, indie band $500 for an evening's performance. It's not the way the rock game works. Rock bands playing original music are paid according to their draw (although, cover bands often do receive union scale).

In theory, union members are supposed to use union contracts and are not permitted to play gigs that pay less than union scale. In reality, many do. The most common way to work for less than scale is to indicate union scale on the contract, and then deduct production and/or promotional costs, like sound and advertising, from the rate. If union scale is $500 but the venue only wants to pay $200, the union contract would read:

$500 union scale for the performance
- $100 promotional expenses
- $200 production charges
_____

=$200 net performance fee

Official union contracts are available free to members. In most places, the union is not a particularly aggressive watch-dog, especially with indie rock players.

Really, the only time you'll encounter wage scales as an original band is for TV appearances. To play on some networks, such as the CBC, you must be a union member. Non-union players can obtain a onetime permit from the union for the performance. Unfortunately, television stations often ask you to sign a contract that lets them out of their obligation to compensate you for your appearance. The idea being that the exposure you receive is payment enough. If you do get paid, it will be union scale.

Strong Arming

If you have a signed union contract for a show and the venue or promoter tries to stiff you at the end of the night, you can call the union. Union workers claim that they've been known to get out of bed at all hours of the night to go down and yell at deadbeats. If verbal abuse doesn't work, the deadbeat can be blacklisted, meaning that the venue will not be allowed to hire union performers until the debt is paid. The union has also been known to assume legal representation for members who become involved in payment disputes.

I don't know how an indie band could ever actually benefit from all this. In the beginning, you'll be making peanuts and working below union scale, so you wouldn't be advised to seek union assistance. Later, when you're a draw powerhouse, you'll probably have some other kind of clout that's much more effective than the union.

Visas

It's virtually impossible for bands to cross the Canada/US border without the right paperwork (visa). It's a bit difficult to just call up the American Consulate and get a visa to perform stateside. However, for all contracted gigs across the border, the union has a direct pipeline to visas for members. This service is extremely valuable for bands looking to expand into neighbouring American cities.

The union works with four different types of visas, each one specifically tailored for different kinds of performers.

- **O-1:** This visa is for internationally known solo artists (i.e. Eric Clapton or Ani DiFranco).
- **P-1:** This visa is for internationally known musical groups that have been together for at least one year (i.e. U2 or The Toronto Symphony Orchestra).
- **P-2:** This visa is for lesser-known musicians entering the United States from Canada.
- **P-3:** This visa is for culturally unique solo artists and musical groups, such as Celtic, Carnatic (Indian) and Latin groups.

The P-2 is probably the visa for you. Applications for P-2 visas are handled through the AFM Canada Office in Toronto (416-391-5161). The union recommends that most applicants allow at least a month for processing time.

Insurance

It can be difficult and also expensive for non-union musicians to insure their gear because many companies won't go near musical instruments and band equipment; it's simply not worth the risk. The union has an arrangement with various insurance companies that allows members to get instrument insurance at very competitive rates. I originally joined the union just to take advantage of the insurance.

Other Services

- **The Pension Fund:** When you retire at sixty-five from a long life as a pro musician, you'll be eligible for a pension.
- **Life Insurance:** Union members receive automatic life insurance coverage that pays $1,000 if you die.
- **Counselling:** There is free legal, administrative, and financial counselling available to union members.
- **The Directory:** A directory of all members is available free to union members.
- **Group Insurance:** Similar to their instrument insurance, the union has relationships with companies that will provide you with group insurance—accidental death, mutilation, disability, accident, sickness and dental—at reasonable rates. It could be worth it for the dental insurance alone.

The Special Payment Fund

The Special Payment Fund is a great bonus for union members who perform on major label albums. Major labels must contribute a percentage of album sales to the AFM Special Payment Fund, which then gets distributed amongst the musicians who appeared on the albums. If you play on such a session, you not only receive your session fees, but yearly payments from the fund. Session players often receive sizable cheques for performing on successful albums.

What is CanCon?

Back in the '70s, the Canadian government decided that radio in Canada was being dominated by foreign (mostly American and British) music in the same way that Canadian movie theatres are still in the grip of non-Canadian, Hollywood movies. At the time, this had a very negative effect on the Canadian recording industry. The public wasn't being exposed to Canadian bands and therefore didn't buy a lot of Canadian albums. Enter Canadian Content Legislation (aka CanCon).

The Canadian Radio, Television and Telecommunications Commission (CRTC) requires that commercial Canadian AM and FM radio stations, as well as music video stations, play a minimum of 35 percent Canadian music over the course of a programming week. It also requires that the CBC play at least 50 percent Canadian content. While some radio programmers resent government control of their playlists, CanCon has proved to be extremely effective in not only protecting existing Canadian music, but also in helping to nurture a whole generation of artists that can (and do) succeed internationally. CanCon is a very positive thing for Canadian bands. The legislation has been so successful, in fact, that the minimums were raised on January 1, 1999 from 30 to 35 percent.

To qualify as a Canadian recording, songs must fulfill at least two of the four conditions of the MAPL test. Albums that qualify are permitted to have the MAPL logo to show radio programmers that they are CanCon. If the MAPL content varies, try to indicate somewhere (preferably by the songwriting/publishing credits) the status of each song (eg. "all tracks MAPL except tracks 3, 4, 8, which are MA"). Study how artists on major labels display this information.

MAPL Conditions
- **M (Music):** The music is composed entirely by a Canadian.
- **A (Artist):** The artist is Canadian.
- **P (Production):** The track is recorded and mixed entirely in Canada. This has nothing to do with whether the producer is Canadian or not (this is a common misconception).
- **L (Lyrics):** The lyrics are entirely written by a Canadian.

Cowriting Condition: The musical selection was performed live or recorded after September 1, 1991 and a Canadian receives at least half of the credit as a composer and lyricist. So, if you're a Canadian artist who recorded an album in the US and cowrote half the music and lyrics with a non-Canadian (and you must have the SOCAN registration to prove the splits) you would qualify as CanCon with one point for "**A**" (Artist) a half point for "**M**" (Music) and a half point for "**L**" (Lyrics). The song's status on the CD label or booklet would be indicated with a variation of the MAPL logo. This concession was won by Bryan Adams in the early '90s who, because he cowrote the *Waking up the Neighbours* album with producer Mutt Lang and recorded outside of Canada, did not qualify as CanCon at the time.

CanCon and You

While qualifying as Canadian content improves the chances of your music being played on the air, there are no guarantees. This is an often misunderstood point. Competition for radio and television airplay in Canada is intense, even among bands whose music passes the MAPL test. Factors such as music quality, production, promotion and album sales play a huge part in determining airplay. CanCon simply gives Canadian bands a fighting chance against international acts.

I should also point out that radio programmers use different definitions for CanCon rotation and international rotation. Heavy rotation for a CanCon artist is equivalent to medium rotation for an international act. This slight of hand allows programmers to give the impression of playing more Canadian music than they actually are. Record companies and managers are always trying to get their Canadian artists bumped up to international rotation levels.

Full MAPL: The recording is 100% Cancon.

The Artist is Canadian.
Recording was produced in Canada.
This usually applies to a cover song.

The extremely rare cowriting condition MAPL logo:
Half a point for Music and Lyrics; a full point for Artist.
Try to avoid this situation, if you can.

The National Library of Canada

If you release an album that has at least some Canadian content, you are required by law to send a copy to be kept on file at the National Library of Canada. If you don't, they will eventually track you down (I'm serious).

Legal Deposit
National Library of Canada
395 Wellington Street
Ottawa, Ontario
K1A 0N4
Tel.: 819-997-9565
www.nlc-bnc.ca/ehome

Chapter Five

Independent Recording

Introduction to Recording

Once your band has strong, original songs together, you'll want to record them. Recording is a skill you'll need to hone as your music career develops. Learning to record your songs in interesting and exciting ways can definitely increase your chances for success. An indie band doesn't have the luxury of big budgets and experienced producers, so you have to be creative and resourceful to get the biggest bang for your buck.

When is it Time to get Serious about Recording?

Bands that write their own original material should always be recording. Use a ghetto blaster in the jam space or make a home recording with a portastudio. Recording your jams is extremely valuable because it really aids in songwriting and arranging; you can listen back and identify effective and not-so-effective elements of your material. Meanwhile, home recording teaches you the basics of the art, such as overdubbing and using effects, and allows you to further refine your songs. In fact, many bands hone their home recording skills to the point where they can make their own, industry-calibre demos and, in some cases, albums. Jam space and home recording work very well together to prepare you for the recording studio.

Before spending the big bucks at a professional studio you should spend some serious time refining your songs, recording them yourself and performing them live. A recording studio will not turn a mediocre song into a smash hit, so get things together first. A successful studio recording requires that your band be tight and confident and that your songs are fully written and arranged. It's all too common for ill-prepared bands to waste a small fortune in the studio.

Demo or Album?

What is the purpose of your recording? Do you want a demo to send out to the music industry and to attract record companies, or an indie album to sell to the public, or both? This is a very important question. While a demo and an album have a lot in common, the primary purpose of a demo is to showcase your songwriting and melodies; to show off your material's strength and potential. On demos, make sure that jams, epic solos and long-winded introductions are kept to a minimum; production is simple and clear. An album, on the other hand, is more of a finished product with all the bells and whistles. It contains more songs than the three required for a demo.

There's a lot of debate about how good a demo should sound in order to generate interest from the industry. Some feel that a great song will shine through just about any production. They argue that A&R execs have finely tuned ears that can pick out a hit a mile away. Others believe that the more professional sounding the demo the better. Most record and publishing companies get stacks of demo tapes every week. Your demo will be one of many, why give yourself a handicap? I tend to agree with the latter argument. I'm not suggesting that you drive your band deeply into debt making a Radiohead calibre record, but it makes sense to put together the most professional package possible. And that goes for the recording, the artwork, and everything. Don't expect a prompt reply from a record label for a ghetto blaster recording on a cassette with a handwritten cover; it just shouts: "This band doesn't have it together. They're not ready."

Home Recording

I'm a huge fan of home recording. Perfecting songwriting and recording skills in a home studio is an important part of your development as a musician. It's great for learning to write cohesive parts and arrangements. There are many different options for home recording, catering to just about any budget. I'm often amazed at the calibre of material that has been tracked on inexpensive multitrack recording gear. You probably won't reach the level of a U2 record by just working in your bedroom, but you can do some amazing things that go towards the goal of mastering the art of capturing your music. Beck's first album *Mellow Gold* was recorded in a home studio.

There are, of course, certain limitations to home recording. While it's relatively easy to get some decent guitar, keyboard, bass and vocal sounds, recording drums is extremely difficult. Even if noise isn't an issue (say you live in a home for the deaf), getting professional-calibre drum sounds without an arsenal of expensive microphones, preamps and compressors is pretty much impossible. Great drum sounds require a great drum room; that is, a large live-sounding room. Mind you, if you decide to try and record drums in your apartment, let me know how it goes.

It's very common to record drums at a real recording studio and then record everything else as overdubs in a home studio. It's also quite common to use a sequencer, where drum loops, which generally consist of one or two bars of a real drum pattern, are played over and over. CDs of various drum loops can be bought at most of the larger musical instrument stores.

There are basically three common varieties of home studio gear: analog portastudios, dedicated digital audio workstations (DAWs), and computer-based digital audio workstations. In addition to these systems there are analog reel-to-reel multitrack systems but they're so expensive, that I'm not going to discuss them. If you want to check out any of the following options, most large music stores carry a variety of each.

Analog Portastudios

When you hear someone talk about a four track, they're likely referring to an analog portastudio. Portastudios combine a mixer and multi-track tape deck into one unit, so they're portable and easy to run. They use standard cassette tapes and come in four and occasionally eight track varieties. Until the arrival of their digital counterparts, analog portastudios were by far the most common format for home use.

The greatest drawback with analog portastudios is the limited number of tracks, combined with the comparatively low quality of cassette tapes as a storage medium. If you're short on cash, however, a used analog portastudio can be bought pretty cheaply. By the way, *Sgt. Pepper's* by the Beatles was recorded using analog four track machines (albeit reel to reel).

Dedicated Digital Audio Workstations (DAWs or Digital Portastudios)

Like analog portastudios, DAWs consist of a mixer and recorder combined in a single unit. DAWs are more akin to a computer; they contain RAM and save audio on digital storage media like mini-disks (as opposed to cassettes). DAWs are available in four to sixteen track models. As a result, digital portastudios are taking over the market. Improved sound quality and audio editing possibilities, such as looping and moving around parts of a song, make them more desirable than their analog counterparts. Most DAWs retail from around $800 to $4,000 (for more tracks, features and better digital converters for better quality sound).

Computer-Based Digital Audio Workstations

Computer-based digital audio workstations are software packages designed for use on PC or Mac computers. These recording platforms range in price from around $800 for a program like Cubase™ by Steinberg, and up into the tens of thousands of dollars range for professional studio packages such as Digidesign's Pro Tools™.

These programs give you a full-service studio with loads of tracks (sixty-four and more) and an arsenal of outboard gear contained in the virtual space of a computer. There is a full mixing board with VU meters and a rack of built-in effects that sit on your computer screen. Fader and knob levels are adjusted with the mouse.

Of the three home recording options, computer-based DAWs have the most features and the greatest flexibility. The main expense comes from buying a fast computer with lots of RAM and large speedy hard drives for storing audio files. Count on spending about $4,000 on computer hardware. Also, unlike dedicated DAWs, they're not really portable (unless you want to haul a computer around town), so you can't easily take them to your rehearsal space to record a jam.

Choosing a Recording Studio

There are many different breeds of studios available. Over the past fifteen years, a veritable explosion of recording technology has made it possible for independent bands to create professional recordings without spending a fortune. In the past, all recording was done on expensive multi-track gear using analog magnetic tape. The expense of these machines meant that low-budget studios seldom offered more than eight or sixteen tracks. However, digital recording platforms such as Pro Tools™ and ADAT™ have allowed the rise of countless basement studios with surprisingly sophisticated equipment and affordable rates (which are always negotiable).

Digital vs Analog Recording

When comparing studios, it's important to understand the differences between analog and digital recording. In a nutshell, analog technology is the studio equivalent to your cassette tape player, while digital corresponds to your CD player. Analog recording has been around since recording was invented. With analog, an audio signal is imprinted on magnetic tape, whereas with digital recording, the audio signal is translated into the 1s and 0s of computer language, and then reconverted to analog for output to the amplifier and speakers.

Each format has inherent strengths and weaknesses. Analog tape is generally considered to produce a warmer, richer, more real-sounding recording than digital. It's often the preferred format for recording drums, bass guitar and lead guitar. Unfortunately, studios offering large numbers of analog tracks tend to be much more expensive than their digital counterparts.

Digital, on the other hand, is cleaner with less noise than analog, but it sounds harder and more sterile. The great advantage of digital format is the capability for audio editing (such as pitch correction and compiling applications), and the often limitless number of tracks available. Many basement or low-budget studios use digital recording platforms and, with a good engineer, it's quite possible to get impressive, professional results. Often, higher budget studios use a combo of digital and analog equipment. This provides the sonic advantages of analog tape coupled with the flexibility of digital.

Analog tape is also quite surprisingly expensive while digital tape is extremely inexpensive, and, if you're recording to a hard drive, free. In addition to lowering your recording budget, digital media allow you greater flexiblilty to keep takes and assess performances. But exercise caution, because having twenty-five takes of a song is more confusing than helpful.

Number of Tracks

Usually, the more tracks a studio offers, the more it charges. This is becoming less true in the age of digital, but it still holds as a general rule. So, how many tracks do you require? The answer depends a lot on the sophistication of the recording you want to make. A song on a full-budget major label album often consists of forty-eight or more tracks. However, a four or five piece indie rock band can get pretty amazing results with sixteen tracks. We recorded half the songs on our first record on a sixteen-track analog machine.

The danger in having too many tracks at your disposal is that you might be tempted to use them all. Recording over-dubs can yield positive results, but each additional track adds time and expense to the recording and mixing. Plus, record producing is an art that takes time to master. While you're still learning, it's best to keep things simple; the results will sound better. Guitarists can be huge overdub menaces (I know, I am one) but too many guitar tracks bog down the mix.

The track list for "Push," recorded sixteen-track analog:

01. Snare
02. Kick drum
03. Floor tom
04. High hat
05. Overhead
06. Room mic left
07. Room mic right
08. Bass guitar
09. Rhythm guitar
10. Rhythm guitar double
11. Guitar solo
12. Organ left
13. Organ right
14. Lead vocal
15. Background vocal 1
16. Background vocal 2

To get into a mid-range studio in this country is not that difficult. We recorded "Last of the Ghetto Astronauts" for $7,000. (Producer) John Shepp did one hell of a job and we worked our asses off to do it, but we just trusted our ears.

*- **Matthew Good** of The Matthew Good Band*

What Makes a Studio Right for You?

There is a fundamental truth about studios that many people don't seem to understand: Studios don't perform miracles. You can record a crap, loose performance of a lame song in any studio in the world and it will still be lame. You could hire the best people in the recording industry to try to mix the crap out of what you've recorded and it would still be crap. A great studio, coupled with a great engineer, can produce great results, but not automatically. Most of your successes or failures in the studio will be because of you.

Think of the studio as a really sharp lens that can clearly reveal your music (in Technicolor, so to speak). Your strengths and your flaws will be there for all to see. The luxury of multi-track means you can go back and fix mistakes, but you can't turn a weak drummer into John Bonham. A reasonable approach is to go in with the goal of capturing what you do live.

Key Issues to Consider When Choosing a Studio

• **Rates:** Studios charge by the hour, day and by the lock-out (several days). Daytime hourly rates are the highest, so ask about package deals and off-peak rates. Find out if the rate includes an engineer. Beware of hidden expenses such as extra gear rentals and audio tape. Engineers can get you amazing deals if they're into your band and want to record you.

- **The Engineer:** The calibre of your engineer can have a dramatic impact on what you accomplish in the studio. Ask for samples of your prospective engineer's work.
- **The Live Room:** The studio should have a live room large enough for the whole band to set up comfortably. Generally, the larger the live room, the bigger the drum sounds will be.
- **Digital vs Analog:** What is the studio's recording format? Ask to hear samples.
- **Number of Tracks:** Does the studio have enough tracks to get the job done (generally consider sixteen tracks to be the minimum). Remember, digital studios usually provide more tracks for less money.
- **Gear:** The gear list should contain a good variety of outboard gear and microphones. It's generally a good sign if the studio has Neumann microphones (i.e. U-47, U-67 or U-87) and Neve preamps and/or recording consoles.
- **A Trial Recording:** If you haven't recorded at a specific studio or worked with a particular engineer before, consider starting with a one-day, one-song recording. That way, if the studio or the engineer are in any way unacceptable, you haven't committed everything you have. It's an unbelievable drag to spend a week and a small fortune recording a bunch of songs, and then hate the results at the end of it.

Preproduction
Getting Ready to Record

Even the simplest things take a long time in the studio. Assume that everything will take ten times longer than you think it will. I'm always amazed how something really simple can take all day and, thinking about it afterwards, I can never quite figure out why. Sometimes it's technical problems; sometimes it's performance issues; sometimes it's last minute changes to the arrangement. I've just had to accept that this is the case.

Time management plays a big part of your success or failure in the studio. One of a producer's big responsibilities is to weigh artistic perfection against time and money constraints. Good producers know when they've gotten the best performance possible in the amount of time available. You have to play the role of producer and force yourselves to move on when something starts to take up too much of your valuable time.

One of the most common studio mistakes is spending 99 percent of the time on beds (particularly guitars) and then rushing the vocals. Keeper vocals are often recorded later in the process, so they always fall victim to time shortages, which is really ironic because vocals are the most important single piece of a demo; A&R people, publishers and managers all listen for melody, vocal hooks and the quality of the lead singer's voice.

The Songs

Before you go into the studio, you'll have to make some tough decisions about your songs and decide which ones are ready to record. Unfortunately, self-criticism is one of the most challenging skills to master. It's tough to step back from your own songs and spot their strengths and weaknesses. It's even sometimes difficult to know which songs are stronger than others; songs you like may not be the songs that everyone else connects with. I usually favour more recent work because the freshness of newer material can give it an edge over older songs. Or you might prefer a song because it showcases your playing when, as a whole, it's not as appealing. It's really difficult to be objective. Play your songs to innocent bystanders to get some outside feedback. Often your favourites will be the popular favourites, but it's great to get a second opinion.

It definitely helps to do a lot of jam space and/or home recording. Listening to yourself on tape gives you a greater degree of objectivity. Road test your songs by playing them live. Once you've performed a song in front of an audience, you play it with a bit more authority and confidence (swagger is a nice word). A road test can also give you a pretty fair indication of how songs are actually working, as opposed to how you think they're working; it's a lot like playing a tape for the innocent bystander—blatantly honest and immediate. If an audience doesn't "get" a song, they don't react—and they don't spare your feelings the way a friend will.

When we were writing our second album, *Creature*, we had a song with the working title "Acid Jazz" that we all thought would be a definite crowd pleaser, a real mosh song. We played a couple of surprise warm-up shows and dropped this little gem into the set. Well, you can guess where this is going— the crowd was rocking all night except during "Acid Jazz" when everyone in the house turned to stone. For a second, we thought it might be awe but, no, they just didn't get it.

How Many Songs?

The number of songs you record depends entirely on your time, money and approach to recording and overdubbing. It's hard to work out a formula for how many songs you can undertake in a visit to the studio. Some musicians use the one song per day calculation, whereas others tackle an entire album in a long weekend. My experiences have always been different, depending on how rehearsed the material is, the studio, the engineer, and our approach. The first time Moist entered the studio, we managed to do nine songs in two days. The second time, we struggled with three songs in five days.

Choose a manageable number of your strongest songs to really focus on. It's much better to record a few songs well than to try to lay down an entire album. It's a huge mistake to undertake too much, particularly if you haven't done very much recording before. And remember, if you're planning to shop the recording to the industry, you only need three songs anyway. Prepare a shortlist of your best songs and prioritize them. That way, if you only manage to record a couple of tracks, at least they'll be your strongest songs.

Preparing Your Songs

Unless you have a fortune to spend on needless studio use, have a collection of finished songs together before you go into the studio. You should be able to play the songs confidently, and the guitar, bass and keyboard parts should work with one another—the songs should gel. Test for conflicts by playing the songs at super-low levels. Sheer volume can mask problems that are soon revealed under the cold light of the studio.

The song arrangements should be finalized so that everyone is clear about how long the intro section or the last chorus is. The lyrics should be finished and written down, if not memorized. It's possible that the studio will give you some last minute inspiration, but don't count on it. Bottom line: go in with finished songs.

There's often a difference between live and studio song arrangements. Some songs will require editorial decisions about the length of sections, particularly when recording a demo. A three minute intro or a ten minute wailing guitar solo may be great live, but they can really bog down a recorded song. One of the first things a serious record producer does is to have the band shorten any long-winded arrangements.

The next thing a serious record producer does is make suggestions for delineating and defining the various sections of a song. Make sure the songs aren't too linear. A linear arrangement offers very little sonic difference between sections and invariably puts the listener to sleep. Define verses, choruses and bridges using dynamics, different sounds and different parts. Examine how the verse actually differs from the chorus, beyond the fact that the chords are different. It's helpful to dip into your CD collection and listen to how bands differentiate between sections on polished, produced recordings.

Tempos

Tempo is not an exact science. Rock bands, even really polished ones, always speed up and slow down. However, it's a good idea to have a set starting tempo. The drummer can listen to a click track or drum machine for a second before you start the song, and tick in at a good starting tempo. Usually, the rest of the song will follow suit. To figure out song tempos, you'll need a good rehearsal tape of the song and a stopwatch. Start the watch on the first beat of the song and count how many beats occur in thirty seconds. Multiply the number of beats by two to determine the beats per minute (bpm). For example, forty-five beats in thirty seconds is a tempo of ninety bpm.

Many bands use a click track in the studio. The click can even be programmed to speed up slightly for choruses or solo sections in order to emulate the feel of free-time playing. It takes a lot of practice to play well to a click. There's a danger that your songs will feel unnatural, sterile and lacking in energy. Unless you practice playing with a click in rehearsal, which means bringing in a drum machine, a multichannel headphone amplifier and headphones for everyone, steer clear of click tracks for awhile. An energetic performance with shifty time is much better than a sterile performance with perfect time.

Gear

Make sure that all your gear is in top working order. Things like crackling volume pots on guitars or grounding problems on amplifiers can be a real hassle. Don't forget, the studio clearly reveals imperfections, so a small crackle in the rehearsal room becomes a big crackle on tape. Put fresh strings on all the instruments and consider getting a new set of drum heads. Sometimes I replace the tubes in my Marshall head before recording, but that's totally your own judgment call (just how old are those tubes?).

Record Producing 101

Before you go near a studio, tape your rehearsals. Choose any particularly vibey, energetic and effective takes to use as reference tapes. Your goal should be to make sonically improved versions of those performances. The first time we ever went into the studio, I asked the engineer how he was planning to record us. His response was simple: "You guys sound great playing live. I want to make the recording sound like you're playing live."

To make a studio recording sound as spontaneous, energetic and vibey as a live performance is actually quite a challenge. In a sterile studio environment the instinct is to tighten up and play everything carefully and perfectly. This mind-set results in recordings that sound mechanical and dull or wooden. This is especially true of overdubbing. Try to capture the live energy and excitement of your band so you don't sound like you're in a recording studio. All through the '60s and early '70s the Rolling Stones recorded live off the floor. They would play a few takes and listen back for that loose, vibey energy. When Keith Richards smiled, they knew they had a keeper.

Recording Approaches

Most recording approaches differ in how to deal with recording bed tracks—the basic rhythm instruments such as the bass, rhythm guitar, keys and, most importantly, the drums. Think of the beds as the basic recording of the band live before overdubs. Every instrument (except the drums) can be easily overdubbed later to fix mistakes or even re-recorded entirely. The drums, however, are a done deal once you've finished the beds; they're the skeleton on which you hang everything else.

Many producers like to keep as much of the bed guitar and bass tracks as possible, particularly with time and money constraints, because overdubbing is so time consuming. Also, bed takes often have that live spark that's difficult to recapture in overdubs. It's always preferable to use an energetic bed take with a some small mistakes than a perfect, but sterile, overdub take.

Approach One: Wham Bam Recording

With the wham bam approach, the entire band (with amplifiers), and possibly even the singer (with monitors or headphones), sets up in a live room and plays. The engineer mics the drum kit and all the amps and uses baffling and partitions to separate the sounds as much as possible. This is the best possible technique for capturing the live feel, because it's exactly like jamming in your rehearsal space. For this reason, it's a pretty good approach for your first studio adventure.

The downside of this technique is sound leakage. Guitars, the snare and cymbals will wash into every microphone at the cost of clarity and separation. This can affect your ability to fix mistakes with overdubbing because that sour keyboard note will be picked up in several different microphones.

Moist has often used the wham bam approach for recording demo versions of songs. It's fast, simple, and can yield decent results. We almost always re-record vocals using a good condenser mic (i.e. a Neumann U-47 or U-67), as opposed to the dynamic mic (i.e. a Shure SM-58) used in the live room. We also overdub additional rhythm guitars and solos after the fact.

By the way, the term wham bam is a term I made up. So if an engineer gives you a funny look when you say you want to record using the wham bam method, you'll know why.

Approach Two: Wham Bam Deluxe

This involves everyone, except the lead singer, playing together in a live room. The singer performs in a vocal booth, basically a sound-proof closet with a window, adjoining the live room. The amplifiers are placed outside the live room (in other booths, in the lounge or in broom closets) while the drummer plays, as before, in the live room. Players wear headphones to hear themselves and the other players. In some studios the engineer can give each player a tailor-made headphone mix, at others you'll have to share mixes (i.e. keyboard and guitar players receive the same headphone mix).

The biggest advantage to the wham bam deluxe approach is that you get separation and clarity, while still enjoying the contact of playing together. Much of the vibe and energy of live performance relates to anticipation and eye contact that can't be duplicated doing overdubs. Also, because of the reduced sound leakage, overdubbing additional instruments and fixing mistakes is a breeze.

The drag is that playing with headphones is very weird and unnatural, and it's often difficult to get a great headphone mix; suddenly you're in a strange listening environment that you're not used to. Adding reverb and/or delay to some of the elements in your headphone mix can help, but headphone playing is not the same as having your amp blasting at you. The big challenge is to ignore the weirdness of the headphones and play normally. Wham bam deluxe is the approach we used to record the first Moist album, *Silver*.

Approach Three: Click-track and Guide Recording

This approach is the most time-consuming, because the instruments are recorded one at a time. It's also the most alien, simply because it's not at all like playing in the familiar environment of your jam space. However, this is the way many big budget recordings achieve perfection.

The process begins by laying a click track to tape. Then, to create guide tracks, the rhythm guitar, bass, and vocals are recorded separately. Finally, the drums are recorded. Once you have the perfect drum take, the bass, guitars and vocals can be retracked. The rest of the instruments and vocals are then recorded one track at a time. If time and money are not an issue, the drums can be painstakingly edited or looped to make every hit consistent. Hit by hit drum editing is often found on big production albums produced by people like Bob Rock.

While this method can lead to perfection, it can also lead to unnatural and sterile recordings. I wouldn't recommend it for your first few trips into the studio. Moist didn't start using this approach until we recorded our second album, *Creature*.

Overdubs

Once you've captured vibey, energetic bed tracks, it's time to consider overdubs. Listen to the beds as a band and decide collectively with the engineer what overdubbing should be done. Boost different instruments up in the mix, listen for mistakes, and decide whether they add character or warrant fixing. Usually the player that made the mistake is the biggest proponent of fixing it. This is why you should all decide together if it's worth screwing with something. If no one else can even hear the mistake, it should probably be left alone.

The luxury of multi-track studio recording is the ability to artificially enhance a band's performance. The limitations of the studio's recording gear will dictate how much overdubbing can be done; it comes down to the number of tracks that are free after the beds are recorded. Usually eight or more tracks are used for the drums, one for bass, one for each guitar, one for lead vocals and two for keyboards, which are generally recorded in stereo. Things like doubling the rhythm guitar or chorus vocals can fatten and improve a recording. But too many overdubs can make a mix sound muddy and confused. Choose your enhancements carefully. We often make a DAT copy of the unimproved bed recording as a reference before we start adding tracks. That way we can go back and make sure it didn't sound better before we started improving it.

Common overdubs include: doubling rhythm guitars; doubling chorus vocals; backing vocals; percussion (tambourine, congas); additional rhythm guitar parts added for texture (acoustic guitars are often effective texture enhancers); additional keyboard parts; and solos.

Write a good song; that's the only way. Yeah, sure you can have bands writing all these riffs all the time, but it just gets boring.

—David MacMillan, marketing manager of EMI Music Canada

The Mix

Mixing is a vital stage of the recording process, where an awful lot can be accomplished. The mix can find or create the sparkle in a fairly mediocre track. The saying "we'll fix it in the mix" does have some truth. It's during the mixing that the final decisions about your recording are made. But beware: This stage can also make a great recording sound truly awful.

Basically, mixing is assigning a level for each individual track in relation to all the other tracks. The engineer sets the levels for each of the individual drums and cymbals, then turns up the bass, guitars, keyboards and the vocals. The goal here is to create a mix that is exciting, dynamic and a realistic impression of a real band playing.

The engineer will use panning controls (the same idea as the balance knob on your home stereo) to position each instrument in the stereo left to right spectrum. Some tracks, like rhythm guitars, might be hard panned to one side, while lead vocals are generally positioned in the middle, coming evenly from the left and right speakers. If the panning is set realistically, you should be able to sit in front of the speakers, close your eyes and see the band playing in front of you.

Along the way, the engineer will EQ the various tracks, because there's often too much going on in specific frequency ranges. For example, the low-mid frequencies might be bogged down because the bass, toms, guitars and keys are all pretty fat sounding. Alone, each instrument sounds great, but together it's too much and sounds muddy. So, the engineer will thin out some of the tracks to reduce the traffic in that area. Another way of making instruments sit well together is by using compression. Compressors moderate the peaks and valleys and fatten thin-sounding tracks to make them more punchy. Effects such as reverb and delay are also commonly used to add a sense of depth or texture and enhance the overall sound of the song.

The Band's Role in the Mix

What is your role in the mixing stage? If you haven't mixed in the studio before, the engineer's knob twiddling can seem a bit mysterious or intimidating—even if you're making your tenth record. Just sit back and observe and, if you're interested, ask questions. If not, take a break until the engineer says the magic words: "Do you want to come in and listen to this?" Until the engineer has a mix more or less up and running, there isn't much to comment on—unless you're a budding engineer.

When you listen to the mix, try to listen to the whole song—don't just focus on your own instrument. This is a very difficult task, believe me. The song might actually sound better with your instrument lower than expected in the mix, but often ego won't let you see that. Scott Litt once said that R.E.M. was the only band he'd ever worked with where everyone was asking to be turned *down* in the mix. Some musicians can get pretty tense during mix discussions (I've been one of them). The more experience you get as a musician, the more you'll learn to serve the song rather than your own parts and ego.

A Long Weekend in the Recording Studio

Let's say you're a four piece (drums, bass, guitar and vocals) booked in for a three day long weekend studio lock-out starting Saturday morning. By the end of the weekend, you want five recorded and mixed songs. For the sake of argument, let's say you're going to use the wham bam deluxe method. The following is a rough road map as to how things might unfold.

Before the Studio

- Have five songs fully written, arranged, and rehearsed.
- Tech your gear: Tune the drums; make sure the amps are working; buy spare nine volt batteries and strings; change the strings on the guitars and basses.
- Ask the studio if you can load in and even set up your gear on Friday night (without paying for Friday night studio time). If not, arrive promptly at the agreed starting time on Saturday morning (remember, time is money).
- Get a good night's sleep and don't arrive hungover.

Day One: The Beds

10:00 AM–11:00 AM: Set up gear.

11:00 AM–12:30 PM: Mic set up: The engineer places microphones on the drums and amplifiers, and double checks the cables and connections. Invariably something doesn't work and the engineer scrambles around replacing stuff.

12:30 PM–2:00 PM: Get sounds: How long this takes depends on how particular you are. The engineer will try different microphones, and adjust their positions to make your gear sound great.

2:00 PM–2:30 PM: Lunch break.

2:30 PM–3:15 PM: Set the headphone mixes and levels.

3:15 PM–4:00 PM: The test pass and listen: Record one pass of a song and listen from the booth to make sure you like the sounds the engineer is getting. Adjust as necessary.

4:00 PM–4:15 PM: Quick psyche-up, smoke break, "we're about to record" moment.

4:15 PM–8:00 PM: Bed recording: You only have about five takes per day for each song before the spark starts to wear off. Assume it takes ten minutes for each pass of a song (that's four minutes for the song and six minutes for getting cued, screwing around and false starts). So, each song will take just under an hour to bed. Resist the temptation to run into the booth and listen back after each take; that hurts your momentum and roughly doubles the length of the process. However, listen to what you've recorded every few passes—particularly if you have limited tape and have to record over inferior takes.

8:00 PM–8:30 PM: Dinner break. Check to make sure you're not getting charged for breaks, otherwise order in food.

8:30 PM–12:30 AM: More bed recording.

Everyone has different tastes when it comes to how much instrumentation should go into a song...Don't assume that every recorded track has to survive the mix. You may find the wiser choice is to let go of some of the tracks that clutter the song and detract from the overall musical vision. Remember, sometimes "less is more!"

- Karen Kane, freelance producer/ engineer working out of Toronto

Day Two: Overdubs

10:00 AM–12:00 PM: Listen to the favourite takes from the previous day. Make final decisions on the versions. Decide what mistakes to fix. Prioritize the songs. Some songs record better than others and it's usually pretty clear which songs are starting to shine. Work on the great ones first. That way, if you run out of time, you can axe songs that aren't working.

12:00 PM–2:00 PM: Bass guitar: Fix any mistakes and/or retrack bass parts. Even fixing only a couple of things can take much longer than you'd think. Matching sounds for the punch-in and cueing up a song takes time.

2:00 PM–2:30 PM: Lunch break.

2:30 PM–8:00 PM: Guitar: Fix any mistakes and/or retrack guitar parts. Overdub solos and double parts as necessary.

8:00 PM–8:30 PM: Dinner break.

8:30 PM–1:00AM: Lead vocal takes. Track keeper vocals. This often involves recording two or more passes of a song and combining the best moments into a single, superior take; this process is called *comping*.

Day Three: Wrapping it Up

10:00 AM–2:30 PM: Record background vocals and anything else that needs to be done.

2:30 PM–3:00 PM: Lunch break.

3:00 PM–4:00 AM: Mix each song. Get cassette copies of each final mix to play on a car stereo to make sure you've got it right. It's amazing how many mixers rely on the car test.

This power weekend of recording won't give you perfection; it takes a lot longer than three days to record five songs to the level of a Metallica or U2 album. Instead, the goal is to capture lively, energetic recordings that allow the strengths of your writing and the sound of your band to shine through. Recognizing the limitations of the process before you start will help you keep everything in perspective.

Mastering

The word "master" is the most heavily used term in recording. There are studio masters, production masters, master tapes, and masters and slaves. The mastering I'm talking about occurs once the mixing stage is complete, but before the tape is sent off to a manufacturer to make CDs or cassettes. Mastering is performed in a dedicated mastering studio by an engineer who specializes in mastering (called, surprisingly enough, the mastering engineer). Mastering creates a master disc (CD-R), 1630 tape (a big Beta cartridge), DAT, or Exabyte™ tape (looks like a small VHS) which is sent to the CD plant for the manufacturing process. All these formats have individual advantages, but CD-R and DAT are the most common. Check with the CD plant first to see if they have any preferences as to what kind of master they want (also known as an "audio source").

The mastering engineer gives your recordings some tender loving care, smoothing the sonic rough edges to give your songs a consistent sound. Mastering also aims to make your recordings neutral. Every studio has a slightly different sonic character, owing to the monitors, amps, shape of the control booth, and what the booth's walls are covered with. So, your recordings may not sound as good when played at home or in the car. By neutralizing your recordings, mastering makes them sound reasonably good just about anywhere.

What Mastering Involves
- **Song sequencing:** This places the songs into the order you want for the CD or cassette.
  Editing: Your chance for any last-minute editing, such as trimming out an overly long solo, smoothing song fades, and determining the pauses between songs and such.
- **Equalization:** The engineer adjusts the EQ for each song so that they're not too bright or bass heavy and so that the overall EQ of all the songs is consistent. Equalization can also be used to add clarity to the vocals or punch to the bass.
- **Compression:** Your songs are put through compressors to maximize the overall volume and add punch and vitality. Peak limiting removes any inaudible level spikes, called transient peaks, which can cause problems during CD manufacturing.

In a perfect world, mastering makes your recordings sound better. In an imperfect world, it's a bit of a dangerous game. Most of the major label releases in North America are mastered by one of a handful of well-known, extremely busy and very expensive mastering engineers. There's always a risk with lesser known, cheaper and/or local mastering. Shoddy mastering can make recordings sound worse than the premastered material. Always compare the pre and post-mastered sound to make sure you've taken a step forward. When you're shopping around, always ask for a list of mastering credits. Check the credits on local CDs you like for leads. Local mastering fees range from $500 to $1500 (sometimes as much, or more, than your actual recording session).

Samples

With the rise of powerful and reasonably inexpensive sampling gear, many artists are getting into sampling, which involves taking a piece of a prerecorded song and incorporating it into your music. The Verve's worldwide smash hit "Bittersweet Symphony" featured a string arrangement sampled from an instrumental version (by the Andrew Loog Oldham Orchestra) of an old Rolling Stones song. However, before you load up your indie album with samples of all the greatest moments of recorded music, there is a catch.

Any time a sample of someone else's music is used, permission must be obtained from the copyright holder of the music. Otherwise, you could be looking at some big-time legal problems (and you don't want to get sued by Zeppelin or the Stones; they have serious lawyers). Using a sample often comes at a price: either a onetime payment or a percentage of the song's earnings.

The cost of using samples tends to rise with the stature of the artist. Some lesser known bands from the past are simply happy to be remembered, while super groups will want the world for the use of their music. The Verve, for instance, gave up 100 percent of the songwriting credits and subsequent earnings from "Bittersweet Symphony" to Allan Klein, the ex-manager of the Stones and owner of the copyrights to their early material (the songwriting credit is listed as Jagger/Richards/Oldham).

Clearing Samples

Obtaining permission to use a sample is called clearing the sample, and the process is quite straightforward. Simply call the publisher listed in the album's liner notes and request permission. You'll have to send them a copy of the song containing the sample. The publisher will then contact the copyright holder, usually the artist, and come back to you with the terms. There's definitely room to negotiate, but a lot depends on the stature of the artist.

Cover Songs

If your album includes a cover song, you have to apply for a mechanical license (basically, getting permission to cover the song) from the Canadian Musical Reproduction Rights Association (CMRRA). As an indie band manufacturing a limited number of CDs, you'll be charged a fee for each song covered and each album manufactured for distribution in Canada. This is called pay as you press, and the fees go to the publisher of the song in question, who will then pay the writers their share. The fee is 7.4¢ per song under five minutes long; each additional minute costs 1.48¢. If you cover one song and press a thousand copies, it will cost you 7.4¢ times 1,000, or $74.

Contact the CMRRA at:

Canadian Musical Reproduction Rights Association Ltd.
56 Wellesley St., #320
Toronto, ON, M5S 2S3
Tel: 416-926-1966   Fax: 416-926-7521
www.cmrra.ca

Outside Canada, your distributor will have arrangements in place with the various agencies, like the Harry Fox agency in the US. Again, this is only if you are covering other people's songs. You can also pay the publisher directly and not go through collection agencies. Either way is fine, as long as you pay the royalties.

Contact the Harry Fox Agency at:

Harry Fox Agency
711 Third Avenue
New York, NY, USA, 10017
Tel: 212-370-5330   Fax: 212-953-2384
Email: clientservice@harryfox.com
www.nmpa.org/hfa

FACTOR Assistance

Recording can be extremely expensive. Bands often spend far more than they can afford for professional calibre demo tapes. However, to record demos and independent albums, Canadian bands can turn to the Foundation to Assist Canadian Talent on Records (FACTOR) for financial help. Assistance is also available for videos and tour support.

FACTOR is a nonprofit organization that provides assistance for "the growth and development of the Canadian independent recording industry." Over the last twelve years FACTOR has provided over sixteen-million dollars towards the production of recordings for distribution in Canada.

FACTOR offers several programs to help independent bands. Three of the most relevant FACTOR programs are: the Professional Demo Award; Independent Artists Recording Loans; and FACTOR Loans for Artists with Distribution. Contact FACTOR to obtain more information, application forms and program deadlines. There are several other programs that might be of interest to you, please ask FACTOR for a complete listing of their current programs. Contact FACTOR at:

FACTOR
125 George Street, 2nd Floor
Toronto, ON
M5A 2N4
Tel: 416-368-8678
www.factor.ca

General Program Information

Applicants to FACTOR's programs must be Canadian citizens or have landed immigrant status, and must live in Canada. The music must satisfy the strict Canadian content regulations. FACTOR recognizes a variety of musical genres and requires applicants to state which category their music falls into. FACTOR-recognized music includes: rock (alternative, pop, hard rock); roots (folk, blues, traditional); country; reggae; easy listening (a.c.) and new age; children's; world music; jazz (traditional, contemporary, acid); classical; and urban (hip-hop, euro/house, R & B, commercial dance).

Applications are reviewed by an evaluation panel that's composed of representatives from the recording and broadcasting industries. They assess applications according to the quality of the music, lyrics, vocals, musicianship, originality, package presentation (bio, promotional material), sales potential, and radio airplay potential.

It's very important to follow all FACTOR application requirements to the letter. They must be legible, complete (with all accompanying documentation) and adhere to FACTOR guidelines. The literature stresses that you'll be disqualified for any omission or aberration from the requirements, so take your time and make sure you get everything right.

There is serious competition for FACTOR assistance; far more bands apply than the foundation can possibly assist. If you're turned down, don't be discouraged. Simply strengthen your package and try again. Persistence is the key.

Professional Demo Award

The Professional Demo Award assists new artists with the production of a professional calibre demo tape to be used for shopping to the music industry. FACTOR will cover 50 percent of your recording costs up to a maximum contribution of $1,000.

Independent Artists Recording Loans

This program assists unsigned Canadian artists in the production, marketing and promotion of independent releases. You must record a minimum of six songs, and the finished master must be made available for commercial sale.

FACTOR will loan you 50 percent of your recording budget up to a maximum loan of $7,500. FACTOR will also loan as much as $2,000 to cover the basic costs of assembling a professional press kit. Again, this is based on FACTOR contributing 50 percent of the total budget. More marketing and promotion funds can be obtained from FACTOR once specific sales levels are achieved. Loans are paid back at a rate of $1.00 per unit sold for a period of two years after release in Canada.

FACTOR Loans for Recording

FACTOR Loans for Recording assist artists, Canadian-controlled labels, production companies, producers and managers by partially financing the production, marketing and promotion costs of EPs or albums for commercial release. To be eligible, applicants must have a fully-executed distribution deal in place with a FACTOR-recognized distributor before applying.

To satisfy distribution requirements you must either:

- Have a licensing agreement with a major label (EMI, Sony, and the rest).
- Have a licensing agreement with a Canadian-owned and controlled independent record company or label that has acceptable distribution (Aquarius Records, Nettwerk and similar).
- Have a distribution agreement with a FACTOR-recognized distributor such as Distribution Fusion III, Festival,or Outside Music. See a complete list at the FACTOR website.

FACTOR will loan 50 percent of the total recording budget, up to a maximum of $30,000. FACTOR will also loan $2,000 to cover basic costs for professional press kits. Marketing and promotion financing of up to $3,000 is also available.

chapter six

The Independent Release

Releasing an Independent Album

Before you decide to release an independent album, ask yourselves a simple question: Why? Releasing an album involves hard costs and investment from the band, so you should have solid reasons for making that investment. Many indie bands spend a ton of money putting together and manufacturing more albums than they can sell. The albums just end up collecting dust in someone's basement. The biggest drag is that a year later these albums probably won't reflect your best work; they'll simply be outdated.

Reasons to release an independent album include: to establish a fan base; to help finance tours; to develop a reputa-

*You can do
extremely well
in this country
independently.
There is no
need to go
farther than a
P&D deal, if
you think you
can do it on
your own. A lot
of people have
this belief that
suddenly
somebody signs
you to a record
deal and a limo
pulls up in your
driveway and
you're living the
high life. I'll tell
you one thing,
you get up on
stage and there's
a packed house
in front of you,
and you know
it's because of
what you did
by yourself, it's
a hell of a lot
more rewarding.
And it's
empowering too.
In the position
that we're in
now, if people
approach us
from labels,
what do I have
to lose?*

tion, thereby making yourself more attractive to the majors; to give yourself clout for negotiating with the industry; and to learn the basics of the record business from the ground up.

Releasing your own album is proactive in that you're not waiting passively for the major labels to magically make your career happen. Releasing an independent album puts you in charge of your destiny; you create your own opportunities.

The Release Scenarios

Once you've decided to release an album, you must determine the type of release it will be. There are many ways to release an album independently, depending on the scale of your distribution. Pressing five-hundred copies and selling them off the stage counts as an independent release. Forming your own record label and distributing your album regionally or even nationally is an independent release. Signing to an independent (non-major) label is still considered an independent release. Depending on the band, each of these scenarios can be very effective, but they all involve varying degrees of risk.

Signing with an Independent Label

Releasing an album through an indie label is similar to dealing with a major, only on a smaller scale. You have to attract the label's attention and get them hyped enough to assume the financial risks to manufacture, distribute and promote your album. This route can be an extremely effective way to release your music and develop a fan base. Indie labels can range in size from basement-operated micro-companies to full-service labels with mainstream distribution and a fair amount of clout.

A particularly attractive feature of indie labels is that they place a greater emphasis on artist development than the majors, who often discard bands that don't immediately reach a certain level of success. Indie labels are more inclined to work with bands to gradually create a fan base. In fact, in today's marketplace where artist development is becoming increasingly rare, many majors view the indie label system as a farm league to develop the big names of the future. Major labels often buy up successful artists' indie label contracts. In recent years, indie labels have fulfilled a valuable industry role by servicing albums in niche music genres like hip-hop, punk, and reggae.

When considering a prospective indie label, it's quite important to look carefully at their track record, roster of artists, distribution and resources. Some labels have full-scale P&D (pressing and distribution) deals with major labels while others use alternative distribution channels. All indies are not created equally, and in many cases, bands might be better off releasing their own album than turning to an unstable, inept indie label.

Major Label Distribution
The Do-it-Yourself, Full-on, National Release

With major label distribution, you're not only the artist, but a full-service record company as well. In essence, you create your own independent record label and assume the workload and financial risks of a national release. Orchestrating a national release requires a considerable amount of infrastructure. You're competing head to head with major label releases, so you have act like your own major label, taking on all the activities yourself. It's not easy, but it's not impossible.

The process starts with a pressing and distribution deal (P&D in industry lingo) to enable you to both manufacture and get albums into stores. With a P&D deal, a label (usually a major) manufactures and distributes your albums through their distribution network. Labels typically commission around 20 to 25 percent of wholesale, deducting manufacturing and shipping costs from your cut. If your album doesn't sell well and is returned, these costs fall back to you; you'll owe the label money. As a result, the majors aren't keen on this kind of deal unless you're a full-fledged indie label like Nettwerk, True North, or Alert. Landing a P&D deal requires a lot of clout.

To avoid the nightmare of massive returns, you have to aggressively market and promote your album to create a demand for it. To get radio play and media coverage, you'll have to hire an indie promoter and publicist or use the major label's promotion and marketing departments. Of course, all these costs are yours. You'll probably need to make a video for your single, further increasing costs. You'll also need to tour extensively to pull the campaign together and to hammer home your presence in cities across Canada.

This approach scares me, and it's not difficult to see why. The chances of spending a bundle, only to have all your CDs returned, are simply too great. Even most major label releases are not successful. In fact, in the US, the average major label CD sold under a thousand albums last year. Labels lose

I have nothing to lose. I can release this independently if I want, it will do better than the last one. More people should do it, really.

–Matthew Good

money on most of the artists they work; fortunately for them, it only takes one smash success to offset those losses. The P&D route means you assume all the same risks faced by the majors without having the same industry contacts, relationships, or manpower. There are success stories, but it's a very dangerous game. You need very deep pockets to record, manufacture and promote an independent album.

If, through extensive touring, you've developed a sizable national fan base that will run out and buy your album as soon as it comes out, the P&D approach might make sense. Bands such as Sloan and Age of Electric had reasonable success with this. However, if you've already reached that level of stature, the labels should be climbing all over themselves to sign you to a big fat deal. It's better to let a label take the financial risks of putting out your album.

The Licensing Deal

A variation of the P&D deal is the licensing deal, where the major does all the promotion and marketing, treating you pretty much like a signed act. You make less money than a P&D deal, but more than a directly signed act. You also retain ownership of your masters. Again, you'll need clout to get a licensing deal as most majors would rather own masters than rent them. Licensing deals were popular in the mid 1980s (Blue Rodeo, for example, have such a deal) when many major labels had to beef up domestic signings due to government legislation. If you find yourself in the middle of a bidding war, concessions such as a licensing deal could be a deal sweetener. Any situation that lets you keep your masters is a good one.

Setting up Your Own Indie Label

Many bands opt to go to the trouble of forming an actual indie record label to release their album, even if the release is limited to selling CDs at the merch table at shows. While forming a label to release your own material is optional, it does offer a couple of advantages: It gives your band added credibility in the eyes of the general public and, to some extent, the music industry, and it offers some tax advantages (such as writing off part of your rent as a business expense).

Setting up an indie label to release your music is very straightforward; you face none of the complexities and legal issues of releasing other people's music. You just register your label as a business, including doing a name search, and open a business chequing account under the label's name (so you can cash cheques made out to your label). Voila, you have a label.

Of course, having a label doesn't really mean anything in itself; your label is only as good as its distribution, marketing and promotion (all of which will be covered in this chapter).

Releasing Other Bands on Your Label

Releasing your music on your own label is not that complicated. Releasing other bands' music on your label is another story altogether. You need to realise that once you sign other bands, you become an actual, working record label, with a lot of the same issues and responsibilities as the majors, only in miniature. However, the complexity of releasing other bands on your label depends a lot on how serious you are and how far you want to take things.

Music-for-Product

If you're looking at your indie label as, at most, a hobby and don't plan to spend or make very much money, then you can keep relations with your bands extremely casual. In this scenario, labels don't tend to use contracts, and bypass the world of advances, budgets, calculating and paying royalties. Labels in this category often work with a music-for-product system that looks something like this:

• The band supplies recordings of their music.
• The label manufactures maybe 1,000 CDs.
• The label pays the band by giving them 200 free CDs (which they can sell at their shows).
• The label keeps 800 CDs to send out as promotional items and distribute to retailers.

Such arrangements serve all parties involved pretty well, as long as things stay at this level. The band is paid up-front in product, and both label and band are responsible for promoting and working to sell the run of CDs. Then, if you actually do experience some success, you can either repeat the exercise with another 1,000 CD run or alter the relationship to fit the changing demands of the situation (at least in theory). Even at this level, where you're probably only releasing CDs by your friends' bands, draw up a very straightforward, one-page contract in your own language (as opposed to legalese) outlining the responsibilities of band and label. Have a lawyer give it the once over to make sure it says what you want it to say.

It's very important to save all your receipts and keep a detailed ledger of money going in and out. As a business partnership or sole-proprietorship (if the label is a solo venture) you can write off your business losses. Conversely, if you actually make money, you're required to pay tax on it, and the government will expect to see accurate records of your business income and expenses.

Beyond Music for Product

Moving beyond the music-for-product arrangement, you graduate from hobby label to a bona fide independent record company. You enter the world of contracts, royalties, recording and promotion budgets, marketing and so on. The bizarre thing is that suddenly you're the one offering contracts.

This might exaggerate the situation a bit. Operating a micro-label that handles a couple of micro-bands doesn't require anywhere near the infrastructure of a major (at least in the beginning) before you feel the momentum of success. However, you do need to plan for success by securing relationships with your bands with recording contracts.

Indie label recording contracts range from simple, one-page agreements up to huge, intricate documents of fifty pages or more. It depends on the size of the label and the scope of its activities. It's safe to say that as your label grows, so will the size and scope of your contracts. (See Chapter 10 for more details)

Key Points of Any Recording Contract

Advance: This is money you give to the artist that will be recouped out of their record royalties. Advances can be given as a signing bonus or more commonly as a recording fund, out of which the costs of making the album are deducted.

Term: This specifies the length of the relationship as a number of albums. A recording contract term is usually one album, with a series of optional albums following that. This means that if the first record fails, you can let the artist go and, conversely, if the album does well, you can hold the artist to the contract.

Royalty Rate: This refers to the artist's share of the income from the retail sales of the albums. (see Record Royalties, p.228)

Territory: This corresponds to the countries in which the label will be representing the artist. It can be as specific as Canada-only, or as sweeping as "the universe."

Resources

Operating a full-on independent label demands a lot more attention than can realistically be provided here; it's an entire book in itself. I've dealt with some of the larger issues, but if you're thinking about starting up a serious label, make sure to educate yourself about the practical and legal realities of operating a label.

Recommended Reading

• *Musicians and the Law in Canada*, by Paul Sanderson, Carswell Tomson Professional Publishing.
• *All You Need to Know About the Music Business* by Donald Passman, Penguin Books.
• *Tim Sweeney's Guide to Releasing Independent Records*, by Tim Sweeney, TSA Books.

Indie Distribution

Distribution moves your CDs from the manufacturer to the record store racks. You're probably already taking full advantage of the most effective indie distribution method, and it doesn't even involve a record store: selling at your shows. Always keep a generous, well-displayed supply of your album on hand when you perform. Beyond this, getting your music into record stores is an important next step for every band.

Consignment

Consignment is the most common indie distribution method. This involves pressing a relatively small number of CDs and getting them into the indie consignment section of stores in every city along your touring circuit. This approach works for many bands because the risks are minimal; it isn't all that expensive to press a small run of CDs, and if your live shows are drawing, you stand a decent chance of actually selling them.

When a label/distributor tries to put albums in a store, they have to convince the store or chain to purchase the copies. The number of copies is determined by the size and track-record of the artist. The store can actually refuse to carry even one copy; the CD would only be ordered if a customer asked for it and was willing to wait for it to arrive. The retailer never really assumes any risk because even though they "purchase" the CDs, they can return any unsold stock to the distributor.

When it comes to an unknown indie band without a distributor, retailers are simply unwilling to risk buying their CDs; it would be nearly impossible to return unsold albums and get their money back. Instead, most stores have an indie consignment rack.

With consignment, independent artists deliver a small number of CDs (i.e. five) and if they sell, the store takes a cut before issuing the band a cheque. If they don't sell, the artist simply takes them back. This is a no-risk situation for the stores, because the artist is left holding any unsold inventory. Consignment, however, does give indie artists the opportunity to sell their albums alongside major label releases.

Consignment will give you a pretty good indication as to the current demand for your music. If you have a strong buzz on, and the albums are flying out of the store, it might be time to change gears and move on to another release approach. Also, selling tons of indie albums through consignment is a tremendous card to play for the major labels who, believe me, are interested in indie bands who can actually sell albums. The Barenaked Ladies sold thousands of copies of their indie tape using this approach.

Dealing with the Retailer

If you've never toured or had national radio or video airplay, don't worry about selling CDs in other cities. Narrow your focus to areas where you've had some exposure. If you stock albums in cities where no one's ever heard of you, you're wasting time and money, because you won't sell any CDs.

Selling CDs on Consignment

- Approach consignment-friendly retailers and ask to speak to the person who takes care of consignment sales.
- You should be armed with a promo pack, five copies of your CD and a store copy for the staff, so they can play your music in the store, if they're into it.
- The store will apply about a 25 percent markup, so keep your asking price low enough that your CD is competitive with other independent albums.
- Get a store receipt for the number of CDs left for sale to

eliminate the chance of any discrepancies later.

- If the CDs sell, you'll periodically receive a cheque for your cut of the proceeds (in reality, you'll have to bug them for it).
- Keep tabs on inventory. Indie CDs are not a huge priority for stores, so if your CD does sell out, you'll have to be on the case and make more copies available. Also, the more the CD sells, the more stores will stock. If they sell out of the initial five, they might take ten the next time. On the flip side, stores won't stock your CD for long if no one is buying it.

Advanced Consignment

If your band is enjoying regional or national exposure, capitalize on it by getting your CD into stores wherever that exposure is happening. If you can demonstrate that you have a buzz on, it's possible to deal directly with the head offices of the major record store chains. This can get your CD into their stores nationwide (some stores have separate racks for local and national indie albums). Promo packs and professionalism are essential when dealing with head offices; showing them there's a buzz on, tour experience and airplay can translate into sales.

Another option is to hire an independent promoter or a professional consignment broker. They'll stock your album in the appropriate stores and track the inventory. This service comes at a fee of about $1.00 to $2.00 per CD, but it makes a lot of sense for indie bands that have exposure outside their local markets. The consignment broker may even be able to get some stores to buy your albums outright. Many bands have had good experiences with Indie Pool, who handles distribution for over 2,000 independent artists in Canada. They can also provide e-commerce, database cataloguing, toll-free mail order, retail special order fulfillment, SoundScan registration and website construction. Visit their website at www.indiepool.com.

On-line Distribution

As I write this, on-line sales of albums in general, and especially for indie albums, are nowhere near the sales figures for conventional channels (i.e. record stores). on-line sales are definitely growing, but we're a few years away from the cyber-domination of retail, so to speak. That said, no outlet for indie album sales should be overlooked.

There are basically two ways to sell albums on the Internet. You can set up a merchandising page on your own

Bands have to have a really clear or a realistic view of what record sales really are like out there. I mean, they are not as big as people think they are. People think that every indie band that puts out a record and has an ad in a magazine sells a thousand copies. It's just, like, not the case. We've got records here that have sold, like, thirty copies, and some that have sold 3,000 and some that have sold 30,000.

– Mark Milne, cofounder of the indie label Sonic Unyon

website, and people can order CDs directly. Get them to send a cheque (wait for it to clear the bank) and then mail them the CD. Charge enough to cover shipping and handling. Don't expect to get rich with sales from your website, because people rarely buy things from indie bands' websites. Without the ability to deal securely with credit card sales, your website can be little more than a glorified mail-order catalogue.

The second way is to sign up with an Internet-based company that works with independent artists. Dealing with companies such as cdbaby.com or theorchard.com can yield impressive results. These companies are all independent music brokers that either create a page at their site for each album they service or get your album onto the large (and successful) retail sites such as Amazon.com and CDNow.com.

Both companies take about 30 percent of retail as payment. New Internet companies pop up everyday, so ask around and conduct a search of web-based indie music retailers.

Independent Distribution Companies

The next step up the distribution ladder is signing on with an indie distribution company. They're mostly concerned with your album's demand. If they get your CD into stores, will anyone want to buy it? Radio play, previous consignment sales, and tour draw are all taken into consideration. Distributors also want to see that you have a professional package. If your album sounds like it was recorded underwater, an indie distributor will probably think twice about working with you.

It's quite common for indie distributors to offer the services of a promotions department to help create demand for your album. Depending on your distribution deal, promotional costs are either included in the distributor's cut or charged back to you as additional expenses. Indie distributors can range quite dramatically in size, clout and resources, so research any of the prospective companies thoroughly. Talk to the managers of cool indie record stores and find out who the best distributors are.

Marketing & Promotion

Promoting an indie record, both locally and nationally, is a pretty challenging task. You're small; your competitors (the major labels) are very large, with numerous field representatives spread out across the country. You have one small release while your competitors have new releases coming out all the time, both domestic and international. Many independent artists have outmaneuvered and outperformed the majors. It can be done, and like someone, somewhere once said, "you can't stop a hit."

To go up against the competition, you have to understand how they think and operate, and use as many of their strategies as possible. Ultimately, it's going to be your unique, creative touches that will make the difference.

Selling Albums Major Style

The strategy of hitting the target audience (demographic) from as many sides as possible is followed to the letter by the majors. Their multipronged campaigns hit the record-buying audience in numerous ways.

Most promotional campaigns will consist of a selection of the following and, depending on the creativity of the label, will also include some unique one-off approaches.

At Record Stores

The marketing department provides stores with point of purchase materials, known as "P.O.P," such as posters, life-size cardboard cutouts, stickers, hanging mobiles and postcards. The sole purpose of P.O.P. is to create an in-store presence for the artist; to make the potential record buyer aware that the album is available. Record labels also spend a great deal of effort and money to front rack new releases (i.e. have them sitting on shelves at the front of the store) and to book the front window space for displays.

Record companies often set up in-store performances and autograph sessions for bands on the road. Usually these appearances are set up in conjunction with radio station support. The local station advertises the event and usually sends their mascot (the bear, the fox, the lizard or whatever) to the store for the appearance. These events can generate a pile of record sales, or in industry language, create a sales spike.

The Indie Angle: Indie bands can't afford front rack or window display space. However, with a little sweet talking, it's possible to get your poster up in stores, particularly those with a strong indie focus. Leaving free stickers and other promotional materials can really help your exposure. Try making a small cash counter display tray to hold your CDs or stickers.

The average major label artist sold 702 CDs last year in the U.S. They received an approximate royalty rate of $1.00 per CD. Since they didn't sell that many, they owe the record company money! However, you can build your own company, record the music you want, make CDs for $1.70, sell them yourself for $12 or to a distributor for $7.00. In either case, you are making more money selling yourself than if you were signed to a major. After all, 93 percent of all major label releases fail in a year. Do you want them to take your career over?

- Tim Sweeney, author of Tim Sweeney's Guide to Releasing Independent Records

On the Street

Street postering and its cousins, street murals and billboards, are popular street level promotional tools. Often, a few weeks before a release, the majors put up teaser posters that are somehow vague or confusing to create conversation, curiosity and later, awareness of a release.

The Indie Angle: This is your turf, use it to your advantage.

Record Launch Parties

Labels hold private record launches, sometimes called listening parties, in cities across the country. Staff from local record stores, the media, including press, TV and radio, and contest winners party in a local night spot and hear the new release. Depending on the city and the nature of the event, the band will be in attendance and occasionally even play a set.

The Indie Angle: An indie band will often hire a publicist to work the media and make the general public aware of an album launch (and the party that goes with it). Unfortunately, the media often get invited to several launches in one week, and consequently tune out and fail to show up. However, originality in creating your event can work to generate interest. Make your launch memorable and different; use your imagination. Use unusual locations, like a laundromat or an art gallery. If possible, use a location that ties in to your group name or album title (if the band is called Whale, try an event with the local aquarium).

Radio

Radio airplay is crucial for promoting a record. If radio gets behind a band or a song, it can have dramatic effects.

Criteria for Radio Play
• The station's music format.
• Local and/or national record sales (SoundScan).
• Politics (they'll play a label's unknown artist in return for the right to present a show by one of the label's bigger name acts).
• Airplay at other radio stations, locally and nationally (radio programmers look at other programmers' charts).
• Audience reaction (called phones) i.e. the telephone lines light up whenever the song's played and/or a lot of callers request it.

- A band is coming to town; the station is presenting the show.
- The band is taking part in a special event, sponsored by the station (these are referred to as radio shows and are common in the summer and at Christmas—you play these for free).
- The badgering of an indie promoter over and above the label's promotions staff (it's common for labels to hire outside promoters to work important songs to radio and then bill 50 percent of the costs back to the artist).
- The record label offers to sponsor a special promotion (win a trip, or other prize), if the song is played.

The Indie Angle: Indie bands always seem to have a tough time getting radio play, especially on mainstream radio. Hiring an indie promoter to service a single to programmers can work, but only if you can give the promoter a story to work with (i.e. strong indie sales or a hot selling tour). Still, competition for spins at commercial radio is intense, so most indie bands focus on campus and community radio instead.

While campus radio formats don't generally lead to piles of album sales, they can play a valuable role in creating exposure for you and your album. Check out *Chart* magazine and its website for information on campus radio playlists (www.chartattack.com).

SoundScan

SoundScan, established in 1991, revolutionized the way the music industry tracks record sales. Prior to SoundScan, sales figures were tied to the number of records shipped. Record labels could exaggerate (or hype) the performance of an album by shipping more product than there was actually a demand for.

Now, every Wednesday, SoundScan releases in-depth statistics on how many albums were actually sold (scanned through at retail) from Sunday midnight to the next Sunday midnight. All retailers aren't yet plugged into SoundScan, so the figures aren't 100 percent accurate, but they definitely provide a very good idea of how albums are performing. SoundScan charts have an enormous impact on the music industry, directly affecting the decisions of everyone from label executives to radio programmers and booking agents. This, by the way, is a very good reason to put a bar code on your indie album, because without it, your release will be invisible to the SoundScan super-computer.

Check out the Jam!MusicCharts at www.canoe.ca for recent (week-old) SoundScan statistics. If you want up to the minute sales figures at your fingertips, you'll have to pay for a SoundScan subscription, which runs at about $14,400 per year (this gives you access to detailed sales on everyone).

Print Media

Print media consists of local and national newspapers and magazines as well as Internet media such as Jam!Showbiz at Canoe.ca and Yahoo.com; these are published either daily, weekly, biweekly, or monthly. The publicity department utilizes print media in three ways (the first two are free).

- **Record reviews:** A label delivers free copies of the new CD (often by hand) to the media and begs for (good) reviews.
- **Articles and interviews with the band:** A label's publicity department works to get print media interested in the band and their CD. Articles coincide with upcoming tour dates or a new release, because the press needs a reason to do a story.
- **Advertising:** Record labels will buy advertising space to announce new releases, tours, or to reinforce sales and airplay in key markets. Often, deals are worked out with a local record store where the store places an ad featuring the album and receives compensation from the label (known in the trade as "co-op" ads). The majors buy advertising in alternative weekly newspapers (like the *Georgia Straight* in Vancouver, *Now* in Toronto, and *Hour* in Montreal), as the readership is more or less the record buying demographic.

The Indie Angle: Most alternative weekly papers and music magazines (like *Chart*) run indie columns and sometimes, in the case of magazines, a section dedicated to indie bands with a buzz. Send a promo pack to the journalist in charge of the column. Again, it helps to have an angle such as a new release or an upcoming show to perk up their interest. Submitting a copy of your album for review (accompanied by a promo pack, of course) is also a good step. Sadly, without a major publicity stunt or particularly exciting story, it's hard to break into the big newspapers and magazines.

Television

Television stations typically require an event, like a well-publicized concert, before doing anything on even a major label band. The publicity department badgers station personnel until they agree to do a quick interview with the band on day of the show. Sometimes, labels buy fifteen or thirty second slots on mainstream television to advertise a record, but this is not very common, unless the ad is for the new Celine Dion record or a K-Tel all hits package.

The Indie Angle: Unless your CD shoots straight to number one on its first day of release, or you organize some crazy-ass publicity stunt that may land you in jail (not recommended), you're probably not going to get a lot of mainstream television coverage. If you're part of a multiband festival or charity event, you may see some airtime, but even then it's rare to get an interview. It's also possible to play local breakfast and daytime magazine shows, if you're persistent and have a buzz going. Otherwise, your television career as an indie will probably be limited to cable access programming, which won't break your band, but is still pretty good practice for future opportunities.

Music Television

MuchMusic, MuchMoreMusic, VH1, MusiquePlus, Musi-Max, MTV, M2, and CMT have a young record-buying viewership and consequently have a real impact on record sales. The majors have a special relationship with these channels, providing promotional opportunities and access to superstars, not to mention the power of the advertising dollar. Music television charts influence radio programmers when they're designing their own playlists.

Music channels promote albums by:
• Playing videos.
• Running ads for albums and concerts.
• Running promotions that tie their sponsors into contests involving artists.
• Presenting concerts.
• Interviewing and running features on bands.

There were no real contracts or anything in the beginning; it was very loose. We look up to a lot of other labels, a lot of which operate without contracts, so we tried to emulate that for a while, but found out that that didn't work the best. I think we were a lot more trusting and naive than we are now. Had some of the bands been signed to contracts properly, like we do now, we would have probably been in a lot better position financially very earlier on.

-Mark Milne,
cofounder of the indie label
Sonic Unyon

The Indie Angle: Your indie video could receive some play during specialty programs. If you're gigging in Toronto, it's quite possible to snag a quick interview on an indie show, which they'll play before your video. Unfortunately, it's usually pretty rare for indie bands to actually get a video into rotation, with or without the services of an indie promoter; it does occasionally happen (i.e. the video for "Push"), but the odds are stacked against you. However, keep the music stations informed of your activities, such as a CD release or gig in their home-base city.

Concerts and Tours

Live performance is the anchor of record promotion. Blowing people away with a killer live show always generates sales. However, your biggest target is the people who don't come to your show. Many of the various avenues of promotion are most effective when tied in with a live performance and/or tour. It's very common to see massive sales spikes follow a band touring across the country. This has as much to do with the media coverage, advertising, increased airplay and any of the other promotional activities as it does with the performance itself. If a thousand people see you live, a hundred times that number probably heard about you coming to town, thought about you and became potential record buyers in the process.

The Indie Angle: It's vital to play cities where your album is available, and conversely to make your album available when you play. That way, all of the micromarketing activities you do in a city will work towards creating CD sales. Also, be sure to take full advantage of the story value of your tour with the media.

Manufacturing

The general rule in manufacturing is that the unit cost of each CD or cassette drops as the size of the order increases. This is particularly true of small orders of less than five-hundred units, where the unit cost can be several times more than that of a larger order. So, before you enter the manufacturing process, you should know what you're going to do with the CDs and/or cassettes that you make.

If you're not on tour and have no airplay, or if you're only going to use your recordings for your promo pack, you should resist the temptation to manufacture too many copies (despite a lower unit cost). In fact, for the purposes of a promo pack, burning your own CDs on a home computer might be the best option. However, if you're going to be aggressively marketing your recordings as an independent album, going for an order of a thousand or more copies can make a lot of sense.

CDs vs Tapes

You'll have to decide whether to release your album on CD, cassette, or both. Over 80 percent of the albums sold in Canada are in CD format. Cassettes may not make sense any more. When vinyl records were phased out and CDs were still fairly new, cassettes held a much larger market share, but no longer. People seem to take indie albums on CD more seriously than those on cassette.

The Manufacturing Process

An album consists of two elements: packaging and recorded music. Accordingly, the manufacturing process consists of two different stages: package printing and audio duplication. Printing involves the printing all of the packaging for the CDs or cassettes, and duplication involves copying the master of your recordings onto blank CDs or cassette tapes.

General Packaging Issues

Beyond the size of the order, several factors affect the cost of printing CD packaging.

- **Printers:** the music industry is served by about four or five printers that have perfected a gang-run method to keep booklet printing prices very low. The company that presses your CD will get you these industry prices. Shop around.
- **Colour:** Full-colour printing, also known as four-colour or CMYK printing, is more expensive than one or two colour printing. However, printers that run CD covers for the music industry will charge an extra fee for two colour printing (black and red, for example) as it deviates from their standard set up. For an additional charge you can even get into fifth colours such as silver and gold. To save money, many bands go for interior black and white printing with full-colour outside.
- **Number of pages/panels:** Some CDs and cassettes come with expensive multipage booklets or pull-outs. The price goes up with each page or panel added, so keep the size of your packaging down to improve your bottom line. Use only what is required.

- **Paper weight and gloss:** There's usually no real choice. Printers use "house stock." Special paper usually costs more.
- **Film costs:** Film for reproducing your artwork is a one time expense that's directly related to the number of pages you're using (i.e. the more pages or more colour, the more film, the larger the cost). You can save film costs by ganging up as many pages as possible onto one large piece of film. By the way, the film we're talking about here is not the kind used for photographs, but rather large negatives that printers use to make printing plates (how the colours get on the paper). Film costs are sometimes added on to the design bill. Many printers are switching to digital printing (plates are made directly from the digital art files), so film is slowly being phased out.

Packaging can have a big effect on how people will perceive your album and, consequently, on sales. Amateur, shoddy artwork and layout may discourage people from buying, because it suggests that the music inside will sound amateur and shoddy. Design and colour can have a big impact on your album's visibility on store shelves; effective packaging catches the eye and prompts people to check out the album. If you're planning to seriously compete with other releases on the store shelves, consider bringing in a graphic designer. Designing effective packaging yourself is quite challenging, particularly if you don't have a background in graphic design.

Graphic artists charge from $35 to $60 an hour; some charge a flat rate. Prices can range from hundreds up into the thousands of dollars, depending on the experience and the reputation of the artist or company. A typical indie design-only rate is around $800. For a little extra, a graphic artist will design posters and stickers based on the same theme as the album artwork. If you opt for a flat rate, be sure to get a detailed list of everything you'll receive.

To find a graphic artist, talk to other bands you know whose graphic look you admire. Check with local music organizations, as sometimes they have directories with contacts for graphic services.

There are two professional directories for the Canadian music industry, *Music Directory Canada* (available at all major bookstores or from www.nor.com). The other is the *CONTACT* directory (this is available at music trade shows or from Dunn-Farrell@home.com).

You can also check your local Yellow Pages™ under

"graphic art," contact the designers at the local cool college paper, or if there's an indie label in town, chances are you could probably hire whoever they use (call and ask). CD manufacturing companies usually offer extremely competitive all-in deals that include graphic design (this is a very competitive area, and you might luck into an amazing deal). Try to really discuss everything up front and see what, if any, limitations there are.

You'll also probably require a photographer to take band shots and any abstract photography you want to use in your design. Photographers range in price from free for a keen amateur (you cover film and processing) to $1,200 for a good local professional and up to $15,000 for a one-day shoot with a top international photographer. Again, make sure to get a detailed list of everything you'll get for the price. Professional photographers usually have a list of stylists and make-up artists that they regularly use, and will include their fees in the price.

The ideal situation is to hire a designer who will also act as a creative director for the project. A good designer is well-connected and knowledgeable, and can usually find the right photographer and other members of the creative team as required. They'll not only coordinate everything, but they'll make sure it all fits stylistically with the image you want, and that costs are kept within your budget.

If you decide to create the design and artwork yourself, ask the printing company or the manufacturing rep to give you the exact size and dimension of the templates for the packaging. CD manufacturers often provide detailed guidebooks or digital files for bands that are designing their own layout. If you're submitting your work on disk, make sure the software program is acceptable to the manufacturer; QuarkXpress™ for Macintosh is industry standard. One big warning about trying to do it all yourself: Make sure you know what you're doing. One very small mistake could eat up any possible do-it-yourself savings. Luckily, a lot of CD manufacturers are very specific about what you have to provide them with. In fact, don't get into the final layout or create final film until you've confirmed all the specs with your manufacturing rep.

This is an old adage: Just because everybody can make a CD, doesn't mean that everybody should.

- Denise Donlon, president of Sony Music Canada (former VP/GM MuchMusic/ MuchMore Music)

Things You Must Include in Your Design

- **UPC bar code:** This is the rectangular bar code you see on most of the things you purchase. Including a bar code means that the sales of your album will show up on SoundScan album sales tabulations (your distributor does the paperwork involved to get you in the system), because your CD will scan at the checkout counter of all record stores. Talk to the CD manufacturing rep about getting a bar code (usually a $30 fee). If you don't have a bar code, some stores may refuse to stock your CD and you may have to sticker it with a bar code (some stores may do it and charge you).

- **MAPL:** If your band and your material is Canadian, include the MAPL icon on your CD. The icon means you comply with CanCon guidelines (see page 102). Include only the letters that apply in the circle artwork. If individual songs require different MAPL icons, try to simplify it on the inside of the booklet (all tracks are MAPL except tracks 3,7,9 which are MAL). The MAPL logo usually goes on the CD label (tray card is ok as well) or anywhere on the packaging, but preferably close to the song publishing information.

- **Compact disc icon:** ▣▣▣▣ This symbol is normally required on the CD label only. The CD rep can get you this.

- **The copyright symbol:** © For publishing (on the inside booklet or on the CD label) followed by the year (optional) and publishing company name (never put "© SOCAN" on your packaging, because that means that SOCAN owns the copyright to your songs). You can put ©2001 Indie Bible Publishing/SOCAN, which indicates your publishing company and your collection society. On the tray card, © indicates copyright on the packaging and artwork.

- **Circle P:** ℗ Followed by year, band name or label, indicates the CD's original year of release (as in published in 2001).

- **Your address:** Put your basic mailing address only on the tray card and more detailed information on the inside. Packaging law in Canada requires this, plus it makes common sense and follows the normal CD tray card layout (look at any major label CD for reference).

- **Catalogue number:** For your CD to be identifiable at CD and printing plants, and for retailers to be able to order it, it must have a catalogue number (normally the UPC number). You can make up whatever you want but try to avoid using 001 as there are thousands of CDs with 001 in the catalogue number. Try to be cooler about it, for example, IBR 66601 (IBR is an abbreviation for Indie Bible Records). The catalogue number must appear on the back cover of the booklet (you can keep it small as long as it's legible), on the tray card and on the CD label. Remember, these are all separate items that will be travelling through various plants and warehouses so if any item gets misplaced, it can be quickly identified.

• **Made in Canada:** If you plan to export copies to other countries you must have "Made in Canada" printed on the back tray card and the CD label, preferably slightly bolder than the other type. If not, CDs may get stuck at the border.

• **All rights reserved, unauthorized duplication is a violation of applicable laws:** This is a warning to potential music pirates.

• **Sample tray card legal line:** ℗©2001 Indie Bible Records, 1650 West 2nd Ave, Vancouver, BC, Canada, V6J 4R3. www.indiebandbible.com All rights reserved. Unauthorized duplication is a violation of applicable laws. MADE IN CANADA. IBR 66601.

Sample Costs

The following prices are meant to give you an idea of the average costs of CD duplicating and printing, and give you an overview of the manufacturing process. Prices refer to the printing of completely prepared, camera-ready artwork. Many printing and duplication companies offer specials and package deals, so be sure to shop around for the best company for you.

Compact Discs

Glass master: This is used in the manufacture of CDs. It involves a onetime charge of $150 to $250 which is often waived for orders of more than 1,000. The glass master is different from the CD-R master. It's a glass plate used to create the metal stamper that presses your CD on the assembly line.

CD Manufacturing: This involves stamping your music onto blank CDs. The price usually includes:

• Silk screening for a two colour CD label (count on about $50 per colour for additional colours).

• Jewel box with black tray (sometimes clear trays are no charge—be sure to ask).

• Insertion of CD folders and tray cards.

• Shrink-wrap.

Price: CD manufacturing prices seem to hover at the $1.30 to $1.45 range, depending on what's included. Some companies lowball the manufacturing price and then charge extra for shrink-wrapping. Make sure prices are all inclusive.

CD Packaging

CDs typically come with either folders or booklets that contain artwork, photos, lyrics and credits. Packaging costs rise as panels or pages are added. A four page booklet with a colour cover and black and white insides costs about $250 to $300 for printing (film costs can add an extra $300). A full colour booklet will usually cost twice as much. Film costs can skyrocket if you don't plan the film setup properly. Try to fit as much of the art as possible on one set of film. An experienced designer can really save you dollars here.

The world of CD manufacturing seems to change daily, especially with the advent of short-run CD burners where getting one to two-hundred CDs is financially feasible.

I cannot stress enough the importance of shopping around for the best deal, and finding a helpful CD sales rep, especially if it's your first CD. Reps who can guide you through the process very easily will be the holy grail of your search.

A typical run of 1,000 CDs with standard four page booklet (colour outside and black and white insides) should cost $1,800 to $2,200.

The World of Cassettes

Do you really need them? Cassettes aren't cheap and may cost about as much as a short run of CDs. Do your research. What are you using them for? Will your audience buy them? You'll need inserts designed and printed. CD sales reps also handle cassettes. Get thorough quotes, and shop around for deals. If the cassettes are for sale (gigs and retail), then you want professional results, not cheap laser-print label jobs.

Duplication: Recording music onto cassettes can involve, in micro runs, using a chain of high-quality cassette recorders and dubbing the cassettes in real time. For larger orders, a process called bin-looping is used. With bin-looping, music is recorded onto cassette tape at high speed and then the tape is wound onto the reels of the cassette.

Other Charges

Running master: This is used to duplicate your cassettes and involves a onetime charge of around $50, which is often waived on larger orders.

Cassette imprint plate: This is used to print labels on the plastic cassette shell, and involves a onetime charge of around $50, which is often waived on larger orders.

Cassette Packaging

Cassette packaging consists of either a J-card (short back flap) or a U-card (large back flap with the two holes punched out) that fits into the plastic cassette case. Like CD packaging, the cost of cassette packaging depends upon the number of panels and the amount of full-colour printing used.

The Bottom Line

These suckers are not as cheap as you'd think, and may not be necessary depending on your genre of music.

chapter seven

Independent Video

Music Videos

In Canada, rock videos are one of the most powerful tools for promoting both a band and an album. Having a video in rotation on MuchMusic and MusiquePlus, or on one of the many televised music programs, can have a huge impact on record sales, tour draw, and general exposure nationwide. Major labels in Canada typically spend anywhere from $30,000 to $150,000 for every video they commission, depending on the artist. In America, major labels spend somewhere in the $100,000 to $500,000 range and up. There is little to no market for selling videos and they often cost more to make than the albums they support, but they are integral to a band's overall marketing plan.

The record company usually pays up front for the entire video, but charges half the costs back to the artist. In other words, you don't have to pay anything out of pocket, but the costs are charged to your royalty account and recouped through record sales. (see Record Royalties, p.228)

Videos are always a gamble for any label. They're an essential part of a promotional campaign, but a large percentage of videos only get played a couple of times and then disappear. The playlist for a station like MuchMusic can only support a limited number of videos, so many big-budget videos simply don't get added. Each week, the programming committee at Much meets to decide which clips are going to be added or dropped. They also assign videos to a rotation, meaning the number of times the video will be played during the week. The rotation levels are buzz (super-heavy), heavy, medium, light and recurrent (very light).

If videos are an investment risk for a major label, they're a super-risk for an indie band. The chances of making a clip that never gets airplay or at most, receives only a couple plays, are extremely high. The fact is, most indie videos don't see the light of day. For this reason, I recommend against indie bands making videos altogether. The costs are too great in relation to the chances of success (i.e. airplay). Funds spent on a video could be used in other places where the risks are far lower and the returns far greater.

Having said that, there are situations where taking the risk of making an indie video could make sense:
• When you have financial backer (anyone from a publishing company to a rich uncle) willing to take the risk.
• You have a song so unbelievably great that the entire music industry is beating down your door (in which case, why not wait for a record deal and get the label to cover the expense).
• Someone offers to make a video at a tremendous discount (i.e. a film student, or a filmmaker who either loves your band or wants to get into video making).
• You manage to get a VideoFact or FACTOR video grant.

In addition, you should have a reason to make a video. If you only play local gigs and don't have an album out, there really isn't any reason to bother with a video. Video airplay can only impact your career if you have the pieces in place to take advantage of the exposure. If people see your video but can't buy your record or see you live, what's the point? Your video will be played for awhile, you'll fail to capitalize on the opportunity and you'll soon be forgotten. And worse, if you get airplay and nothing happens, video programmers will be less interested in the next video you send their way.

We made our first video (for "Push") before we had a major record deal; however, we had a publishing deal with EMI Music Publishing, who helped foot the bill. Therefore, our risks were considerably lower than if we'd been totally independent. The video, which was initially added into medium rotation and then moved up to heavy, played a huge role in breaking Moist in Canada. It greatly impacted the sales of our indie album *Silver*, and suddenly our shows started to sell out right across the whole country.

The Video Process

If making a video makes sense for you, you'll have to find a director who is willing to take on a low-budget project. Have a professional-calibre promo pack ready to give to prospective directors to give them an idea of what your band is about and to show that you're serious. Most seasoned directors won't be willing to make an indie video, so focus on young directors attending film school and rookie professionals. Film students often have access to free cameras, lighting kits, and editing facilities, while rookie professionals are often members of film cooperatives that offer inexpensive rates on gear and editing facilities.

Posting signs at local film schools and film cooperatives is a good way to start your director search. Check with major video production companies, because they handle scores of directors with varying levels of experience. And don't forget to talk to other bands about people they've worked with in the past.

Choosing a Director

Major label artists, who enjoy the luxuries of a sizable video budget and a well-connected A&R department, sift through a collection of various directors' demo reels. They then establish a shortlist, and approach each director to write a creative proposal or treatment for the video.

The process isn't quite as simple for indie bands, because the pool of good, capable directors is much smaller. Not only do you have to find someone with interesting ideas, but you have to gauge their ability to get the job done. Rookie directors may not have experience drawing up and working-within a budget or shooting an appropriate amount of footage. They may not even be that expert at loading film into a camera.

How to Gauge Whether a Director is Appropriate

- Check out the director's reel. Is it original? Entertaining? Do you like the work? How is the director's sense of composition and lighting?
- Talk to prospective directors about ideas to see if their vision is in line with what you think is cool.
- Video directors should be up-to-date and well-acquainted with videos so they have an idea of what's been done before and what's actually original. It's a drag to unknowingly make the "el cheapo" version of a big budget idea.
- A video director should have some experience working with synch sound.
- Do you like the director? You do have to work together.

Video Treatments

A video treatment outlines the video concept and look. Some bands like to collaborate on the treatment or even come up with the concept themselves, while others prefer to leave video-making to the filmmaker. Either way, it's important to have a good idea of what the director will be going for when the cameras start rolling.

Some treatments are incredibly detailed, describing the video shot by shot, start to finish. From your standpoint as the artist and project financier, the more detailed a treatment is, the better. Different directors approach video creation in different ways. Some stick closely to a detailed shot list, while others may prefer to fly by the seat of their pants and take advantage of shooting-day inspiration. While both of these approaches can yield successful results, the fly-by-the-seat-of-your-pants option takes a lot of the creative control away from the artist. Quite simply, you won't know what you're getting until after the shoot. This makes me a little uneasy, particularly when working with an inexperienced director.

The Top Ten Indie Video Tips

- Work and think within your budget. Low budget videos have many artistic and logistical limitations. Understand these limitations. Treatments involving dolphins or helicopters, for example, cannot be considered.
- Successful low-budget videos always have simple, tight concepts. Keep the idea simple and memorable.
- Identify the video's hooks. What elements or moments are

unique and stand out? Like a hit song, a good video treatment revolves around clear, well-defined hooks.

- Originality is your biggest asset when you compete with mega-budget videos. A cheap, bush-league facsimile of an expensive video won't get played. Programmers love clever, fresh video concepts.
- Strong video concepts usually contain a strong sense of development, tension and/or climax. Does the idea tell a story, either literally or figuratively? What changes occur over the course of the video?
- Avoid content that may handicap your chances of airtime.
- Personality is a powerful tool. Conveying the band's or lead singer's unique personality through the use of close-ups is an effective way to reach the viewer.
- When playing to the camera, especially in close-ups, small expressions and movements become huge and large expressions become ridiculous. Don't overdo it. Relax, be yourself.
- The more cuts you have, the more time-consuming and expensive your edit will be (the video for "Push" contains a handful of cuts).
- Big budget videos are shot on 35mm film, giving them a sharper image and better colour. Lower budget videos are usually shot on 16 mm film or even Super 8mm. Even 16mm film yields a much better image than shooting on video (unless your concept calls for that look).

Video Content Standards

MuchMusic, as a broadcaster, must adhere to the Canadian Broadcast Standards Code in addition to their own internal standards. Violence, sex, guns, and drug use can severely handicap your chances of receiving airplay. MuchMusic has a second screening committee that convenes on Thursdays to rule on potentially problematic videos. For an indie band, it's highly advisable to avoid including problematic content in your video. The video selection committee has to consider so many videos that they often have to look for reasons why not to play a video.

Is there a double standard? Yes. Can Madonna get away with stuff that a little baby indie band can't? Yes. Am I going to be hung out to dry by some indie band that has pushed the envelope and suddenly I am writing letters to the commission? Is it worth it for me to push it, on a business level? Probably not. Is it worth it for me to push it for Madonna? Probably.

–Denise Donlon, president of Sony Music Canada (former VP/GM MuchMusic/ MuchMore Music)

After the Shoot

Once the footage is complete, it's time to create your four minute video. The following happens:

- **Film processing:** The film is developed at a professional processing lab.
- **Transfer to video:** As the film is transferred to video, you and your director see all the footage from the shoot (known as the rushes) for the first time. This stage is important because the colour and exposure (the darkness or lightness) of the footage is adjusted and made consistent. You'll be given broadcast standard Beta cassettes of the rushes. Ask for VHS copies as well so you can watch them at home and better familiarize yourself with the footage you have to work with. High-end transfer suites can charge as much as $900/hr for transfer time.
- **Rough transfer (aka one-light transfer):** This is a cheaper alternative to a big budget transfer. Unfortunately, it doesn't give you the opportunity to adjust and balance the footage which, in turn, makes editing much more difficult.
- **Off-line edit:** The rushes are loaded into a computer for editing, using computer editing software (Avid, for example). You and your director, along with a technician, assemble (cut) the footage into the video clip. The new generations of computers are making separate off-line/on-line stages a thing of the past. Full resolution images can now be compiled in real time.
- **On-line edit:** Based on the time coding of the cuts done in the computer, the Beta footage is compiled into the finished video. You'll receive both broadcast-quality Beta cassettes and VHS copies of your video (for home viewing enjoyment).

Delivering the Goods

Now that you have your finished video in hand, it's time to deliver it to music video programmers such as MuchMusic, MuchMoreMusic, MusiquePlus, MusiMax, MTV, M2, and VH1.

When sending your video to programmers, put together a package that consists of:

- A one-page cover letter, addressed to the program director or the host of an indie video show. Introduce the band, mention

any great accomplishments, (especially radio airplay and sales), and provide details about your video.
• Your promo pack.
• A copy of your CD.
• A Beta copy of your video.

If the program is based in your city, hand-deliver the package. If not, send it by courier (people tend to take couriers such as FedEx more seriously than regular mail). Wait a few days and then make a follow-up call to whoever you sent the package to. Ask if they've received it and had a chance to watch the video. Be professional and courteous.

Another way to deliver your video to programmers is to hire an independent promoter who has an ongoing relationship with the various video stations. While this route is more expensive and in no way guarantees that your video will be played, it can improve your chances of at least getting a fair shot. (See Independent Promoters and Publicists, p.211)

Advice from Denise Donlon, President, Sony Music Canada (former VP/GM MuchMusic/MuchMoreMusic)

When you're on the video selection committee, you could get sixty to eighty videos every single week. Maybe you can add five or six into meaningful rotation, and some of the other stuff will go onto specialty shows like *The Electric Circus, Da Mix, Rap City, The Wedge,* or *Indie Spotlight.* And then you really need some response to come in. You need the viewers to be reacting to it. There are all kinds of ways we have of measuring that on the channel—phone, fax, email, all that stuff.

Once you put a video up to bat, you really do need to see that it's working on some level. You need to hear from the band's management that there's a tour coming up, that there's distribution and that they've done their job and distributed the single to radio, so that four or five weeks down the road when you're going "okay am I still going to bank on this video because I've got pressure to add fifty other ones" you have all these other factors to look at.

You really have to assess what point you're at in your career. Do you want national exposure if you don't have enough money to pay for gas to get from Red Deer to Medicine Hat?

You shouldn't shoot on video. I don't care how many "film buttons" you push in the actual post production, it just doesn't look the same. Don't scrimp on your film stock. It's the carrier, the pipe of your idea. And to shoot on video puts you behind the 8 ball; you've already compromised the total look of the piece.

There's a lot of creativity that comes out of the old do-it-yourself idea where you break rules, not for the point of breaking them, but because you can. When you get into the outer limits of a Whitney Houston video a lot of times the creativity gets a bit stunted because there's so much at stake now. You'd think that more money equals better video, but it doesn't always work that way. Sometimes the best idea is just a brilliant performance that's true to the band.

If it's a good video, the timing is right and there's space, we'll play it. We love to champion indie stuff. We get huge kicks out of taking an unknown video, putting it up to bat and watching it come home. That makes us happier than almost anything.

Call the Much library and talk to the librarians. They'll send you you paperwork to be filled out as to whether your video is CanCon, who the producer is, who the band is, and so on. Send in some biographical material: your recent concert reviews, pictures of the band, tour schedules, whatever you've got going, because we add that into the library and it helps the VJs talk about it on the air. Send in your Beta copy or the best quality format the video exists in. And get it in in time for the Tuesday meeting. The video programmers sit in a room all day Tuesday and watch every single video that comes in, in no particular order. It doesn't matter if it's major, minor, indie, U.S. or what, every video, solicited or not, gets a viewing by the selection committee.

Video Grants

Awhile ago, I was talking with the bass player of an American indie band who couldn't believe that Canada has organizations that help bands finance their careers. In the U.S. indie bands are much more on their own. Well, here's to Canada. There are two organizations in Canada that provide financial assistance to indie bands for music videos: VideoFact and FACTOR.

VideoFact

VideoFact was established in 1984 by MuchMusic to "increase the number and quality of music videos produced in Canada." Since then, MusiquePlus, MuchMoreMusic and MusiMax have joined with MuchMusic as sponsors. VideoFact assists artists, record companies, music producers and video directors by covering up to 50 percent of the cost of producing a music video, up to a maximum contribution of $15,000. And the good news is that VideoFact funding is an award and doesn't have to be repaid.

Applying to VideoFact

Applications are assessed by the VideoFact board of directors. The board is primarily looking for strong songs, creative video concepts and realistic budgets. Bands will often complete the VideoFact application with the video director because of the detailed production budgets and scripts that are required. In fact, many of the up-and-coming video directors specialize in completing VideoFact applications for their videos.

The competition for VideoFact funding is pretty intense; the foundation receives as many as one-hundred and fifty applications for each two-month funding period with only a handful being accepted. So, don't get discouraged if you don't receive funding the first time you apply.

VideoFact Eligibility Criteria
• Satisfy at least two components of the MAPL test.
• Use closed-captioning for the hearing impaired in the video.
• Not have already made the video.

Required Materials
• A completed VideoFact application form.
• A copy of the song to be used.
• A lyric sheet.
• A video synopsis.
• A video treatment.
• A storyboard and/or script (three to five pages).
• Previous music videos if applicable.
• A promotional photograph of the artist.
• A production budget (including all financial sources).

For information and application forms:
VideoFact
Suite 501, 260 Richmond Street West
Toronto, ON
M5V 1W5
Tel: 416-596-8696
Fax: 416-596-6891
Email: videofac@passport.ca

FACTOR Video Grant Program

The FACTOR Video Fund provides video financing for currently-released albums by Canadian artists. FACTOR provides 50 percent of the video budget up to a maximum contribution of $12,000. FACTOR requires that applicants submit a detailed marketing plan for the album and video along with the application. As with all FACTOR programs, there are very stringent Canadian content regulations governing applicants, the album and the video production process.

FACTOR's board of directors assesses applications by the strength of the album's marketing and promotion plan, and, if the album has already been released, its current success.

Video Grant Eligibility Criteria
• Applicants must be Canadian artists, labels or record production companies.
• Applicants must own the Canadian copyright to the video and the master sound recording of the song.
• The album the video supports must have FACTOR-recognized distribution (see the list at www.factor.ca).
• The CD that the video supports must be released within twelve months of the date on which FACTOR receives the application.
• The video must be shot in Canada.

For information and applications, contact FACTOR at:
FACTOR
125 George Street, 2nd Floor
Toronto, ON
M5A 2N4
416-368-8678
www.factor.ca

Final Word from Denise Donlon

There is a lot of competition out there. Videofact meets five times per year now and there's about two-hundred and fifty applications that go through every single jury meeting. And we only end up funding around forty in each individual meeting. So there's a lot of good stuff that doesn't get funding that should come back and try again.

When you get into the short strokes, and I've got sixty videos and I want to fund them all but I can only fund forty, that's when I start looking at factors like: Do they have a buzz going on in their local town? Do they have an independent CD out that's already available that maybe is making some noise already? Do they have some good club reviews where they've gone and played already? How is their promo picture? Is the rest of the package set up so that, if the video gets made, the band has the other elements in place to take advantage of the opportunity?

A good advantage to a VideoFact application is to have a known director or a known production company fill out the applictation. The other great thing about VideoFact is that we are as much about encouraging new directors as we are about encouraging new bands. We take chances on new video directors often.

chapter eight

The Road

Introduction to Touring

If you've never done it before, touring can seem like a pretty romantic undertaking. Hitting the road means you're quite literally going places. A band that's toured inherits a status slightly above those that haven't. And a touring band usually plays with a new confidence and swagger that can only come from sweating it out on the road.

During your career, you'll probably spend months touring, playing shows all over the country or even the world. When you talk to any successful band, you inevitably find out that extensive touring played a huge role in creating that success.

Touring Advantages

- It's the perfect solution to the gigging paradox; you can play almost every night without burning out your draw. Playing every night, in turn, makes you a better band, guaranteed.

- It's an amazing test for personality and commitment in the band. If you can get along and gel as a social unit on the road, your band can survive just about anything.
- It can generate money; it's the biggest income source for many bands (including Moist).
- It's a great way to make contacts, particularly if your band isn't based in a big music industry hub like Toronto.

Before you start packing your bags, there are some important issues to consider. Touring has to be part of a larger strategy for breaking your band. It has very little to offer an unknown band with no radio and video play, media coverage or even records in the stores. Alone, touring will probably only succeed in breaking up your band.

You already know how hard it can be to develop a draw in your hometown. You have to repeatedly hit people from multiple angles. The draw game is exactly the same in other cities, except that you won't have the luxury of doing the extensive leg work to get people out. The result: empty houses. There's nothing more soul-destroying than playing night after night away from home to no one. It feels like a waste of time and guess what—it probably is.

Touring is expensive. You need some pretty strong dollars coming in to offset the pile of dollars going out. There are expenses like fuel, accommodations, musical supplies (strings, drum heads, batteries), per diems (the daily allowance each band and crew member receives for food, smokes—if you can afford them) the list goes on. If you're not drawing, there's no money coming in. This quickly creates a bit of a problem.

I remember sitting on the Black Bull patio in Toronto in early September 1993 puzzling over our little problem. It was the first time Moist ever toured across Canada and we managed to play every city from Vancouver to Toronto. Unfortunately, that's where the gigs and the money ran out. We were literally marooned a continent away from home with no real means of getting back. We ended up borrowing money from a friend's father and driving nonstop from Toronto to Vancouver via Thunder Bay. It was just lucky that the van hadn't yet reached the break-down-every-700 km stage (that was waiting for us on our second tour).

Independent bands can and do undertake successful tours. Touring can break a band and introduce them to the national stage. But before that can happen, you've got to create a plan and lay some groundwork. Think about touring the same way you think about grassroots promotion and apply the logic of micromarketing. It's a bad idea to just rush out and tour; like your hometown draw, you've got to develop the tools you need for successful, smart touring.

Setting up Your Tour

The goal of touring is to develop your following and notoriety beyond your hometown's city limits. It's best to build your touring circuit over time, starting with small tours and gradually expanding to new cities as your draw (and tour income) grows. Start with a more modest tour of two or three cities in your area. If you're lucky enough to live in Ontario or Quebec, there are many cities located reasonably close to each other. In fact, you could book quite a lengthy tour without even leaving your province. Unfortunately, for those in the west, epic drives are something you'll get to know very well—even on short tours.

A national tour only makes sense if you're getting video or radio airplay nationally, you're offered an opening spot on the coast-to-coast tour of a national band, or you're driving across the country to an industry conference such as New Music West in Vancouver or NXNE in Toronto. Otherwise, expanding your circuit in concentric circles is the most effective way to get out on the road.

The Types of Gigs

A touring indie band can't afford to be too picky about gigs. You have to be ready and willing to play just about anywhere that will have you. The more you play, the more exposure you get and the more effective your tour will be.

The Most Common Kinds of Tour Gigs
• Opening slots for popular local/national bands.
• Opening slots on a small indie package tour.
• Clubs and all-ages venues that feature original bands (opening slots or spots on new talent nights).
• Music festivals (Edgefest, Indiefest, Wolffest).

I personally don't think a band should be out doing a national tour, doing any kind of sizable tour unless there's a reason for it. Canada's an absolutely massive country and it's very expensive to go on tour.

– Jack Ross of The Agency Group

- Music conferences (like NXNE, New MusicWest).
- College/university events like a multi-band festival put on by the student union or campus radio station (often tied into orientation week or homecoming).
- College/university venues.
- Conferences: There is a yearly conference of post-secondary entertainment coordinators called COCA (Canadian Organization of Campus Activities). Getting your promo pack circulated or doing a showcase can really help to get school shows. Check out the COCA website at www.coca.org.

One way to identify possible venues for an indie tour is to read *Exclaim* and *Chart* and look at the tour advertising for bands at or near your level. These ads list all venues the bands are playing in each city; use these as a guide to get you started. You can also check out band websites for tour itineraries.

Booking Tour Dates

To book an indie tour requires a lot of time and persistence. It gets easier as more people get to know you, particularly once you start to develop a draw in other cities. This is another reason why gradually expanding your touring circuit makes sense. Here are some basic things you can do to find gigs on the road:

- Send out promo packs to venues that feature original bands playing your style of music.
- Talk to larger booking agencies such as Feldman & Associates and The Agency and see if they have openings on any bills.
- Talk to local agents and try to get on bills as an opening act. Indie agents often have small package tours going out and They might even help you book a few shows.
- Team up with other bands as a package for some shows.
- Send entertainment agencies promo packs.

Routing

Tour routing can have an enormous impact not only on your tour's success, but on your health as well. Routing is particularly important in the west, where the distances between cities averages around 600 to 700 kms. It's important to be realistic about the distance you can travel in the allotted time. Plan for delays, van breakdowns, bad weather, bathroom stops, food stops, road kill stops—anything that could impede your progress. Don't plan to average 130 km per hour for ten hours—it's not going to happen. It's disastrous to cancel shows that you've begged as a favour because of poor planning.

It's pretty difficult to book a tour that moves in a very logical way, because you often have to take whatever gigs you can get. Few low-budget tours run smoothly from place to place. Instead, you'll likely end up driving a Vancouver–Saskatoon–Edmonton–Winnipeg–Calgary–Thunder Bay–Medicine Hat star-like pattern. You get the idea. Until you command a sizable draw, you have to go where the gigs are, but again, be realistic about the distance.

Days Off

Days off are basically days with the usual tour expenses but no income, so the fewer days off the better. Figure out your limitations: How many nights in a row can you play before your show starts to suffer? Usually the stamina of your singer's voice will determine that number. After a certain point, all singers hit a wall, after which they'll blow out their voices—which is the one thing that can force you to cancel shows. Every singer has different limitations. Some voices are damn near bulletproof while others are quite fragile. Our rule, for example, is four days on, one day off.

Contracts and Money

If you're driving nine hours in the dead of night, tired, just to get to the next show, you want some guarantee that the show, and the agreed-upon fee for playing that show, will be waiting for you when you arrive. Handshake deals for gigs in your hometown are fine; if there's a misunderstanding and the gig evaporates, you'll swear a bit and go for a beer. If you're 3,000 kms from home and on a razor thin budget, the loss of your show could be catastrophic. Having a signed contract for a performance is, therefore, pretty important. The musicians' union has contract blanks for members, free of charge. (See the Union, p.98) When you do have to play road shows without a contract, you must be doubly vigilant with your show advance and make sure the verbal agreement is crystal clear.

Contracts outline the venue, time, date, and fee for the performance, including the number of sets you're expected to play and minimum length of your performance. They also lay out the terms of payment.

Once you've got a following in your city—as soon as you can attract two-hundred to three-hundred people to your shows—then you should start working other markets, other cities close by.

– Sheri Jones, comanager of Laura Smith, Mary Jane Lamond

Four Different Ways to be Paid for a Performance

- **Flat guarantee:** The band receives a guaranteed fee for the performance regardless of attendance; it's basically risk-free for the band. The promoter is responsible for all expenses and risk for the show. When you're supporting another act, the deal is usually a flat guarantee.
- **Guarantee plus bonuses:** The security of a guarantee, with bonuses if attendance surpasses specified levels.
- **Guarantee plus split:** You take a percentage of the door (or ticket sales) after a specified minimum attendance or dollar figure has been reached. For example, you might receive a $500 guarantee plus 75 percent of gig receipts once you reach 85 percent of a sellout.
- **Split:** Your pay is completely based on the door/ticket sales, so you share the risk with the promoter. If you command a strong draw, splits are usually the most lucrative. Since you share the risk, you make more if the show is a success. In an 80/20 percent split, for example, the band receives 80 percent of the net of the show after expenses while the promoter receives 20 percent. You really have to be very on top of the show expenses; dishonest promoters will try to artificially inflate expenses and invent costs that don't exist, in order to increase their profits. By the way, you often have to pay opening acts out of your share of the split. And as an opening act, note that your pay could be coming from the headliner.

A Union Contract for an indie-level show should have the following in the Terms and Conditions box:

- The capacity of the venue and ticket price(s).
- Any change in the agreed upon ticket price must be approved.
- The specified advance on the guarantee for the performance.
- All cheques must be payable to _____.
- Gross potential receipts.
- Net receipts, to be defined as the gross gate receipts less all approved/vouchered expenses.
- All expenses must have corresponding receipts.
- Who pays and provides the supporting act(s)?
- Who pays for the sound and lighting?
- The attached rider is an integral part of this contract.
- The employer must sign the contract and rider and fax it back to _____.

S.L. Feldman & Associates, a div. of A & F Music Ltd.
200-1505 West 2nd Avenue, Vancouver, B.C. V6H 3Y4
Phone: (604) 734-5945 Fax: (604) 732-0922
"CANADA'S NATIONAL TOURING NETWORK"

THIS CONTRACT for the personal services of musicians, made this __4__ day of __Nov__ , 19 __98__ , between the und

purchaser (hereinafter called the "purchaser") and ____1____ musicians (hereinafter called "emplo
(including the Leader)

WITNESSETH, That the purchaser hires the employees as musicians severally on the terms and conditions below. The leader repres
employees already designated have agreed to be bound by said terms and conditions. Each employee yet to be chosen shall be so boun
terms and conditions upon agreeing to accept his employment. Each employee may enforce this agreement. The employees severally
render collectively to the purchaser services as musicians in the orchestra under the

leadership of _____ as f

Name and Address of Place of Engagement   WINSPEAR CENTRE Rehearsal Hall

9720 102 Ave. SW, Edmonton, AB

Date(s) of Employment   Dec 31 98

Hours of Employment   Sets: 2 x 45 Min Sets, Set times: Approx 6:45 & 10:

Type of Engagement   Concert

Name of Sponsoring Organization   L Brenneman-Snider/ FIRST NIGHT FESTIVAL

FEE AGREED UPON $ $800.00 Flat Fee

Capacity: 1,750 Ticket price: $8.00 advance/$10.00 at door (gross)

(See reverse for Terms & Conditions)
This fee includes expenses agreed to be reimbursed by the purchaser in accordance with the attached schedule, or a schedule to be furnished
purchaser on or before the date of engagement.
To be paid   balance to leader by cash or certified cheque prior to the engagement.
(Specify when the payments are to be made)
Upon request by the American Federation of Musicians of the United States and Canada (herein called the "Federation") or the local
jurisdiction the employees shall perform hereunder, the purchaser either shall make advance payment hereunder or shall post an appro

SEE REVERSE SIDE FOR ADDITIONAL TERMS AND CONDITIONS

**Any change in ticket price must be approved by Artist and/or Artist Rep.
**Employer to provide house sound and lights at no cost to artist.
**The attached rider is an integral part of this contract.
**Employer to sign contract & rider & fax to S.L.F.A. immediately. Original
contracts to follow. Please sign all 3 copies & rider & mail to S.L.F.A.
**Employer to provide at no cost to Artist: Accommodations of 1 double.
**$400.00 DEPOSIT DUE BY CERTIFIED CHEQUE TO S.L.F.A. BY Nov 30 98.

Money

In the early stages of your touring career, always try for guarantees, because then you can actually do some hard budgeting. Risk is not a good thing when you're struggling to have your tour break even. Later, once you have a sizable draw, splits will make a lot more sense. Unfortunately, as an unknown band on the road for the first time, you'll have to fight to get guarantees. Club owners and promoters will be happy to offer you a cut of the door (a basic split) because it means they'll likely have to pay you less. Ironically, once splits start to make sense, promoters will start throwing loads of guarantees your way (because, again, they make more and you make less).

If you do manage to wrangle some guarantees, expect them to be in the neighbourhood of $75 to $150. As you've undoubtedly discovered from playing the club circuit in your city, a cut of the door can be much lower than that.

And remember, just because you have a pretty sizable draw in your hometown doesn't mean people will come out to see you in other centres (even neighbouring towns). It takes time to develop draw in other places.

Riders

A rider outlines, in detail, all your requirements for playing a show. A rider is attached to the contract you fill out for the buyer (promoter, bar owner, event manager). Your riders will change over the course of your career; arena band riders are considerably more exhaustive than bar band riders. There are more variables and more things to exercise control over when you headline an arena show.

When you finally get to the arena level, the tour and production staff will have very specific ideas about your rider. Meanwhile, I'll touch on some of the things you should include at the indie level.

It's important to be reasonable and demand things appropriate to your level (size of venue, draw). When playing a two-hundred seat bar in Manitoba, your technical rider should not demand follow spotlights and operators. It ain't gonna happen. If your rider is reasonable and appropriate, the buyer might actually pay attention to it.

Riders don't usually exist at the first level of gigging (you're lucky to get a free beer), but once you start to play larger venues, riders will become an important part of your organizational process.

General Rider Issues (Arena Level)

Most issues covered in the general contract rider deal with the way things work in a split, to limit the ways in which you can be ripped off by unscrupulous, careless, or incompetent promoters. Most important is the ticket accounting.

Tickets are numbered sequentially (i.e. 01, 02, 03...). Have the promoter provide you with an invoice from the ticket printing company that states the number of tickets printed, and a box office statement that lists the number of tickets sold, the number given away, and the number left unsold. The promoter should also give you any unsold tickets, to prove they weren't actually sold. This way, you'll be able to account for every dollar of show income. If things don't add up, you should reserve the right to count the ticket stubs (known as ticket drops) that get torn off at the door.

General Rider Issues

- **Tickets:** Outline the acceptable procedures for printing tickets, the number of tickets to be sold and the number to be given away.
- **Guest list/free tickets:** Indicate acceptable numbers of guest list and free tickets for you, the promoter, and any supporting bands on the bill.
- **Promoter expenses:** Ask the promoter to provide a detailed accounting of expenses with receipts; indicate maximum amounts to be spent in each category (i.e. advertising).
- **Advertising:** Reserve the right to approve the presentation and look of advertising and posters for the show. Many riders contain predesigned and approved ad mat artwork. This way, the promoter has all the materials necessary to make posters and advertisements for the show. Local details such as venue, date, and time can be added separately. The promoter should submit tear sheets (newspaper clippings of the ads) and invoices for print and radio advertising.
- **Press:** You must approve all band promotions and interviews set up by the promoter.
- **Recording/photos:** You must approve any recordings (audio or video) and photos of your performance.
- **Merchandise:** Outline the terms of merchandise sales at the venue, such as the house/promoter cut.
- **Legal provisions:** This outlines cancellation provisions and liabilities, i.e. sickness, acts of God.

Technical Rider

Not surprisingly, the technical rider outlines your technical requirements. Until you develop a thousand plus draw and start playing larger venues, you'll usually have very little control over the house sound and lighting equipment. It belongs to the house. It's not going anywhere. You're going to use it and be grateful. The technical rider lists your specific requirements for things such as sound system power, lighting specifications, monitor specifications, and the stage dimensions.

Hospitality Rider

The hospitality rider spells out your requirements for meals (vegetarian, allergies) beverages, and the dressing room. When you hear about bands demanding a bowl of Smarties with the green ones removed, that's the hospitality rider. Until you're a pretty big deal, keep your rider simple (i.e. bottled water, beer, wine and/or spirits). Bear in mind that, with splits, most of the hospitality rider's costs come out of your pay.

Advancing on the Road

Advancing shows on the road is pretty much the same as for local gigs (see Advancing Shows, p.62). The real difference is the sheer volume of work it takes to track down buyers to advance gigs on consecutive nights. Organization and strict note taking are absolutely essential, because misunderstandings on the road can make the difference between a successful tour and a money loser. It's important to leave a good impression. There isn't an excess of suitable venues across Canada and you want to be asked back.

Don't underestimate the value or the challenge of advancing shows. It's an unbelievably frustrating exercise of tracking down people who are never in. Get a telephone calling card to make long distance calls from highway rest stops and motel rooms. Never charge long distance calls to your room, because the rates are outrageous. Use email when you have access to a computer. It's cheap, and raises the odds of your band name being spelled correctly on venues' promotional materials. A cell phone to catch return calls when you're driving can really help, although be very careful about long distance rates. Some cell phone providers now have plans that offer amazing savings on long distance, so shop around. Also be aware that some cell networks do not offer very much coverage outside of major cities.

If you're acting as your own tour manager, it'll be a daily battle to squeeze performance, promotion, accounting, sleep, driving and advancing into just twenty-four hours. Tour managers are well-known for their ability to function on only a few hours of sleep a night.

A Lost Weekend in Edmonton

It was going to be our second ever trip out of Vancouver to play a show. We'd befriended a band called The Smalls that were doing great, pulling in a lot of people to their shows from Alberta to Manitoba. They offered us a weekend gig opening up for them at a club in Edmonton, and we jumped on it. We were just starting to taste the road and wanted as many gigs as we could find, even if it meant driving twelve hours to play two shows. Everyone booked time off work and we were set. I put through a call to The Smalls the day before we were all set to leave and it was, like, "Oh, no dude it's not this weekend it's next weekend." Thank God I called. I would've been a pretty popular guy in the van on the way back to Vancouver if I hadn't done the advance, I'll tell you. There's a lot of miles for endless torment between Edmonton and Vancouver.

Computers on the Road

Almost everyone on a big tour nowadays has a laptop computer; this goes for tour managers, band members, sound engineers, everyone. Computers are amazing for writing, organizing, note taking, accounting, and printing schedules and set lists. They're also indispensable for staying in contact with your management, booking agent, buyers, promoters and even your friends and family back home via email. An inexpensive Internet/email account with one of the big service providers like AOL or CompuServe means you can log on in any city for the price of a local call and have immediate cyber-contact with anyone; it goes a long way to reduce the often crippling long distance charges that bands regularly rack up on the road.

If you don't already own a laptop computer, you can pick up a used one that has more than enough under the hood to perform the basics for cheap (like under $500). The newest and fastest machine with all the bells and whistles will cost more like $3,000 plus. You can also take advantage of Internet cafes, university computer labs, and perhaps even the computer at the house you're crashing in (if you go this route, get a free account at Hotmail.com or Yahoo.com and check your mail via their websites).

Micromarketing on the Road

Before you enter a new market, ask yourself the most important question: Why? What sort of groundwork has been laid already and what are you going to do when you get there? The number one goal of early touring is to develop a buzz. Each time you return to a city, you want to see a larger crowd. This is the process of developing your fan base.

With micromarketing, you try to exploit every possible avenue of promotion and thereby maximize the impact of your visit. The first few times you perform in a new city, you'll probably be stuck with the worst spot on a multi-band night or be opening for a more popular band. Either way, you likely won't enjoy the luxury of a full house; you may not even get the luxury of playing to a crowd that numbers in the double digits. This kind of reality makes micromarketing all the more important. In terms of your career and the growth of a fan base, promotion is often more important than your actual performance. In the beginning, you just want people to hear your name.

Micromarketing requires that you spend a lot of time laying the groundwork for a tour. Start small with short, regional tours and slowly build outward. By concentrating on a few centres, you can maximize your presence and actually see some results. If you develop a draw of two to three-hundred people in three or four cities, you'll have a great foundation for larger tours. You'll also have a story and start to see an industry buzz. Not many independent bands can boast a strong three or four city following.

Before you tour, you should have a consistent draw of at least two-hundred people, and a decent tape or a CD to sell. Without one, you cut off many possible areas of promotion (and to some extent, income).

In Advance

A lot of the following contact information can be obtained from the club you're booked at. Clubs are usually more than helpful in giving you a list of media contacts for their city. Some even have media info sheets they'll fax on request. Feel free to ask for their help; it shows you're ready and willing to promote the gig with them.

- **Media:** Well before your tour, send your promo pack to the various newspapers, magazines and college, community and commercial radio stations in the cities you'll be playing. Contact the local record stores and send them copies of your tape or CD for consignment (speak to a store manager first).

• **Local Radio:** A few days before you arrive, contact the program directors of the campus radio stations. You can try the local commercial stations as well but don't expect the red carpet treatment. Let them know you're coming and where and when you'll be playing. Ask them to play your CD and let them know you're available for telephone interviews (called phoners) or live, in-studio appearances and visits.

• **Press:** Well before your tour, send your promo pack to the local weekly entertainment newspapers and dailies. A couple of weeks before you arrive, call and speak to the entertainment editor. Try to secure an interview, or failing that, try to get a mention in the "what's on" column. Invite a reviewer out to your show. Be prepared for some difficulty in getting editors on the phone; they're notoriously difficult to snag.

• **Postering:** If you have a spot on a multiband night, it's quite possible the venue will put up posters. This isn't guaranteed, so ask about it when booking the gig. Having your name printed on a poster along with a collection of other unknown bands may not count for much, but it's a start. If you managed to score a spot supporting a popular local or national artist, your name might be printed on the posters. Check ahead.

Once You Arrive

• **Busking:** If you have a few free hours on show day, busk. Set up downtown with some stickers and/or flyers and a sign saying who you are and where you're playing that night and drum up some audience.
• **Radio drop-ins:** Handshaking and interviews, if arranged.
• **Guerrilla stickering:** Sticker everything.
• **Record stores:** Visit both chain and independent stores. If they don't have your indie tape or CD, hand deliver some for consignment. Meet the manager and talk to the staff. Drop off some stickers and flyers.
• **One-on-one:** The most effective way to promote a show is by actually telling people about it. If you arrive in a city the night before you play, go out on the town armed with stickers and flyers for the show. Go to bars, clubs, bookstores— whatever. Talk to people; give them a sticker or a flyer. Some people are naturals at frontline promoting and some aren't. Our drummer Paul is an absolute natural. He can do more

A day off is a bad day. You never want to be off when you're on tour. If we're not playing, we do an in-store somewhere; we try to convince a store to let us come play for free. It's just better to be doing something, because as soon as you're not doing something, you're spending money.

– Tim Potocic,
of the band Tristan Psionic and cofounder of the indie label Sonic Unyon

with a pile of stickers and a vodka and tonic than an entire record company promotions department. The big trick is to be outgoing. You have to make it happen.

On our second tour across Canada, we arrived in Banff the night before we were to play and found out where all the locals were partying; we managed to drum up a sold-out show for the following night. (We did have to deal with some pretty severe hangovers at sound check, mind you.)

• **Alliances with other bands at your level:** Try to develop a relationship with local bands in other cities. A great strategy is to develop a relationship where you open for them in their city and they open up for you in yours.

• **Merch at the show:** Sell your tape or CD and cool T-shirts. Maximizing your presence in a city is exhausting and time-consuming. You have to be very outgoing, aggressive and charming. Welcome to show business. And this isn't sarcasm. Signed touring bands spend a lot more time on the road shaking hands than actually playing. Get used to it and get good at it.

Transportation

Unless you're lucky enough to own suitable wheels, you'll have to arrange for some sort of appropriate transportation (which can actually turn into a big issue). I've seen some pretty bizarre machines on the road. We once toured with a band named FurnaceFace that had a yellow short bus modified to be a sort of Mad Max camper. They stopped before installing the gun turret, but you get the picture. We saw a Partridge Family-style bus once at the side of the road with all these burnt-out looking dudes walking around it, smoking cigarettes and kicking tires—which leads me to probably one of the most important transportation concerns: reliability.

Touring in Canada requires that you must cover an unbelievable amount of ground. Outside southern Ontario and Quebec, eight to ten hour drives are the norm. You absolutely have to be able to trust your vehicle. Breakdowns screw with your gigs, your health and your safety.

We once suffered a breakdown about three hours south of Thunder Bay, Ontario in the dead of winter. It was quite easily 30 degrees below zero, and freezing to death was definitely not out of the question. Luckily for us, a cop drove past and gave a couple of us a lift into the next town, where we called for road assistance. But if it weren't for that cop... So, remember, cool, bizarre, rustic or vintage vehicles are only as good as their reliability.

Another transportation issue is size. The size of the vehicle you need is completely related to the size of your band, your crew and your gear (aren't you glad you bought a combo rather than a stack?). We played a few shows with Zolty Cracker, a three-piece band that used a djembe drum instead of a regular kit and had no crew. They could tour quite happily in a Buick LeSabre. This, unfortunately, is pretty unusual. Most bands have four or five members and travel with at least one or two crew members. This arrangement requires at least a full-size van—probably a fifteen passenger long van. A lot of people buy the biggest van they can find and build a bed in the back, around, over or beside the gear. With night drives being the norm in the west, sleep is a key consideration.

To radically improve the overall comfort and sleep-ablity of your van, get a trailer for your equipment. As soon as you clear the gear out of the living area, touring becomes much more pleasant. All it takes is a U-Haul style single or double axle trailer (depending again on the size and weight of your gear).

Half of any given year, we're chained together in a tour bus, which is like a submarine with wheels. We surface only when we have to.

- Gord Sinclair, bass player with The Tragically Hip

The Transportation Evolution

Most bands go through the transportation evolution below:

Phase One: Start with an "el cheapo" junker van bought for a song out of the paper. It's a lovable enough set of wheels. You and your gear just manage to squeeze in, and everyone gets pretty good at sleeping sitting up. Unfortunately, the phase one van soon suffers a horrible breakdown that costs more to fix than you paid for the piece of crap in the first place.

Phase Two: Splurge on a new or newish van. Empty the band treasury and maybe drive the band into debt with a bank loan or leasing arrangement. Van two is a huge step forward: It's reliable and a lot of the options (like the radio or even tape deck) still work. It's all pretty luxurious. Soon, however, you run into some other bands on the road who have already moved on to phase three—the van plus trailer combo. You see how these bands have done the excellent big bed modification to the back

How could it possibly be this far to Kansas City? I'm gonna go insane. And by the end of the tour it's like, fifteen hours in the van, okay.

- John Munson, of the band Semisonic

of their vans and arrive to shows well rested and ready to play. They seem so happy.

Phase Three: You either buy (or rent) a trailer and some lumber to build a queen-size bed in the back of your van. I should point out that home-made van beds are both dangerous and illegal, but most bands seem to build them anyway (we did). Phase three is the best possible arrangement until you, at long last, move on to phase four, the tour bus.

Phase Four: Enter the tour bus. Beware, unless you're going to start touring in a tour bus right away, never, ever step on board one. Don't let curiosity get the better of you. Stay away. You can be happy for years in phase three unless you brush up against phase four. And unless you have a pretty big draw or you're signed to a generous label, you can't afford to travel in a tour bus. It's a Pandora's box: once you travel in a tour bus, there's no going back. Put it off as long as you can. Tour buses cost a fortune.

Financing Your Wheels
Four Basic Ways to Get Your Hands on a Vehicle
- **Borrowing:** This is the cheapest option if you know a van benefactor (ie. a generous friend or family member). Make sure that the insurance covers your use of the vehicle.
- **Renting:** Good for short tours or if you don't tour very often. Rental vehicles are very reliable and usually come with that new car smell. However, if you plan to become a serious road warrior, renting quickly gets very expensive. The rental charges with over-mileage penalties for a couple of lengthy tours will more than pay for an "el cheapo" used vehicle that you can call your very own.
- **Leasing:** In a standard vehicle leasing agreement, you pay a monthly fee for a period of three to five years, at which time you have to give the vehicle back or pay a lump sum to buy it outright. If you want out of the lease before the term is up, you have to pay out the remainder owing on the lease. Leasing agreements will often have expensive over-mileage penalties. Still, leasing can make sense because you get a new, reliable vehicle and if you're making money, you can write-off the leasing charges against your business profits.
- **Buying:** New vans are too expensive for most bands to consider. Used vans, on the other hand, range quite dramati-

cally in price, depending on the age and condition of the vehicle. Just remember that reliable transportation is essential and ancient vehicles may not measure up. The adage "you get what you pay for" definitely applies to the used vehicle world. Consumer Reports publishes extensive ratings of all sorts of used vehicles.

Tour Buses

The first time I stepped onto a tour bus, I knew there was no turning back. Before that step, we toured around North America for a couple of years in a van with the modified bed in the back, and we had no serious complaints. We'd certainly seen tour buses before, but we couldn't have guessed how they transform life on the road. We were pretty happy in our ignorance.

Tour buses come equipped with all the luxuries of home, including TVs, VCRs, video games, a fridge, couches, a kitchen table and, most importantly, a bunk for each person.

Oh yeah—they're extremely expensive. I only know a couple of bands that have bought buses; almost everyone rents them. This is not a surprise—a new tour bus can cost more than half a million dollars and you still have to hire a driver with the proper training and license. Tour buses usually rent for between $500 and $650 per day. Add the cost of the driver, a driver hotel room every twenty-four hours, and fuel, and it all adds up to around $1,000 per day. So don't even think about a tour bus until you're playing some pretty big rooms or you sign onto a label that will shell out sizable tour support.

Most Canadian bands rent from HalJoe Custom Coach in Toronto. There are also several reputable bus outfits working in various areas of the United States. But, by the time you get to this level, someone else will be doing this stuff for you.

The coolest bus I've ever seen belongs to Neil Young. He tours in an modified forty-five foot coach dating back to his days with Buffalo Springfield. There are two 1943 Buick car roofs welded to the top of the bus to increase the headroom inside, a spare bedroom where the storage bays used to be, a fully functional shower and satellite TV. Watch for it on an expressway near you.

Never drive tired. Make everyone in the band get their license. If you get tired at all, just pull over. If everybody's tired and you can't drive, then sleep for a couple of hours until somebody can drive. There's no point in killing yourself getting to shows.

- Tim Potocic, of the band Tristan Psionic and cofounder of the indie label Sonic Unyon

The Great White Van

After we'd been together for awhile and got a bit of a buzz going around Vancouver, we decided to undertake our first big tour—Vancouver to Montreal and back again. We're talking about a lot of miles here. We booked the shows and got ourselves ready to go. We were a young band with about fifteen songs, so we learned some covers and played some songs twice—once at the beginning of the first set and again at the end of the last set. Anything would do. It was our first tour and nothing was going to stop us. Unfortunately, we had no van or transportation of any kind. At first, we figured a solution would present itself. But one week before the tour was to start a solution still hadn't arrived. We did have band tax at the time, but the band treasury was seriously hurting after all the tour preparations (printing T-shirts and stickers).

Then, someone spotted the Great White Van in the classifieds. It was perfect—a twelve year old Ford Econoline fifteen-passenger van. By removing the two rear bench seats, it could hold all our gear, our bags, our soundman and us. Great! Problem solved! Except for one thing: it cost $4,500. Cheap for a van I guess, but a fortune for us. We simply had no money. So, we agreed to borrow money from everybody we knew, for a stupidly high interest rate (50 percent). Everybody went mad with borrowing. Fifty here, a hundred and fifty there. It was insane for us to go so deep into debt with our friends, families, and neighbours, but we had no choice. We even promised to do a private show for the guy selling the van if he would chop some dollars off the price tag.

Well, it worked. The van was ours, and we played the tour; although we ran out of money and gigs in Toronto and had to drive straight home to Vancouver without stopping. By the way, it took us more than a year to pay everyone back, which is hardly surprising at 50 percent interest. What were we thinking?

Accommodations

Sleep is a treasured commodity when you're touring across Canada in a van. Without sleep, you get sick, you can't perform properly, and you don't have the stamina to do the intensive micromarketing that the road demands. In Moist, we've always followed the golden rule: If a band mate is sleeping—leave him alone.

Two factors that can impair your ability to sleep on the road are time and money. Even if you have places to crash, long distances between cities demand all-night drives to arrive on time for sound check. On the road you usually do a lot more driving than sleeping.

Depending on the kind of venues or events you play, accommodations ("band rooms") might be included in your contract. If so, you'll typically be put up in a club owned and operated guest house or a cheap rock 'n' roll motel the club has a deal with. Sometimes the rock 'n' roll motel is located upstairs from the venue, which is very convenient, albeit noisy.

You usually need to command some draw in order to cross the threshold into the world of provided accommodation. If you've begged the first slot of six bands on alternative night, don't expect the club to shell out for beds. In this case, I'm afraid you're on your own.

There are companies that specialize in booking rooms in different cities at a discount. They cater to entertainers on the road, and can often get cheap corporate rates or find rooms in a city that's all booked up. They operate like travel agents and don't charge you for their services because hotel/motels pay them a commission. Most touring bands in Canada use En Tour. In the United States, Tzell Travel is widely recommended.

En Tour
Box 30, Site 6, RR 2
Winterburn, AB
T0E 4J7
Tel: 800-440-0853
or 780-987-2830
Fax: 780-987-2832

Tzell Travel
8383 Wilshire Blvd.,
Suite 922
Beverly Hills, CA
90211
Tel: 213-651-5557
Fax: 213-651-5454

Typically, there's a natural road accommodations evolution that can be boiled down to six stages.

- **The van:** Sleeping in the van or tents beside the van. You basically can't afford to rent anything for the night and nobody likes you. If you're playing back-to-back shows in certain western cities (like Vancouver and Edmonton), you'll probably have to sleep in the van while you endure a dreaded all-night drive. Sleeping bags are essential during this stage and showering can be a little tricky. Comfort factor: 0–2.

- **Floors:** Well, you're not so wretched anymore, although you still haven't generated enough draw (and therefore cash) for a motel room. Fortunately, some university students you meet after the show let you crash on their floor, as long as you don't mind empty beer bottles and their amorous cat. You jump at the chance. Many bands actively canvas the venue after their show, looking for potential landlords for the night. Sleeping bags and maybe air mattresses, while not required, are still seriously recommended for this stage. Comfort factor: 2–4.

- **The all-in-one motel room:** Congratulations. You now draw enough to afford real commercial accommodations, cleanish sheets, and a colour TV for those all-important, late night reruns of Kung-Fu. The down side is that six of you are sharing a room that's designed to sleep two comfortably. Motels/hotels can be funny about you sleeping six to a room, so don't say anything. Most places charge extra for the use of a cot. Sleeping bags optional. Comfort factor: 4-5.

- **The guest house:** At one time or another, we've stayed in almost all the venue-owned guest houses, and most of them are pretty decent: clean, comfortable and equipped with a TV and kitchen. They always have quite a few beds, so everyone should get a good night's sleep. A few have cats, so if anyone is the "boy in the plastic bubble" when it comes to animals, you'd better ask. Sleeping bags are not required. We've only had one bad experience with a guest house. We arrived to find blood splattered all over the bathroom, bugs in two of the beds and a used condom in the third. (We broke out the sleeping bags.) Comfort factor: 4-6.

- **Full rooms:** Well, now you've finally made it: two to a room. Everyone gets their own bed and the luxury is only limited by your pocket book. You'll find two glasses wrapped in plastic (for your protection) in every room. And as an additional bonus for the band's big spenders, you usually have the option of ordering in-room movies (aka Spectravision). Ahhh. It doesn't get much better than this. Comfort factor: 6–9.

• **Day rooms-tour bus combo:** Everyone sleeps on the bus as it drives between cities. Upon arrival, the bus pulls up to a hotel where a couple of day rooms are rented for showering and hanging out in during the day. After the show, everyone piles on the bus and the cycle repeats. Comfort factor: 8-10.

Sneaky Accommodation and Travel Tips

If you're opening for a band on the "tour bus plus day room" plan, ask their tour manager if you can crash in their day rooms after they're done with them. Most bands on the tour bus plan depart right after the show, leaving a couple of hotel rooms vacant for the night. Beware, this arrangement will quickly fall apart if you damage the room or incur any charges.

If you have the opening slot on a large tour with separate buses for the band and crew, it's often possible (with some sweet talking) to travel on the headliner's crew bus.

If you tour in the off-season (i.e. winter), it's also possible to get killer deals on the older buses in a company's fleet.

Tim Potocic of the band Tristan Psionic suggests: "Every university has a change room somewhere. So you go into the locker room and take a shower like you're going to the gym. If you're smart, you get there before the interview, so you smell good when you do it."

The Crew

When you go on the road, you'll almost certainly need to hire at least one crew person. Early in the game, when funds are somewhat low, consider hiring a "rookie roadie"—a friend who's interested in volunteering their time in exchange for valuable road experience. Touring can be unbelievably tiring, especially if you're making the most of micromarketing, so that having an extra hand to tune guitars, move gear and help with the driving can really reduce road fatigue and help make your tour more successful.

The size and experience of your crew depends on the scale of your tour. Larger tours generate more money, and the expectations are correspondingly higher, both for the band and the paying audience. When you pay $40 plus to see a show at

GM Place, you expect a great show without technical screw-ups. On the other hand, when you pay eight bucks to see a down and dirty rock show at a local dive, perfection isn't really what you're looking for. Small tours generate less money and require smaller, less experienced crews. It's a simple equation: The bigger you are, the more crew you need (and the bigger their salaries).

Small/Micro Tours

Every additional person on the road costs money. Smaller tours typically require your crew members to perform several roles. For example, often a tour manager doubles as a soundman. This combination makes sense when a band can't afford more than one or two crew members. It covers the most important bases: sound, money and organization. Make sure you hire someone with decent chops and experience; it will have a huge impact on the success of your tour. Get recommendations from bands and people you know in the industry.

Moist always tours with a crew of at least three, although, on our first couple of tours, that was probably a little excessive. It cost us money and precious sleeping space in the van. Our crew consisted of our tour manager/lighting operator/merch guy Stan, our sound engineer Mark (aka Mr. Fink) and our stage manager/tech/driver Graeme. We stuck with the Stan/Mark/Graeme combination until the size of our shows demanded that we bring a monitor engineer and a full-fledged lighting designer onto the team.

The Moist core crew now consists of a tour manager, a stage manager, two stage technicians, a lighting designer, a sound engineer and a monitor engineer. For our full tours, we add additional crew as necessary. On the *Creature* and *Mercedes* tours, we played arenas and towed (brought along) the stage, sound and lighting systems, so we added a production manager, merch manager, sound and lighting technicians, a rigger and a swing guy.

Crew Wages

Professional crew members make anywhere from $600 to $2,000 per week and beyond, depending on their experience, the scale of the tour and their positions (i.e. tour managers make more than roadies). They also receive a per diem of $15 to

$40 a day for meal/living expenses. Count on paying at least $700 a week plus accommodations for professional crew members. It isn't unheard of to strike deals with people if they really like or believe in the band, but as a rule you have to pay more for experienced, professional people.

Hiring Friends

Okay, I have a few points to make about hiring your friends for roadwork. If you're on the road for your first time, making almost no money, sleeping on floors, and experiencing the big adventure, hiring a friend to tune guitars or help with the driving is a pretty good idea. You can trust your friends; they're fun to have around. You can pay them peanuts and they'll probably be okay with that. Also, if it's a low budget, low pressure tour, you won't have to be too demanding and expect the highest professionalism.

Which brings me to the downside of touring with friends. While it's great to share the party action, things start to get pretty uncomfortable when something screws up and someone has to take the heat. It's no fun reaming out your friends, because suddenly now you're not friends anymore; you're employer/employee. That can be hard on any friendship. Things can also get awkward when friends ask for more money.

This is not to say that staffing your crew with friends can't work; we've done it for years. Our first manager, tour manager and stage manager were all longtime friends. They grew with us, and by the time we reached the level where we needed a totally professional crew, they were totally professional.

The Whole Crew

This is a list of typical crew members and their job descriptions. Only full-size arena tours would have individuals for all of these positions. Again, it's very common to see crew members working in a number of different roles.

Tour Manager

Tour managers seldom sleep because they're responsible for everything. They oversee all other crew members; take care of show settlement, payroll, tour support and tour accounting; book transportation, accommodations and catering/hospitality; liaise with label and press; look after safety and security; advance upcoming shows; and perform every other job that's not taken care of by someone else.

Thankfully, it works out well. Usually your first tour is when you're younger and more resilient. You can go through hell and can still play the next night. But when you get a bit older, you definitely start to ease back.

-Geoffrey Kelly, of Spirit of the West

You just have to mentally prepare yourself for not a hell of a lot of privacy when you go on tour, that's just a given. We're pretty private people on the road and kind of stay out of each other's way, just because we know what it's like.

- Andrew Scott, of Sloan

Production Manager

The production manager oversees the technical production of the show, including the sound system, rigging, lights, barricades, and stage sets.

Sound Personnel

- The Front-of-House Sound Engineer mixes the sound that comes through the main speakers and also takes care of the general tech of the sound system.
- The Monitor Engineer controls the band's monitor mix, techs the monitor system, and oversees microphone placement.
- The System Technician, usually supplied by the company that supplies the sound system, is responsible for the system's overall maintenance and set up.

Lighting Personnel

- The Lighting Designer designs the lighting scheme, sets up and focuses the lights; operates the lighting for the show.
- The Lighting Technician, usually provided by the lighting company, is responsible for the overall maintenance and set up of the lighting rig, and operates lighting for the performance.
- The Rigger hangs the lights, speakers, and props.
- The Spot Operator, usually a local contracted for the night, operates the follow spotlights during the performance.

Stage Personnel

- The Stage Manager oversees all equipment and personnel on the stage, and coordinates band changeovers and the sound check schedules.
- Stage Technicians (including Back Line Tech, Drum Tech, Guitar Tech) oversee maintenance and set up of the band's gear on stage.

Other Personnel

- The Merchandising Manager orders merchandise, takes care of merch accounting, oversees the design and operation of merchandise stands and oversees merch sellers.
- The Swing Man has various sound and lighting responsibilities.
- Security, usually locals provided by a security company, is concerned with safety of the band, crew and audience at the show and maintains the security of the stage/backstage areas.
- Drivers drive the buses or transport trucks.
- Roadies, usually locals contracted for the night, load and unload gear from the transport trucks and assist with setting up and tearing down equipment for the performance.

- Emergency Medical Personnel attend to the sick and injured at the show and are usually locals contracted for the night.

Health

It's tough to stay healthy on the road. When you mix lack of sleep and bad nutrition with constant exposure to new people and their cold and flu viruses, you're pretty much fated to get sick. Being sick on the road sucks for a million reasons. It's tough to get decent rest and, as they say, the show must go on. You have to be pretty damn sick to cancel a show.

When we toured England a couple of years ago, Jeff, our bass player, caught an unbelievably nasty flu virus. He was so feverish and weak that he played a show sitting on a stool because he would get dizzy if he stood up. We were all travelling together in close quarters, so each of us caught the evil disease and then passed it on to the next guy in the chain. By the end, once everyone had taken their turn in the sick bed, the flu had mutated to the point where Jeff actually caught it again.

Things to do to Stay Healthy on Tour
- Drink at least eight glasses of water per day (veteran road warriors are never without their bottle of Naya spring water).
- Eat quality, nutritious food (Big Mac combos don't count).
- Take lots of vitamins, particularly vitamin C.
- Don't get loaded every night after the show.
- Wash your hands frequently, because shaking hands with people and then rubbing your eyes is a leading cause of sickness.
- Get as much sleep as possible.

Vocals on the Road

Lead singers get the best and the worst deal of anyone in the band. They enjoy the spotlight. They receive the most attention and the greatest visibility and, later, the most fame. The conventional wisdom in rock videos, for example, is to sell the singer and make it seem as if they're telling the viewer a story, which adds up to mountains of screen time. And compared to us guitar players, singers barely even have to practice their skills (okay I'm exaggerating). But there's the flip side.

Unfortunately, singers have to live a pretty sheltered life on the road. The human voice is a very delicate instrument that demands an inordinate amount of loving care and attention

I think there's this kind of attitude in rock 'n' roll that if you get instruction or training, it runs counter to the concept and I was of that mind. I never thought that Bob Dylan ever took any lessons, so you try not to do that. My advice is that if people are doing it a lot, there comes a time that it's really good to just get a bit of training so you learn to use your voice a little more properly.

– Barney Bentall, Canadian solo artist

or it simply blows out. A blown voice is about the only show-cancelling ailment I know of, and cancelled shows are a disaster on the road. They hurt your reputation with promoters and fans, and they're devastating to the balance sheet. So, while drummers and guitar players can stay out after shows and abuse themselves with all manner of vices, work on a few hours sleep and still get up on stage the next night, singers have to stay behind and drink herbal tea. This isn't much of an exaggeration.

The Top Ten Things Singers Should Avoid
(Brace yourself, it isn't pretty.)
1. Alcohol
2. Tobacco
3. Drugs
4. Late nights/sleep deprivation
5. Caffeine
6. Casual sex (a sure way to catch colds, and other nasties)
7. Stress
8. Dairy products (it's a mucous thing)
9. Talking (yelling in noisy bars wears out the voice)
10. Fun

Okay, I'm painting a pretty bleak picture of the singer's life on the road. There's always the odd bullet-proof singer who breaks every rule but, believe me, they're very few and far between. An ambitious band can spend months on the road at a stretch. That pace and lifestyle can wear down even the toughest voices. Sooner or later, every singer turns to herbal tea and quiet evenings on the tour bus. Singing lessons, even for experienced singers, are highly recommended for learning basic voice preservation techniques.

Tour Karma

The road can sometimes do crazy things to people. Maybe it's the feeling of being away from home on an adventure; maybe it's the loneliness; maybe it's sleep deprivation, I don't know. I've seen faithful guys cheat on girlfriends; sober guys drink to extinction; people turn into savages; savages go quiet; it can be a wonder and a horror to behold. You and your band will change and grow on the road, and you need to remember the fundamental concept of karma. Basically, if you screw someone around, sooner or later, you'll be screwed around by someone else. The music industry is an unbelievably small organism and word travels fast.

At a gig in Banff, Alberta, all the bar manager could talk about was this band that got drunk and broke one of those monster jars of pickles. I know it sounds bizarre and it's not exactly the crime of the century or anything, but I can still remember the guy saying he was pretty sure they'd done it on purpose and "those #@!%$&@! better not come near this place again." Beyond the fact that some guys are really attached to their pickles, I think this is a pretty good example of how a lot of bands screw themselves. You're going to play in some pretty weird places and meet some pretty unusual people, so really try to respect the people and the spaces you encounter.

Also, try to be supportive of other bands. On one of our first tours we opened for a band that was pretty popular at the time. We were totally unknown and absolutely no threat to these guys, but they, or someone in their organization, decided to "spike the graph." Graph spiking is a form of volume control sabotage, where a couple of frequencies on the house graphic EQ are massively boosted up. When you try to get any volume out of the system, you get huge shrieks of feedback from the boosted frequencies. Our soundman, of course, was not allowed to touch the EQ and it really spoiled our show. We've never forgotten that and never agreed to play with them again. It was a good lesson for us, though, in that we always give opening bands full use of the sound system. Of course, if a supporting act's soundman turns the system up louder than we would play, our tour manager usually gives him a little tap on the shoulder. Fair is fair.

Thank the bar staff—these are working people, and you're coming into their environment. You're doing your job, and respect that they have a job to do. I always encourage the artists I work with to ask their customers to tip those people. It's amazing, if you make friends with the bar staff in Winnipeg on your way out to Toronto, there might be a gig for you there on the way back, just because you were good people to have around.

- Jack Ross, of The Agency Group

chapter nine
The Next Level

So, what is the next level, you might ask? Up until now you've probably been taking care of just about everything yourself, from booking gigs to basic accounting and general management responsibilities. At the next level, you begin to establish relationships with the various professionals who will ultimately act as your representatives in the many areas of your band's business life. In essence, you start to assemble a team.

It's time for you to focus on what you do best and to delegate responsibilities to others who do what they do best. This is not to say that you should close your eyes and hope that strangers do a good job with your career. You definitely have to stay on top of things. However, if your band is starting to break, you simply won't have time to do all the jobs you once did, and you'll ultimately owe a considerable part of your success to your team. This is beginning of your journey away from being a true indie band.

Your team usually consists of a personal manager, an entertainment lawyer, a booking agent, an accountant or business manager, and sometimes an independent publicist.

Think of the team as an extension of yourself. These are professionals who help you make your career happen, and all of them ultimately answer to you. Each team member brings unique skills to the table, so listen to their advice and guidance, but always bear in mind that it's your career. You're the boss and you should never have to do anything you don't feel right about doing. It's sometimes easy to forget this when you're sitting in some power broker's office, being wowed by their apparent knowledge and savvy.

Assembling your team doesn't happen overnight. It takes time to find people you like and trust, and who like and trust you. Be skeptical of a slick shpiel. Look for a solid track record and a straightforward approach, because inept or corrupt team members can hold you back. There is no real prescribed order for assembling your team. Often, working with one team member, like a manager or a lawyer, will lead you to others.

Necessity and availability dictate who you need first. For a self-managed indie band trying to book a national tour, working with an agent is extremely helpful. As with everything else, the bigger your band, the more established (and usually better) the professionals are that will talk to you. It's difficult to get a foot in the door, but perseverance will lead to good people. Resist the temptation to sign on until you actually require their services; every additional team member costs money.

I recommend finding a good lawyer before talking to anyone else. It's easier to find a decent lawyer who will return your calls, than a top manager, for example. Lawyers regularly deal with scores of industry professionals and can recommend and introduce you to prospective team members. Also, the issue of contracts has a habit of popping up whenever you start talking to people in the industry and, to deal with that, you must have a lawyer in place.

Assembling the Moist Team

After being together roughly three months, we convinced our friend Keith to manage the band. A few months later, we started working with a lawyer (he was recommended by a couple of other bands). Almost immediately after, we thought about booking a national tour to get out and showcase for labels in Toronto, so we contacted a booking agency. After recording our independent album, Silver, we hired an indie promoter. When we finally started to sell some albums and make money from touring, we got a business manager. We brought team members on board as we needed them, and not before.

The Industry Showcase

The surest sign that you've moved to the next level is that every time you turn around you're playing an industry showcase. Any time someone from the industry, such as a prospective manager, agent or record label, comes out to see you perform, it's an industry showcase. These puppies can be tremendously important, because a great showcase brings you exciting new opportunities, while a lame one can close doors. News travels fast, whether it's positive or negative, and it can be difficult to counteract a bad first impression. I'm not trying to scare you, but it's essential to play the showcase game right.

The Big Showcase Issues

- **The venue:** Choose a familiar venue, where you'll feel comfortable and confident playing. It also helps if the venue is a well-known spot, as opposed to the basement of your buddy's house or the seediest dive in town.
- **The crowd:** The bigger the audience the better. Playing for an enthusiastic crowd has a profound effect on both your show and the perception the industry player will have of you. Bands always look and play better in front of a good crowd; it makes the show much more credible. It's much easier to like a band and imagine bigger success for them when they're playing to a responsive crowd. Also, I know from experience that it's extremely unnerving to play a show when only the industry is present; they stand at the back and never react (it's almost as if they have clipboards with score sheets). It's essential to get everyone you know to come out to the show.
- **The set:** Limit your set to forty-five minutes or less. Play your strongest material, slay them, and get off stage. The adage about leaving them wanting more applies perfectly to an industry showcase.

Everyone wants to do "the showcase."
They're not prepared to think along the lines of let's build and develop. What they're looking for is for the record labels to come out and sign them. That's always a mistake I find with young bands; they've made their basement CD which sounds pretty good and sent it out to the labels and they haven't even got a crowd. I've always encouraged bands to build their audience, because as soon as you're filling the clubs, the industry will come looking for you.

- Yvonne Matsell, veteran talent buyer for various Toronto clubs

- **Presentation:** Pull out all the stops to make your show as memorable as possible. Simple things like backdrops and cool lighting can make a big difference. It's vital to have good sound in the house, so use a good sound engineer who's familiar with your set and makes you sound great. This could be a house engineer you've worked with before, or a hired gun who knows your sound.
- **How much industry?** There are different schools of thought on how many industry people to invite. If you put on a great show to a sold-out house with the whole music industry there, the effects can be quite dramatic. Each industry player will see the other players there and figure that something big is going on. However, if you put on a substandard show to an empty house or something goes wrong, it can really set you back. You'll manage to turn off the entire industry in one fell swoop. It's the eggs in one basket scenario. So, "do you feel lucky, punk?"
- **Doing the shmooze:** When you manage to get industry people out to your show, create a personal connection with them. Industry showcases are not the nights to get drunk and try to pick up a date. If possible, arrange to go out for dinner with your invitee(s) before the show and hang with them afterward. Pick a couple of band members to go straight to the shmooze while the rest do the stage strike and load out.

Be charming and show off your sparkling personality. Most industry people say that the personality of a band is often a huge factor in deciding whether or not to work with them. By the way, if you invite too many industry folks to the same show it's difficult to make personal contact with everyone.

• **Relax:** Now that I've gotten you all uptight about the importance of making a great impression, just sit back, relax and have a good time. Do what you do and be yourself.

Radio Shows

There's another type of industry showcase you'll encounter many times throughout your career—the radio show. Radio stations frequently sponsor performances by new and up and coming artists, providing on air promotion and ticket give-aways. Sometimes radio shows only feature one or two bands at a small local venue, and other times stations stage huge multi-band festivals. In either scenario, lesser-known bands play for free in exchange for publicity and often increased airplay (i.e. heavier rotation) on the station.

Like other industry showcases, it's vital to make the most of radio shows and establish valuable relationships with the station. Bands often receive airplay as a direct result of having played a free show for the station. When you examine the strategies that led successful artists to the top of the charts, you invariably see a long string of radio shows and industry shmoozes.

Entertainment Lawyers

There's an entire field of law, called entertainment law, that focuses on the intricacies of artist contracts, copyrights and trademarks (a broad area known as intellectual property) and band agreements (partnerships and corporations). When working in the music industry, you'll definitely require the services of a good lawyer.

A good entertainment lawyer must be up-to-date on current industry norms and practices, which are always changing because of the circulation of new artists, new technologies, and new laws. When a band manages to get an ugly contract clause omitted, it becomes easier for you to do the same, if your lawyer is on the ball. Likewise, when a new technology like the Internet emerges, it's vital that your lawyer knows what changes it's causing (and is likely to cause) in the industry.

Music and business are so far apart from each other. Sometimes when I talk to young bands, they haven't got a clue. They just think that it's all going to fall in their laps and they don't realize how much work is involved. And a lot of them will say, "I'm no good at shmoozing," but that whole networking thing is so important. I would place that after your ability to write and play; that has to be the next criteria.

– Yvonne Matsell, veteran talent buyer for various Toronto clubs

Lawyers play a key role in several specific tasks such as: drawing up band agreements; administrating partnership and incorporation arrangements; copyrighting band names; making the right introductions to other potential team members, such as managers and booking agents; shopping for and negotiating record contracts, publishing deals and management agreements; licensing agreements; escaping contractual relationships; and providing guidance in business affairs.

There are all kinds of entertainment lawyers out there, ranging from small independent lawyers who work out of their home office, to power brokers who work out of large, powerful firms. Like all music industry players, entertainment lawyers come with varying degrees of clout. Veteran lawyers are familiar with most of those record executives who won't return your calls. Lawyers who represent important clients can wield some impressive clout, and often get you a better deal than a younger, less experienced lawyer. Of course, the downside to powerful, established lawyers is that they're expensive, busy, and often won't even consider representing a fledgling band.

Who are You?

When considering a prospective lawyer, it's very important to have a good sense of their personality. Different bands prefer to work with different personalities, from the soft spoken to the flamboyant. Any style of lawyer can be effective, but you should feel comfortable with the kind of representation you'll be getting.

Lawyers often specialize in one genre of music, and will have their best connections on that particular side of the business. Ask about your lawyer's client roster. Is it appropriate for your band? Also, many lawyers perform work for labels and other industry organizations, so try to be on the lookout for any possible conflicts of interest. If your lawyer frequently works for a company you are negotiating with, it creates obvious conflicts. Ethical lawyers will always steer clear of such situations, but it's prudent to ask.

Ask prospective lawyers for references; ask others about their reputation. Lawyers are often extremely attentive during the honeymoon period and virtually unreachable after. Sometimes bands are passed off to less experienced underlings in the firm and/or basically forgotten about, so it's definitely wise to find out as much as you can before working together.

Legal Fees

Like all lawyers, entertainment lawyers charge some pretty steep fees. A young, relatively inexperienced lawyer charges in the neighbourhood of $100 to $200 an hour, while an established power broker's fees are usually more than double that. Obviously, most young, unknown bands don't have that kind of money, so it's quite common for lawyers to work for a percentage, usually 5 percent, of the deal. The legal fee on a recording advance of $150,000, for example, would be $7,500. While this might seem steep, it usually covers not only the lawyer's work on the contract but all future legal services to be provided for the duration of that contract (which could go on for many, many years, if you're successful).

Personal Management

A personal manager is the most important member of your team. They're involved in every aspect of your career and are usually the first contact industry players will have with your band. Your opportunities will be greatly impacted by the kind of relationship your manager develops with these key people. In a sense, the manager's role can be described as overseeing everything that can be achieved on the telephone. Business and deal making are the manager's gig.

What Does Management Do?

Your manager coordinates and oversees the activities of your team members, and usually plays a large role in putting that team together. The manager can also take on the responsibilities of team members you haven't found yet, and then act as manager, business manager, accountant, booking agent, publicist —whatever it takes. Once you've assembled your entire team, a good manager will continue to play a part in all aspects of your business life. A personal manager's direct responsibilities can include: negotiating gig/tour contracts; booking/organizing gigs and tours; fielding calls about the band; cold calling and establishing contacts in the industry; coordinating publicity and chasing down press coverage; promoting songs to radio and video stations; engineering publicity and buzz on the band; soliciting publishing companies; soliciting record companies; negotiating record and publishing deals; overseeing the activities of your record and publishing companies; working to promote your interests in foreign territories; providing their input to the

[Find] someone you trust who will give you a fair quote and estimate on fees, and who sticks by those quotes and estimates and delivers the work on a timely basis.

- Paul Sanderson, Toronto-based entertainment lawyer and author of the book Musicians and the Law in Canada

creative process (i.e. helping to choose producers, singles and video directors); acting as a buffer to the outside world; and bookkeeping (accounting).

The Manager/Artist Relationship

In the classic artist/management relationship the artist concentrates on the music while management takes care of business. Until recently there was often a huge separation between business and music; bands stayed out of the business completely and relied on management to guide their careers.

Today, many bands come from strong indie backgrounds and have a great deal of business savvy. They want to be involved and take an active role in guiding their own careers. Remember, it's your career. Your job may not be to work the telephone, but the band is your livelihood. So, regardless of who your manager is, stay in the loop. Take an active interest in the band's day-to-day business.

The band should work out short and long-term goals with the manager, who can then develop plans and strategies to realize those goals, search for opportunities, and make recommendations for your approval. "Guys, we have the opening slot on the Bloody Urine tour if we want it. I think it's a good move, because these guys are selling seats like mad and their albums are flying out of the stores."

It's wise to listen to management's recommendations, but you should always reserve the final say because, ultimately, they are administering your career and reputation. If you don't feel comfortable with something, don't do it. A healthy relationship always has loads of communication, so you should be able to justify why you're uncomfortable with a given move. "Sorry, but Bloody Urine are death surf Nazis. They draw huge audiences, but we're not comfortable being associated with them."

In a perfect world, the band and management are a machine, working together to realize very specific objectives. Of course, in the real world, things don't always work quite this smoothly, but it's something to strive for.

When is it Time to Get Management?

There are no hard and fast rules as to when you should seek out professional, personal management. If you're starting to sell out venues in your hometown, it could be time, although some bands wait until they can no longer do the job efficiently themselves. Some industry players say that you should go after management as early in your career as possible. A lot depends on the your band's specific circumstances. It's probably time to get a personal manager when you can find someone good who wants to manage you; taking care of business starts to seriously cut into your music time; or you're beginning to squander contacts and opportunities because you're too busy or disorganized.

Choosing a Personal Manager

There are five primary criteria to consider when you're looking for a manager. The perfect manager should meet all the criteria, but you'll likely have to weigh each potential manager's relative strengths and weaknesses.

1. Expertise
• Do they know what they're doing?
• Are they plugged into what's going on?
• Do they have a track record of success?
• Do they have a proven strategy for breaking bands in Canada and/or the U.S.?

2. Clout
• Are they connected?
• Do they get their phone calls answered?
• Who else do they manage? A lot of their clout comes from the success of other bands they manage. Managers with top international acts have international pull; when they talk, people listen. They can use the other bands to leverage you into opportunities you might not otherwise have been able to get.

3. Manpower/Time
• Do they have the manpower and therefore the time to really effectively take you on? Powerful managers are only an asset if they actually have the personnel and time to make things happen for you. It often takes more time to break a band than it does to administer the success of an established band. Powerful managers remain powerful by developing a stable of

new artists (their power tomorrow, as it were); just make sure they're not overloaded. Find out how many bands they manage. If they're carrying too big a roster, who do you think will get the focus—the big, established, money-generating band or your band? This is important, because it's a big drag when you can't get your manager to return your phone calls.

4. Drive

• Does your manager have the drive and determination to pull out all the stops and thrust you onto the world's stage? Young bands often sign with managers who just don't seem to care about them. Bands in this position rarely find their manager pulling strings or hassling people to get them onto tours. Talk to other bands on their roster, or better yet, bands that have left their roster, and investigate the manager's dedication to the smaller artists.

5. Personality

• What's your gut feeling? You don't have to be best of buddies, but you do need to be able to work together and share some basic views. (There are some real knobs out there. Being tough and being a knob are two different things).

• Trust is a big issue. Are they honest, and straight shooters? Get the opinion of others who've dealt with them in the past.

• Good managers should impress you and be convincing, but beware; many shady individuals can give a great interview, dropping names and blowing your doors off with impressive sure-fire strategies for breaking new artists. Look for sensible and thorough game plans, rather than big promises without real substance.

The Five Garden Varieties of Managers

Let's look at five different hypothetical management possibilities and assess them according to the five criteria.

1. A Big, Established Manager With Big, Established Acts

Managers in this category generally have lots of expertise, clout and a sizable staff. Find out if they've ever actually broken a band, or if they're simply capable administrators of existing success. The real danger areas are roster size and drive. Once you're on board, will they have the time and inclination to return your calls?

Unless your band's generated a major buzz, it'll be hard to interest a big league manager. There are only about four or five big international managers in Canada, and they're all amazingly busy and don't spend a lot of time hanging around local bars on talent night. Occasionally, a bigwig does fall in love with an unknown band, but it's rare.

2. Someone Who Works in the Office of a Category One Manager

People who work for big management companies often find and manage their own pet projects. This can be very good for a young unknown band. Underlings inherit valuable expertise, clout and resources and are driven to prove themselves. Make sure they're genuinely excited about you and that they'll be dedicated to making your band happen. And you should get a good vibe from them.

3. A Smaller, Less Powerful Management Company

There are many more of these managers and management companies than those in category one. Depending on their size, they'll have a certain amount of regional/national clout and can offer certain advantages. Sometimes a smaller management company can break new bands more effectively than the biggies because they're more connected to the grassroots level of the industry.

Check for roster size and talk to bands that may have dealt with them in the past. This category contains the greatest number of sharks, so be careful. Slime seldom rises to the top, it wraps itself around you and keeps you on the bottom. (Nice image, eh?) Bear in mind that you don't need any qualifications to call yourself a manager.

4. A Music Industry Person Who Hasn't, Until Now, Managed Bands

This category includes lawyers, agents, promoters and others who often have industry contacts and expertise, but lack a management track record and, perhaps, clout. If you know and like someone like this, try approaching them about management. They may not give up their day job right away, but they could be a capable manager waiting to happen.

Don't jump at anyone who comes to you and says he wants to manage you, because you can end up tied down to somebody who has no more experience than you do. For a band, I think it's always good for them to do the one-on-one with people like me, for instance. I'd rather deal with the band in the beginning, because that's when you develop your relationship with the band. And that's when I'm going to be willing to help you, rather than some green manager. I'm more responsive to helping the band themselves.

– Yvonne Matsell, veteran talent buyer for various Toronto clubs

The downside is that they usually lack the necessary infrastructure (i.e. a management office with some assistants) that comes with the managers in the previous categories. Also, if they still continue to work full-time at their day job, then time and dedication could be a problem. Still, this category could be a very reasonable option, because contacts and an understanding of the music industry are a real asset.

5. The Rookie

Don't underestimate the potential of the rookie. Consider people you already know who are smart, aggressive, carry themselves well and, most importantly, will go to the wall for you. This type of manager doesn't come with contacts, but their drive and determination can create opportunities. Make sure they have sufficient time to dedicate to your band, because effective management is extremely time consuming, particularly when it takes multiple tries to get people on the phone.

The shortcomings of this category are pretty obvious (inexperience and a lack of clout, for instance), but they can be overcome. The biggest issue is the type of person you choose; a capable, driven rookie can do more for you than a disinterested power manager who takes three weeks to return your calls.

Management Commissions

Management makes money by taking a cut of every dollar you make. Typically, management will commission 15 to 25 percent of your gross income across the board (including your SOCAN payments). The only exceptions are tour support and record company advances that are spent on recording, because they're not really band income. The commission percentage depends on factors such as the category of manager, and your clout (i.e. following, draw, record sales, and airplay). Exact percentages must be negotiated before you start working together; some managers are flexible and open to negotiation and some have rock-solid, unyielding commission policies.

Management Contracts

Some managers require contracts and some don't. Smaller management companies tend to demand contracts more often than superstar managers because bands often jump to a huge mega-manager as soon as they reach a certain level of success. This phenomenon can really screw a smaller company

over. They take a chance on you, spend thirty hours a day trying to break you, make almost no money in the process and then get dumped as soon as things start to happen. Business can be cruel. Management contracts are, therefore, usually very specific about sunset clauses, which outline what happens in the case of a band/management divorce. Be careful about sunset clauses. They can gravely affect your ability to leave a bad situation or can require that you keep paying managers years after you've stopped working together. If a manager demands a signed contract, suggest a pre-signing probation period to determine if you can actually work together. Try to make sure that the contract contains success minimums that allow you to get out of the relationship if you don't reach specified levels of success. Of course, it goes without saying you should have an entertainment lawyer explain the content of any proposed agreement.

A handshake management deal involves a verbal agreement as to the manager's cut. It's really that simple. The band and management work so tightly together that the machine can't function if either party is unhappy or held against their will. If either party wants to leave the relationship, then so be it.

Booking Agents

A booking agent's primary role is to find and book gigs. Agents have working relationships with venue owners, managers, promoters and management companies, and can get gigs you probably don't have the connections to get on your own. They look for appropriate venues and the right audience. They can often get you more money or guaranteed fees, rather than a percentage of the door.

An agent works with you and your management to formulate gigging and touring strategies, such as determining the cities or regions you should concentrate on when building up your fan base. A good agent knows the mechanics of drawing a crowd, and understands what kinds of shows you should be playing and how often. This kind of strategizing can play a key role in breaking your band, because the right combination of opening slots and your own small headline gigs can produce some amazing results.

When to Get an Agent

When gigging in your hometown, working with an agent is useful but not really essential. Once you start touring regionally or nationally, an agent can make a huge difference. A booking agency has a team of people that will get you higher guarantees, better gigs, a solid touring itinerary backed up with contracts, opportunities for opening slots on important shows, use of the agency promotion team and resources, and access to showcase opportunities. Working with an agent sends a message to record labels, clubs, and industry people that you are serious contenders. Once you've developed a draw on your own, it's time to look for an agent.

By the way, to work with a legitimate, franchised booking agent, you must be a member of the musician's union. Booking agencies have to be franchised by the AFM, meaning that the agency can only work with union bands and must use union contracts.

How to Get an Agent

There are basically two approaches to hooking up with an agent: a passive approach and an active approach.

The Passive Approach

If you book your own hometown shows and have a bit of a buzz going, it's quite likely that the booking agents will eventually come to you. Agents actively recruit good, new bands. This approach will only connect you with agents based in your area, so if you live outside of Toronto or Vancouver, you're not as likely to get the attention of the national agents.

The Active Approach

If you're too ambitious for the passive approach then you'll have to let the agents know who you are. Send your promo pack (or get your lawyer to do it) to both the small local agents and the major national agents. A few weeks later make follow-up calls, and try to get a representative out to see one of your shows.

It's much easier to get an agent out to see you if you live in an major center where the large agencies are based. If you're based somewhere else, consider playing at a music conference. If that's not possible, make follow-up calls, because you never know when an agent might be coming through your town (although, if you live in a one-horse town, you might be waiting for a long time).

If an agent agrees to come to your show, make sure you follow the rules for putting on a successful showcase. It's important to show off your potential. Agents are very interested in the calibre of your live show. After all, they'll be harassing bars across the country, telling them how great you are. Their reputation is directly tied to your live performance and your professionalism, so giving a good first impression is important.

Choosing an Agent

There are several different varieties of agents in Canada: large national booking agents (of which there are only a handful); smaller national indie agents; and regional agents (dealing primarily with a city or region). They can all be quite effective, depending on the kind of touring you intend to do. A smaller regional agency that specializes in indie rock bands can often be the most effective if you're just starting to play outside of your hometown.

You can tell a lot about an agency by checking out its artist roster. Focus on agents that deal with bands similar to yours. If you're a death metal band, Frank Fogerty's Country Talent Agency probably won't be able to service your needs. Also, look at the size of the agent's roster. A large national agency can handle a substantial roster because they have enough staff and considerable clout, while a small agency with a large roster might not have the manpower and resources to provide the service you need.

What do Agents Charge?

Agents' fees are charged as a percentage of the gross income received for playing shows. The AFM stipulates that agencies can't charge more than 10 percent, plus expenses, such as long distance and courier charges incurred on your behalf. It's possible to negotiate the agent's percentage down to less than 10 percent, but don't count on it. Read your booking agent deal very carefully to make sure they're not commissioning any other income, like record or publishing royalties.

Agent Contracts

In most cases, agents require exclusive agreements. Sometimes bands manage to avoid signing agency contracts, but unless you wield some sizable clout, expect to be looking at a two or three year contract, during which time the agent will commission every show you play within the applicable territory. The idea is that the agency should have a hand in soliciting and setting up every show you play.

It's in the agency's best interests to hold an exclusive agreement with you for as long as possible, and in your best interests to sign for as short a term as possible. Thanks to the AFM, agency contracts contain a performance clause that allows you to get out of the deal if the agent fails to find you work for ninety days, but it's still a good idea to limit the term of the agreement. If the agency is useless you can run, and if your band goes ballistic, you can reduce the agency's percentage. If at all possible, test the waters with a trial period first. If you feel they're attentive and effective, then sign on.

Managing Your Money

At some point, your band will require a professional accountant and/or bookkeeper. Many bands seek outside help with their finances once they become full-fledged, incorporated businesses, or when there's enough money coming in to warrant the expense of paying an outsider. Keeping professional books (i.e. ledgers of all money flowing in and out of the band), organizing receipts and filing accurate, solid tax returns are important part of maintaining a healthy band business. Once you become a corporation, keeping organized records and books is not only prudent—it's the law.

Having an outsider oversee your finances comes with a few concerns, because you're handing over access to your money. It's extremely important to know as much as possible about all potential candidates. Ask for references and review their qualifications. Always reserve the right to audit their work. Audits are prohibitively expensive (thousands of dollars), but it's important to at least have the option. Ask for detailed financial reports to keep you up-to-date. You certainly don't want any nasty financial surprises.

There are typically three different choices when it comes to finances: you can sign on with a full-service business manager; hire a certified accountant (CA) and a bookkeeper; or, if you work with a management company, their accounting department can oversee your affairs. Each scenario comes with its own set of advantages and drawbacks.

1. The Business Manager

Business managers are usually either employees of large financial management and investment institutions or are affiliated in some way with a large institution. Personally, the idea of entrusting money to a completely independent business manager makes me more than a little uneasy. There are a lot of horror stories about business managers swindling money from successful music clients, and these bad apples spoil it for the legitimate independent consultants. Do your homework very carefully. I personally feel better knowing my business manager is part of an established team that he reports to, and that there are resources if something goes wrong. I know it's a cliche, but money changes everything. The more vigilant you are, the less opportunity for any mistakes. A good business manager should also be an accredited certified accountant (CA) or, in the US, a certified public accountant (CPA), because they've taken an oath of ethics and generally know what they're doing (anyone with access to your accounts should have some qualifications).

A business manager's role is to oversee and take care of your entire financial life, both professionally and personally. Responsibilities include: corporate books; corporate accounts (writing and cashing cheques, paying band bills); payroll; tour accounting (in conjunction with the tour manager); year-end statements; financial projections; corporate tax planning; and corporate taxes (business managers might charge extra for this).

On the personal side, a business manager will take care of each band member's personal finances including: paying bills (like VISA or rent, which can be very handy when you're on

Most artists can't afford to have a separate business manager. We act for our clients as personal manager and as business manager. We have a chartered accountant in the office, we look after the bookkeeping, the year-end statements and financial projections for all of our artists' different companies.

- Sheri Jones, comanager of Laura Smith, Mary Jane Lamond

the road); overseeing personal accounts; tax planning; filing your personal income tax (again, often for an extra charge); and investment counselling.

Business managers typically charge a 5 percent commission on your gross income. Like all these percentage deals, 5 percent of nothing is a pretty low fee, so many business managers set a minimum fee of around $500 or more. By the same token, you should agree to a maximum fee in case your income goes stratospheric; 5 percent of a couple of million dollars is quite a chunk.

2. Accountant/Bookkeeper

In this scenario, a bookkeeper, either an independent or someone from your management company, takes care of the day-to-day maintenance of the corporate books. A bookkeeper should have accounting experience, but doesn't need to have a professional designation. A professional accountant can then be hired to periodically check over the bookkeeper's work, file year-end statements and prepare your personal and corporate taxes. The advantage to this arrangement is that a bookkeeper's fees are considerably less than a certified accountant's fees. Band members, however, must look after their own personal finances.

Bookkeepers' fees vary depending on their experience and credentials. A capable bookkeeper will usually charge $20 an hour or less. Accounting professionals fees are typically more in line with legal fees, depending on their experience and expertise (i.e. tax specialists are more expensive). A partner in a large public accounting firm can charge in the area of $400 an hour, while a junior accountant or sole practitioner may charge in the $100 an hour range. Most accountants will offer flat fees for preparing corporate taxes and financial statements. Expect these fees to fall between $500 and $1,500, assuming that the accounting is reasonably straightforward. Don't be afraid to ask how much it will cost before they do the work.

3. Personal Management

Some bands choose to entrust the administration of their finances completely to their personal management. In this scenario, management assumes the role of a business manager. Having management and business management under one roof is efficient and cost effective, but there are certain risks in concentrating too much control of your business life in one place.

There is an inherent conflict of interest when your manager acts as your business manager. A business manager oversees your financial relationship with your management, making certain that all their commissions are fair and correct. It's doubtful that your management will police itself with the same vigour as a third party. Also, having all your finances tied up with your management can become seriously complicated if you ever want to leave. My preference is to have an outside accountant oversee the process, with management taking care of day-to-day bookkeeping.

Independent Promoters & Publicists

An unsigned band with an independent record has to take care of all the jobs performed by the various departments at a major record label. Two key roles are promotions and publicity; labels have large departments with field reps all across the country. The promotions department focuses on radio and video stations, while publicity works on getting press coverage. The staff deals with the media every day, servicing the needs of a roster of bands and nurturing strong relationships with the various media.

An unsigned band doesn't enjoy the luxury of having a host of media relationships, so getting radio play or landing the front cover of a music magazine can be extremely difficult. Cold calling a program director and saying "you don't know me but I manage this great band..." is just that—cold calling. This can put you at a disadvantage when you're competing with the majors.

If you're planning an indie release, consider hiring an independent promoter and/or publicist. They'll work with both signed and independent artists and, assuming they're reasonably established, will have good media contacts and relationships. Like their label counterparts, the indie publicists work to get your face into the media, while indie promoters try to get your music on the air. While most indie promoters and publicists can't match the manpower of the major labels, they can often be surprisingly effective, and a valuable addition to your team.

Choosing a Promoter/Publicist

Choosing an independent promoter or publicist is similar to tracking down a booking agent or lawyer. You want someone who is well-versed in dealing with your style of band, so check their client roster. You also want them to be fairly

A band that's humble and doesn't try to hype me on them; let me make the decision whether I like them or not. I don't want to work with anybody who just wants to be a rock star. I want to work with people who take their career seriously and I know that when I'm doing my part of the teamwork, that they're doing the other part.

- Paula Danylevich, publicist with HYPEMusic

They should give you a written proposal of exactly what they're going to do, what their plan is, who they're going to service with your product and what they can expect, whether it's weekly reports or copies of the press clippings, etc.

- Paula Danylevich, publicist with HYPEMusic

established with the necessary relationships; a rookie would make the same cold calls as you.

You'll probably have to sell yourself to prospective promoters/publicists, because many will only take on clients they think will make it. People want to guard their reputations. Good promoters won't push songs they know radio won't play. Also, professionals expect professionalism. They want to see that you have it together, that you're organized and have a plan in place for marketing your record.

The Process

When hiring a promoter or publicist, ask for a media plan that outlines their strategy, a timeline, and the various media they're going to approach. Work out a system for how they're going to show you what they've done (or tried to do). You're hiring a team member, and you'll want to stay in close contact to coordinate marketing and touring strategies around their activities. If a promoter manages gets your songs added to the playlist of a Vancouver rock station, it might affect the time-frame for booking tour dates.

Expense

Promoters and publicists charge either by the day, the week, or the project. Fees range between $2,500 and $5,000 for a three-month campaign, plus expenses such as courier and photocopying costs (which can really add up). You can also hire a publicist for shorter periods, at around $150 to $300 per day.

Don't Waste Your Money

Hiring a promoter or publicist can yield some pretty dramatic results, but only if you have a larger plan together to capitalize on their activities. Many bands blow $1,000 or more a month on a publicist when they don't even have a story yet. If there's no story, then there's very little to work with and the campaign will be a flop; these people can't work miracles. If you're not launching a CD or organizing a sizable tour, hiring a promoter or publicist doesn't really make sense.

Incorporation

At some point, you'll need to consider turning your partnership into an actual corporation. If the band has achieved net earnings of over $50,000, it could very well be time. However, before taking the plunge, you need to have a grasp of the advantages that incorporation has to offer, as well as the maintenance and expenses.

The Advantages of Incorporating

Incorporation primarily offers many advantages over partnership in the areas of liability and taxation.

Liability: Incorporation protects band members against band debts and lawsuits. If your band is sued, the band's corporate assets are at stake, but your personal assets are protected. In a partnership, a lawsuit could go after everything that you have personally. Incorporation doesn't give you a personal out from record contracts or publishing deals. These agreements have clauses that tie members personally into the deal. As such, you can't simply break up your company to get out of a contract.

Tax: There are many potential tax advantages to incorporating. In a partnership, all band income is divided among the partners and the tax is dealt with on your personal returns. With a corporation, taxation can be spread out between corporate taxes and whatever the corporation pays the band members. You can set up the corporation to pay the band members salaries as employees or dividends as shareholders depending on your tax situation. All this paper shuffling can save you a fair chunk of change. Of course, you have to be making money in order for this to make a real difference. You'll have to file a corporate tax return, which requires the services of a professional accountant (corporate tax returns are pretty involved).

Setup and Maintenance

Setting up a corporation can cost anywhere from $750 to $1,500 or more, depending on how complex things are. This includes a $350 governmental fee, $50 for a corporate name search (in Canada, this is called NUANS, which stands for New Upgraded Automated Name Search) and legal fees for drawing up the articles of incorporation and other paperwork. You'll also need a shareholders agreement, which is basically equivalent to your partnership agreement. Converting your partnership

The singer will have to go; the BBC won't like him.

- Manager **Eric Easton** *on hearing The Rolling Stones for the first time*

agreement into a shareholder's agreement can be relatively straightforward if you're not radically changing the contents.

The maintenance of your corporation involves keeping professional financial books and filing a corporate tax return, for which you will require an experienced bookkeeper and/or accountant. Corporations are also required to keep a minute book, which must be updated once a year. Maintaining a minute book isn't all that complex or time-consuming, but does require a lawyer. The minute book contains corporate records, articles of incorporation, corporate resolutions (such as decisions to enter into recording deals), the appointment of officers (on paper, band members will be listed as president, vice-president, treasurer or secretary), a shareholder's register (a list of the company shareholders, i.e. the band members), the corporate bylaws, and shareholder's agreements.

The Reality of Incorporation

Incorporation may seem pretty foreign and complex, but don't let it intimidate you. For a band, the maintenance of a corporation is just a bunch of paperwork that really doesn't affect you very much. An accountant and a lawyer will help you save some money on taxes and dot the i's and the lower case j's, so operating the corporation boils down to signing a few papers once a year, and deciding whose turn it is to be president.

GST

If your band has more than $30,000 of revenue in the year, you'll have to register for GST and charge GST on any revenue. This can be a little awkward at the merch table, so just carry on charging the nice round prices that people like, except now the prices include GST. You'll now have to report the GST collected annually, but there are many tax advantages, such as the GST you paid when you had your T-shirts made can be deducted from the GST you collect on when you sell them (this is a simplified explanation). The GST can actually work in your favour, but please consult with your accountant or business manager for your specific situation.

The Fundamental Flaw

In today's music scene, almost any genre of band can achieve success. In the last ten years, punk, metal, gangsta rap, swing, boy bands, girl bands, grunge, ska, electronica, art rock, Gregorian chant music—just about every type of music that's imaginable has made the *Billboard* Top 200. Depending on the prevailing flavour of the month, it could be harder to break one style than another; breaking a hair metal band in 1993, when Nirvana was just reaching its peak, would have been a little challenging. But generally speaking, there's an audience for almost any type of band.

Still, many bands have great difficulty getting any real groundswell happening. Often, a band will have some weakness that prevents them from progressing beyond a certain level, whether that level is establishing a local draw or moving from regional to national success. Many bands hit a wall that they just can't move beyond. The more severe the flaw, the sooner a band will encounter the wall.

To see potential flaws in your own band, you have to think like an A&R rep. (You'll quickly discover that it's a lot easier to say why you don't like something than why you do like it.) Try the A&R game—go out to see local bands and decide whether or not you would sign them. Remember, as Joe A&R, your career is on the line for every band you get behind, so be super-critical. After doing this exercise a few times, apply it to your own band. What's not working?

It's a big challenge for a struggling band to diagnose why things aren't working. Self-appraisal is always difficult because you're too close to be objective. If a flaw is holding you back, it's often pretty apparent to those around you. Fundamental flaws generally fall into one of three categories: songwriting; faulty member; and presentation.

Songwriting

Songs are basic currency for any band. Sooner or later, without compelling original songs, the band will hit a wall. I've seen bands achieve success on the national live circuit through sheer charisma and determination, but without songs you can't sell records and it's difficult to land and keep a record deal.

I love what John Lennon said once when someone said "Hey John, what do you think the next force in music is going to be?" and he said, "The next great song you hear."

–David MacMillan, marketing manager, EMI Music Canada

- **Diagnosing the problem:** Have people outside the group (preferably not parents or girl/boy friends who love everything you do) listen to your songs. Get their feedback. Watch for songs that everyone reacts to and, conversely, songs that no one seems to get.
- **Remedy:** Keep writing songs and be open to new ideas. Analyze songs by your favourite artists and outline their unique formulas and tricks. If you write on your own, try writing with someone else or even as a full band or, if you write as a full band, try breaking down into subgroups. Perhaps even bringing in an outside songwriter or joining a songwriting workshop would help. Songwriters can submit songs to critique sessions that are offered during various music conferences, where professionals go over the strengths and weaknesses of submitted material. Remember, songwriting is a skill that takes time to develop; the more you write, the better you'll become. (See Songwriting, page 12)

Faulty Member

This is a very unpleasant flaw to deal with. A faulty member is someone who either doesn't fit in or isn't up to the standard of the other band members. This can be the singer who always sings off-key or in some other tooth-clenching way, the drummer who can't keep time, the guitarist who can't play rhythm, or the one who repeatedly skips gigs and rehearsals.

- **Diagnosing the problem:** If a faulty member problem is serious enough that it's holding back the band, then it's really going to be pretty obvious to everyone.
- **Remedy:** Only you can decide if it's time for the ax to fall on someone. However, you should be extremely careful. Group chemistry can be a very nebulous thing that's difficult to fully understand. Getting rid of a bandmate can sometimes have unanticipated negative results. Band members sometimes contribute to the overall life of the band in ways you can overlook. Many successful bands have stuck by a weaker member, even though outsiders were recommending a change, and things have worked out in the end.

Presentation

Fundamental presentation flaws are generally pretty superficial and, therefore, easy to correct. Usually they're simply image problems where a band's look or presence is unappealing or just doesn't make sense. Even if the problem is something as fundamental as a lack of charisma, it can often be overcome with persistence and more performance experience. It's a little more serious if your band is just too damn old for the target audience. If you're a boy band, and all your members are forty-five years old, you may find it difficult to connect with the teenage girl audience that tends to buy your genre of music.

- **Diagnosing the problem:** Ask friends, industry allies and strangers, what they think of your presentation. If everyone comes back with the same criticisms, then you might have a problem. Try videotaping a couple of shows; you might be amazed at what suddenly comes clear.
- **Remedy:** It could be as simple as buying a few gig shirts or making sure you interact with each other on stage.

chapter ten

Record Deals

Approaching the Labels

When approaching or dealing with people at the major labels, it's important to understand how they think and what they want to hear. You have to speak their language, as they say, to understand where they're coming from and how they evaluate prospective artists.

Major labels tend to be very cautious, because for every signing there are reputations and jobs on the line. The competition between labels for market share is intense. Label executives constantly watch radio, video and sales charts, because their superiors are constantly watching those same charts. If a label's market share starts to drop, someone has to answer for it. In this often cutthroat environment, labels can't afford to make too many costly mistakes with new signings.

Everyone has heard Cinderella stories about an A&R exec discovering a band in a bar and signing them on the spot. I'm sure it's happened, but it's pretty rare. Labels tend to hem and haw for months when considering signing a band, playing demos for people, watching showcases and making sure the signing makes sense. After all, there's a lot of stuff to consider. To put yourself in A&R's shoes, consider the characteristics that could lead a band to success.

What A&R Looks For

- **Strong original songs (i.e. hits):** The most important thing.
- **Personality:** Nobody wants to work with a jerk. This point always comes up when you talk to industry players.
- **Star-quality/charisma:** This is a nebulous thing. It's hard to define but easy to spot.
- **Indie success:** Strong sales, radio play, press and live draw tell A&R a lot about your potential.
- **Work ethic:** The label has to believe you'll work incredibly hard to make success happen.
- **A clear sense of your musical genre.** Labels have to be able to put you in a bin, so to speak, in order to market you to a specific demographic. Being a blues-punk-country act is not necessarily an asset in the minds of the A&R community. You have to categorize your sound so people can understand where your music fits in. In interviews, many bands waffle when asked to do this. But if people haven't heard your music before the first question they'll ask is invariably: "Who do you sound like?" If you respond with something intriguing, then you're ahead; if not, you may have lost an opportunity to get someone interested.

The Buzz Factor

The best way to get signed is to create such a buzz that the labels simply can't ignore you. In a sense, this sets you up as a sure bet—or as close as a sure bet as there is in the music industry. If you can generate that label-attracting buzz, you'll probably end up being courted by several of the majors which is a great position to be in. It gives you the bargaining power to negotiate a deal with better terms, including higher royalty percentages, bigger advances, more creative control, and control of your masters. On the flip side, if you sort of have one label executive kind of half interested, you probably aren't going to get a great deal.

If several labels are interested, it's possible to play them off against one another and create a bidding war. An indie album with fantastic sales, a demo with undeniable hits, or even an indie video in rotation on MuchMusic or MusiquePlus can make the labels lose their cool. It's amazing how much more interested labels become when they find out that other labels are interested.

Solicited Materials

Major labels usually only accept packages from people they have a relationship with, such as an established manager or lawyer; A&R departments are so swamped with demos that this is neccessary to even get a listen. (See Promo Pack, p.90)

If an A&R executive thinks your demo has potential, they'll want to hear more material and will likely want to see you perform live. When they phone, be confident, friendly and professional, and set up a killer industry showcase as soon as possible. (See Industry Showcase, p.195)

Investigating the Labels

All record labels were not created equal. Each label has different strengths and weaknesses and some labels are better equipped to sell your band than others. As you begin to create a dialogue with the labels, put together a list of labels you would like to sign with. Talking to industry allies and reading music industry magazines like *Billboard, Canadian Music Network,* and *Canadian Musician* are good places to start your investigation.

Things to Consider When Assessing Record Labels
- **The recent success of the label:** Record labels go through hot and cold spells due to personnel changes, A&R decisions, or changes in company focus. Signing with a cold label could reduce your chances of success.
- **Roster:** Check out each label's band roster to see if the label is overloaded, particularly in your genre of music. Some labels carry massive rosters while others narrow the focus down to a limited number of bands. It's important to consider the manpower of the label, because mega-labels can often deal more effectively with large rosters.
- **Genre:** Some labels are better with certain styles of music than others. A metal band, for example, signed to a label that's only had success in the last two or three years with pop and r&b, might not be in the right place.
- **Breaking bands:** What is the label's track record in breaking new bands? Breaking a new band is very different from sustaining the success of an established artist. Some labels are simply better at creating success than others.
- **Artist development:** Is this specific label dedicated to artist development? Some labels have a reputation for "throwing it

Want to know what the single most unintelligent thing you could possibly say to an A&R person is? Are you on the edge of your seat? Well then, here it is: "I write (or have songs) in many different styles." Seems innocuous enough, but it's very lethal... If you tell an A&R person that you write rock, pop and r&b, they'll run the other way. How could they effectively pitch you to a radio station? You're a rock artist, kind of. You're an R&B artist, kind of. Oh yeah, you're a pop artist... kind of. You get the idea.

- Michael Laskow, founder and president of TAXI (www.taxi.com) an organization dedicated to working with unsigned bands

against the wall and seeing if it sticks"; that is, they pour money into one single and if it's not a hit, they stop working the record. A new artist is best served by a label that sticks with artists and allows time for their fan base to grow.

Deal Memos and Contracts

Throughout this guide, I've tried to warn you about the dangers of signing anything without having a lawyer go over it first. Contracts are almost always designed by someone else to protect their interests, not yours. The same is true with recording contracts. When you're in the process of getting signed, someone will send you the longest, most convoluted and possibly dangerous contract you're likely to encounter in your career. Unfortunately, this the one of the few cases where a handshake deal won't do. If you want to work with a label, you have to sign a recording contract.

Often, a label will present you with something called a deal memo. A deal memo outlines, in broad strokes, the basic terms of a recording deal and confirms that, following negotiations, a deal will take place. Deal memos don't usually contain a time limit for negotiations, so if an impasse is reached you can't just walk away. Deal memos are just as binding as contracts, so having a lawyer give the memo a once-over is essential.

Development Deals

Sometimes a label may think a band has potential, but for one reason or another they'll be unsure about taking the risk of signing them. The label doesn't, however, want any other labels to steal the band away in the meantime. Enter the development deal (also known as a demo deal). With a development deal, the artist receives a small sum of money (around $1,000 to $2,000) to be used for demoing additional material. The artist must then submit the demos only to the label in question. If, after a certain period of time ranging from a few weeks to as much as a year, the label decides not to sign the band, the band can take the demos (and their future) to other labels. If another label wants to sign the band, the original label has the right to match the offer and sign them; this is referred to as the right of last refusal.

I'm not a big fan of this kind of a deal. Sure you're establishing a relationship with a label, but you're also giving away a ton of freedom for peanuts. Also, the right of last refusal can be a very unattractive feature in the eyes of other labels. A development deal is great for the label, because it can hold you with no obligations and at virtually no cost.

Deal Shoppers

Indie bands often work with deal shoppers, who shop their demos to potential labels. Labels usually don't accept unsolicited material, so working with someone who can get your music heard makes a lot of sense. Potential deal shoppers include lawyers, managers, publicists; anyone who has enough of a reputation in the music industry to get your foot in the door. However, these individuals rarely work for free and you need to make sure you understand the cost of their help.

The first thing you should bear in mind is that shopping your band to labels is a highly speculative activity; in other words, there are no guarantees that anyone will want to sign you (even if deal shoppers swear that they can get you a record deal). So, never pay someone a flat rate for their services. Instead, shoppers should receive payment out of the record deal they find for you; this can work in one of two possible ways.

Shoppers may ask for a percentage of the income (i.e. advances) from the record deal. In this case, 10 to 25 percent is pretty common; never give up more than 25 percent. The downside of this arrangement is that you're paying money out of funds that are meant to cover your recording and living expenses.

A better arrangement is to compensate the deal shopper with two or three points on your album. In other words, the label pays 2 or 3 percent of the retail sales of your album directly to the shopper. These points are deducted from your twelve to fifteen points, so it's unwise to give up more than three points. Try to limit the number of albums for which you have to give up points; anything beyond your second album is excessive.

Shopping deals should be spelled out in writing and be nonexclusive, which means that other people are allowed to shop your band as well. With an exclusive shopping agreement, if you're discovered by a label without the aid of the shopper, you still have to pay the shopper. As with all agreements, have a lawyer look it over and explain it to you.

If I hear half a great song on a demo, I'll check the band out live.

– Steve Jordan, A&R at Warner Records Canada

TAXI

TAXI is a high-profile shopping service that brings bands and labels together. Labels send in descriptions of the kinds of artists they're looking for and TAXI posts the information on their website. Bands send in promo packs in response to the postings and TAXI A&R experts screen them and pass on the appropriate ones to the label. The system works a lot like a dating service. Promo packs that fail the screening are critiqued and returned to the band; so even if you don't get connected, you at least get some constructive criticism.

There is a yearly fee of $299 US to join TAXI, with an additional $15 US each time you submit a promo pack (answer one of the "band wanted" postings). Because of the expense, make sure you have everything together before joining. Contact TAXI at:

TAXI
21450 Burbank Blvd., Suite #307
Woodland Hills, CA 91367
Tel. 818-888-2111
www.taxi.com

The Anatomy of a Record Label

Major labels have various departments that each specialize in one particular area of making and selling music. Smaller and independent labels have less separation between departments because they have less people. An indie label might have one department take care of work that would be allotted to three or four departments at a major label. Sometimes a small label will have a relationship with a major where they use some of the major's departments. The process and organization of putting out albums remains basically the same in each scenario.

- **The President:** The president of a record company oversees and is ultimately responsible for everything that happens at the label. You don't get signed or release a record unless the president approves.

Creating Albums/Videos

- **A&R:** The Artists and Repertoire (A&R) department acts as a talent scout, finding, courting and signing new artists. A&R then works with artists through the creative process of writing and recording albums and shooting videos. The degree of

A&R involvement in the creative process differs from band to band, depending upon the needs and track record of the artist. New, unproven artists, for example, generally receive more guidance and input than established artists.

Selling and Promoting your Music

- **Product Manager:** The product manager acts as the quarterback, overseeing the marketing, sales, promotion and artist development departments, and making sure that everyone's in synch. Your musical genre and label affiliation will determine who your individual product manager is.

- **Marketing/Creative Services:** The marketing and creative services departments take care of album artwork, point of purchase materials like posters and life-size band cutouts for record stores, and other promotional materials. They're also responsible for coordinating publicity and advertising.

- **Sales:** The sales department deals with record stores, getting buyers to stock albums. They also set up special in-store events such as performances and autograph signings.

- **Promotions:** The promotions department deals directly with radio and music television stations, badgering programmers to play material. They also coordinate tour-related activities such as visits and performances at radio and video stations.

- **International:** The international department is responsible for getting your album released and promoted by affiliated labels in foreign countries.

Business & Accounting

- **Finance:** The finance department is responsible for taking care of label accounting, including your royalty account.

- **Business Affairs:** The business affairs department is staffed by lawyers or legal people who work on artist contracts and any other legal phenomena that might arise.

Manufacturing & Distribution

- **Production:** The production department organizes the manufacturing, printing, assembly and shipping of your albums into the waiting hands of the distributor.

- **Distribution:** Generally speaking, distribution isn't really a department at most labels; it's more of an arm. All major labels own and control their own distribution arm in Canada and also handle the distribution for many smaller labels.

If it doesn't work out, and they don't sell a lot of records, especially if they spend a lot of money, you're probably not going to get to make another one. You've got to realize, once you're signed to a label, it's all about profit. If you don't make the profit, maybe they'll make two records, but maybe they'll only make one. Maybe they'll even make one, put out one single, then bail on you. Then you're fucked. A signed band can't sell consistently ten, fifteen or twenty thousand records and expect to stay signed.

*- **Ken McNeil**, of the band Rusty*

How a Record Deal Works

A typical record deal with a major label is a complex business relationship that affects every aspect of your band's working life. A record deal gives you the money to make your music, and access to a marketing, promotion and distribution network to get your music to an audience. The label advances you funds to make albums and videos that are later repaid (recouped) out of your cut (royalty) of the sale of your albums. If your album stiffs (i.e. doesn't sell), you don't have to pay back the advances; advances are not loans; they are recoupable, but you are not personally liable to repay this.

What a Record Deal Gives You

- Money for recording, which is recoupable.
- Money for making videos; usually 50 percent recoupable.
- The manpower and resources of a promotional department; money spent on promotion, in most cases, is not recoupable.
- The manpower and full resources of the marketing and sales departments; money is not recoupable.
- Distribution, the costs for which are not recoupable.
- Tour support, which is recoupable.

The Major Label Album Cycle

Think of a band's life in terms of album cycles. Each album cycle consists of a series of stages that begins with the writing a new album and concludes when you're finished working that album and start writing a new one.

Stage One: Writing

- Depending on the size of the recording fund you're entitled to, the label will advance you money to live on while you're writing new material, which is then deducted from your recording fund. Some managers take a commission on this income. Some labels request that managers not do so.
- You will be expected to submit demos of new songs to the label periodically throughout this process; the label will usually advance you additional funds to cover any demoing costs.

Stage Two: Making Product

- Once you have enough material for an album, with a few potential hits, the label will help you find a producer.

- The producer, the label, and you (and/or your management), will draw up a detailed recording budget that's in line with the scale of your recording fund.
- You record and mix the album. During this time, A&R reps will drop in from time to time to check on your progress.
- Once you get label approval for what you've created, the mixes are mastered and the CD is manufactured.
- You do an expensive photo shoot, which is not recoupable.
- In conjunction with an art director, often from the label, you design your album's artwork and packaging, the costs of which are not recoupable. Photo shoots and album design are not usually recoupable and labels will often put a cap on what they'll spend. Expenses that exceed the cap are recoupable.
- You and the label choose a video director and shoot a music video to support the first single from the album, the costs of which are 50 percent recoupable.
- A hired writer (often a music journalist) writes your bio.

Stage Three: Selling the Album
- The promotion department works to get your single added to the playlists of every applicable radio station and submits your video to music television outlets.
- The marketing and sales departments work to give your album a large presence at retail.
- The publicity department generates a major media blitz to coincide with the launch of your album.
- To this end, the artist is expected to tour and be available for interviews, record launches and personal appearances. Labels will often provide you with tour support to offset a money losing tour. Tour support is recoupable from album sales.

Stage Four: The Grind
- Basically, you spend months on end away from home going from city to city selling yourself and your music.
- The label organizes sales promotions that coincide with tour dates to sustain the sales of the album.
- The less successful you are, the shorter this stage is because most labels will pull the plug on the promotion and marketing to cut their losses when an album stiffs. Some will stand by and develop an artist, but only if they see some positive signs of potential.
- If your album is released in various foreign territories such as

Sometimes I work with bands that have no clue what's on their album jacket, which blows me away. It depends on the individuals, but I always want input. I never want to do things without input from the bands. But it's all down to the individuals and how much they want to get involved with things. Look at Moist. You guys are the most hands-on band I have ever dealt with in my life, to the point, and I'll be quite honest with you, it drove me crazy.

–David MacMillan, marketing manager, EMI Music Canada

America, England and beyond, the label's foreign affiliates will expect you to promote the album in their territories. Foreign tours usually lose money, so you'll likely get tour support from the label, which is recoupable.

- After every last dollar has been squeezed out of touring and album sales, the album is put to bed. The cycle is complete; return to stage one.

Stage One: Writing the Next Record
- The cycle continues until your albums stop selling and the record company no longer wants to advance you money to make new ones.

Show me the Money

Most recording funds are used up by making an album. Video expenses are usually charged back to your royalty account, so the reality is that most artists never actually see money from the sale of their records. Money generated from album sales essentially goes to make and promote the album. Artists, however, do receive money from several other sources: live performance; merchandising; and publishing, including mechanical, synchronization and performance royalties.

Record Royalties

A record royalty is a sum of money paid on each album sold. Royalties are calculated as a percentage of the retail selling price of each CD or tape. Common percentages (known as the royalty rate) for non-superstar artists range from 11 percent on the low side, up to 16 percent on the high side. International superstars like Madonna, who negotiate with considerable leverage, receive higher rates, but until you sell albums in the tens of millions, count on 11 to 16 percent. So, with a 14 percent royalty rate, your cut of a CD selling for $19.99 is $2.80 before deductions.

People are often surprised to hear how little the artist actually receives from the sale of a CD. And to tell you the truth, after getting my calculator out to write this section, I was more than a little surprised myself. Every record contract contains a list of diabolical little clauses that gradually chip away at the amount of money an artist actually receives for each album sold. For the purposes of illustration, I've drawn up a rough list of the most common deductions you'll encounter. This list

should give you a good idea of what you could actually make for every CD sold, at retail, by a major label.
The standard list price of a CD in Canada is $19.99. A 14 percent royalty on $19.99 is $2.80 per album sold. However, before the artist royalty is calculated, there's a standard packaging deduction (to cover the costs of the CD design and booklet printing) of 20 percent, which comes out of your cut. According to our exercise, this amounts to $4.00. The $19.99 shrinks to $15.99.

The $15.99 is called the royalty base and it's used to calculate the 14 percent artist royalty, which is $2.24, down from the first figure of $2.80. Now comes the new technology deduction.

New Technology: It's common practice to pay only 80 percent of the royalty rate on CDs, due to a clause that states that a reduced royalty is paid for albums reproduced using a new technology. The fact that CDs are hardly a new technology, and are in fact the number one format for music reproduction, is more than a bit ironic. Fortunately, this deduction is starting to be phased out. The new technology deduction reduces the artist share from $2.24 to $1.79.

Enter the free goods deduction. It's customary for labels to give away 15 percent of the albums shipped free to retailers. The artist is not paid royalties for albums given away, so this effectively reduces your cut. Simply, you are paid royalties on only eighty-five out of one hundred albums shipped. The artist share is now ($1.79 multiplied by 85 percent) so the artist share is now $1.52.

The original $2.80 has shrunk by almost 46 percent. And there's still another deduction lurking. You have to pay your producer.

Producer Royalty: The 14 percent royalty is an all-in royalty, so the producer's cut comes out of your 14 percent. A good producer might take three of your fourteen percentage points (in industry speak, you'd say the producer is getting "three points"). So, we now multiply the $1.52 by ¾₄ to get the $0.33 producer's cut. This 33¢ is subtracted from your $1.52 leaving you with $1.19.

This is equivalent to a net royalty rate of 6 percent. Ouch. Now, assume your album is a smash hit and sells triple platinum in Canada; that's 300,000 copies. The band would receive $363,000. For a five member band that's a whopping $72,600 each. Not bad money, but of course there's a catch.

The $19.95 from the retail sale of a CD might break down as follows:

Artist
$1.31

Producer
$ 0.44

Songwriters
$ 0.69

Distributor
$ 4.39

Manufacturing
$ 1.00

Retailer
$ 5.95

Record Label
$ 6.17

Total
$19.95

- Chris Taylor, music attorney with Toronto law firm Paul Sanderson & Associates

You've already received an advance from the record company to make the album. Recording costs come out of your cut.

Let's say the album cost $150,000 to make. This might seem like a fortune to most people, but it's not that expensive by major label standards. Also, if it's a hit record, the record company will have paid for three videos. According to your recording contract, you pay half the costs of each video. Let's say $65,000 per video times 3 videos = $195,000 x 50% = $97,500. As well, you took $40,000 in tour support to offset your tour losses before you started drawing like a demon. All these figures constitute money you were advanced and that you must pay back out of your album royalties.

Record royalties	**$363,000**
Less recording costs	**-$150,000**
Less video costs	**-$ 97,500**
Less tour support	**-$ 40,000**
Net royalties due	**$ 75,500**

Instead of the big $345,000 cash windfall, you'd actually only see $75,500. But before you start dividing up the spoils, remember that you owe your manager 20 percent and your business manager another 5 percent. So, you're left with $56,625, or $11,325 per member for an album with gross sales of $5,985,000. Pretty intense, huh? There are likely even more recoupable costs than detailed here, and it's possible that you won't see one dollar of your record royalties. By the way, in this scenario a major label with its own manufacturing and distribution arms could pull in around $2.4 million. But to be fair, consider what they spent on promotions, marketing, advertisements, salaries, videos and so on.

Before you go back to your day job

Of course, having sold 300,000 albums, you'd be able to make pretty decent money from touring, merchandising, performance royalties (SOCAN), and one other flavour of royalty: the mechanical royalty, which is paid by the record label to the songwriters on the album. Of the amount due, 25 percent goes your publishing company, 20 percent to your management and another 5 percent to your business manager, so the amount due on 300,000 albums sold is around $85,000, which is split amongst the songwriters in the band.

Music Publishing

Music publishing is essential to the financial well-being of bands. Publishing, coupled with touring, is the main source of most bands' income, so understanding the role and operation of publishing is quite important. Unlike the royalties generated from record sales, which are mostly used up creating albums and videos, publishing royalties are funds that you can actually live on.

Years ago, most artists performed songs written by other people, so publishers acted as the bridge between artists and writers. Publishers signed songwriters and pitched their songs to artists who were looking for material. Nowadays, music publishers act more like a bank, taking care of accounting for songwriting royalties and, most importantly, advancing money to songwriters. Publishers still sign non-performing writers, particularly in the genre of country music; it's just not as common as it used to be.

Publishing deals are usually structured so that the publisher pays a portion of the artist's advance upon "acceptance of the masters" and the remainder when the album is released in a given territory (i.e. Canada). This structure allows the artist to actually have some money to live on prior to the album's release. Additional advances are then paid upon the release of the album in other territories (i.e. the US or the UK), if applicable.

How Publishing Works

Music publishers are concerned with four types of income paid to songwriters: synchronization fees, mechanical royalties, performance royalties and print portfolio royalties. Performance royalties are covered in detail in the section on SOCAN. With performance royalties, the publisher does the paperwork, such as song registrations, for SOCAN on behalf of the artist, but can't interfere with or collect the writer's royalties. If the publisher has a copublishing agreement with the artist, then they can collect the artist's share of the publisher's performance royalties, but not the writer's share.

One of our bands got offered a publishing deal early on and we said well it's not a lot of money and it might help you guys and you're not worth a lot of money yet, but our advice is don't go for it. Two years down the line if you guys work really hard, you could be worth a lot more.

*– **Mark Milne**, cofounder of the indie label Sonic Unyon*

Mechanicals

When an album is sold, the record label pays a standard record royalty of around 12 to 16 percent of retail to the artist. In addition to this, the label pays a mechanical royalty to the songwriter(s) of 7.4 cents per song for compositions less than five minutes long; more if a song exceeds five minutes. In Canada, this rate is called the industry standard rate and is set by the Canadian Musical Reproduction Rights Association (CMRRA). Unlike the US, where the rate is statutory (dictated by law), the Canadian industry standard rate is not dictated by law, but still honoured by most labels and publishers. Note that most record deals contain a reduced controlled composition clause (see below) that limits the number of songs on which the label has to pay mechanicals to twelve songs per album in Canada and ten songs per album in the US.

In Canada, the CMRRA works on behalf of publishers to collect and police the accounting and collection of mechanical royalties from labels; the US equivalent of CMRRA is the Harry Fox Agency. CMRRA is the same kind of collection agency as SOCAN with the exception that CMRRA doesn't pay collected royalties directly to the artist.

Controlled Compositions

"Controlled composition" is a term used by record labels to refer to songs on an album that belong to the artist, as opposed to cover songs which belong to a writer outside the group. It's not uncommon for labels to pay only 75 percent of the industry standard (or statutory rate in the US) on controlled compositions (particularly American labels). This reduction appears in the controlled composition clause contained in most record contracts, so watch out for it when going over your record deal. Also, I have heard that some labels will occasionally try to use the controlled composition clause as a way to leverage you into signing with their affiliated publishing arm instead of with an outside publisher.

To include a cover song (non-controlled composition) on your album, you'll have to apply to the CMRRA for a mechanical license. Once the license has been issued, the CMRRA will collect mechanical royalties at the industry standard rate on behalf of the writer(s) of the song.

Synchronization & Print Portfolios

Music publishers actively try to place their writer's songs in movies, television shows and sometimes commercials. They pitch the songs to movie and television producers and issue synchronization licenses for the songs that are used. Synchronization income can usually range anywhere from a few hundred up to millions of dollars, depending on the artist, the song and the type of use. Once an artist reaches a reasonable level of success, publishers try to get their music released as sheet music and songbooks (aka print portfolios).

When Does Publishing Make Sense?

Music publishers sometimes act in the same way as A&R departments at record labels, and actively seek out unsigned and undiscovered bands. They'll sign a band, and advance them money for demo recording, music videos and sometimes even touring. The publisher will also solicit demo tapes to record labels and other industry players to help the band secure a recording contract.

Many bands sign to a publishing company after they've secured a recording contract. Often they'll sign to their label's publishing company. In most cases, publishers aren't all that interested in unsigned bands because, without a record label flogging albums, it's unlikely that the publisher will be able to recoup advances. Bands that wait until they have a recording contract before signing on with a publishing company have more clout and are able to demand larger publishing advances.

Publishing Companies

Music publishers come in a variety of sizes, from tiny, one-person operations to large multinationals affiliated with major record labels. Publishing companies such as Warner/ Chappell and EMI are owned by the same parent companies as their counterparts in the label world. While it may be easier to get a smaller publisher interested, the heavyweights offer two main advantages: money and contacts. The major publishers have deeper pockets and can often out-advance their smaller competitors; publishing advances are very important to your financial well-being. Big publishers are more effective at getting your music into high profile movies and television programs.

Publishing Deals

The traditional publishing deal is basically a 50/50 split between the songwriter and the publisher. The idea is that a successful song requires an even split of artistic and business activity and, in the case of nonperforming songwriters, this does make some sense. However, for artists writing and performing their own material, an even split of songwriting royalties is a bit unfair. Therefore, a more common arrangement is a copublishing agreement, where the artist is labelled a copublisher and receives about half of the publisher's share in addition to the songwriter's share, which adds up to around 75 percent (sometimes copublishing splits are 70/30 or 80/20, depending on your clout).

INDEX

S

T

ACKNOWLEDGEMENTS

All interviews for this book conducted by Mark Makoway with the following exceptions (in order of appearance):

Quotes attributed to Dan Lanois, Gord Sinclair, Joey Serlin, Jann Arden, Michael Laskow, Matthew Good, Brad Merritt, Karen Kane, Mif, Tim Sweeney, Allan Weinrib, Tim Potocic, Danny Greaves, Geoffrey Kelly, Andrew Scott, Trevor Hurst, Barney Bentall, Holly McNarland, Jack Ross, Paul Sanderson, Bruce Allen, Sheri Jones, Ralph James, Paula Danylevich, Steve Jordan, Ken McNeil and Chris Taylor were originally published in *Canadian Musician* and are reprinted here with the kind permission of the publisher, Norris-Whitney Communications (www.nor.com).

Keith Richards and Eric Easton are quoted from the book *Blown Away* by A.E. Hotchner, Fireside (Simon & Shuster Inc.), New York, 1990.

Grace Jones is quoted from the liner notes of her album, *Living my Life* (Island Records).

Irving Berlin quote is from the public record.

Dr. Marilyn S. Miller is quoted from the SOCAN newsletter, *Words and Music*.

All photographs, posters, contracts and ephemera pertaining to the group Moist are courtesy Mark Makoway and the Moist archives.